S0-ADH-235

An African Tree
of Life

The American Society of Missiology Series, in collaboration with Orbis Books, seeks to publish scholarly works of high merit and wide interest on numerous aspects of missiology—the study of mission. Able presentations on new and creative approaches to the practice and understanding of mission will receive close attention.

**Previously published in
The American Society of Missiology Series**

American Society of Missiology Series, No. 14

AN AFRICAN TREE OF LIFE

Thomas G. Christensen

CABRINI COLLEGE LIBRARY
610 KING OF PRUSSIA ROAD
RADNOR, PA 19087

*Illustrations by
Richard R. Caemmerer, Jr.*

ORBIS BOOKS

Maryknoll, New York 10545

#20853069

The Catholic Foreign Mission Society of America (Maryknoll) recruits and trains people for overseas missionary service. Through Orbis Books, Maryknoll aims to foster the international dialogue that is essential to mission. The books published, however, reflect the opinions of their authors and are not meant to represent the official position of the society.

Copyright © 1990 by Thomas G. Christensen
Bible quotations are taken from the Revised Standard Version.
All rights reserved
Printed in the United States of America
Published by Orbis Books, Maryknoll, N.Y. 10545

Library of Congress Cataloging-in-Publication Data

Christensen, Thomas G.
   An African tree of life / Thomas G. Christensen; illustrations by
Richard R. Caemmerer, Jr.
     p. cm. — (American Society of Missiology series; no. 14)
   Includes bibliographical references.
   ISBN 0-88344-656-1
   1. Gbaya (African people) — Religion. I. Title. II. Series.
BL2480.G36C47 1990
299'.6836 — dc20
                                        89-72148
                                        CIP

For Sharyn, Nyla, Matthew, and Mari

Contents

x   CONTENTS

Preface to the Series

The purpose of the ASM Series—now in existence since 1980—is to publish, without regard for disciplinary, national, or denominational boundaries, scholarly works of high quality and wide interest on missiological themes from the entire spectrum of scholarly pursuits, e.g., biblical studies, theology, history, history of religions, cultural anthropology, linguistics, art, education, political science, economics, and development, to name only the major components. Always the focus will be on Christian mission.

By "mission" in this context is meant a passage over the boundary between faith in Jesus Christ and its absence. In this understanding of mission, the basic functions of Christian proclamation, dialogue, witness, service, worship, and nurture are of special concern. How does the transition from one cultural context to another influence the shape and interaction between these dynamic functions? Cultural and religious plurality are recognized as fundamental characteristics of the six-continent missionary context in East and West, North and South.

Missiologists know that they need the other disciplines. And those in other disciplines need missiology, perhaps more than they sometimes realize. Neither the insider's nor the outsider's view is complete in itself. The world Christian mission has through two millennia amassed a rich and well-documented body of experience to share with other disciplines. The complementary relation between missiology and other learned disciplines is a key of this Series, and interaction will be its hallmark.

The promotion of scholarly dialogue among missiologists may, at times, involve the publication of views and positions that other missiologists cannot accept, and with which members of the Editorial Committee do not agree. Manuscripts published in this series reflect the opinions of their authors and are not meant to represent the position of the American Society of Missiology or of the Editorial Committee for the ASM Series. The committee's selection of texts is guided by such criteria as intrinsic worth, readability, relative brevity, freedom from excessive scholarly apparatus, and accessibility to a broad range of interested persons and not merely to experts or specialists.

On behalf of the membership of the American Society of Missiology we express our deep thanks to the staff of Orbis Books, whose steadfast support over a decade for this joint publishing venture has enabled it to mature and bear scholarly fruit.

James A. Scherer, Chair
Sister Mary Motte, FMM
Charles R. Taber
ASM Series Editorial Committee

Acknowledgments

The first pages of this book bear the names of people who have been a tree of life for me. I have difficulty knowing how to begin describing this tree and fear that I shall not do it adequately, but I thank God greatly for each of these people.

Dr. William Danker, former American Society of Missiology Series Editor, Lutheran School of Theology at Chicago, has tirelessly supported and guided this manuscript through all the tedious steps leading to publication. As my Gbaya friends say, "When your brother is at the mouth of the honeycomb, you can be sure you'll have more than wax to eat!" Dr. Danker has indeed been most effective and persistent in representing my quest for making available in print a Gbaya feast of life-giving symbols.

No one has poured more hours of care into the preparation of the final manuscript than Rachel Reeder, Executive Director and Editor of *Liturgy*, the journal of the Liturgical Conference. She freely offered her superb editorial gifts to complete the transformation of a doctoral dissertation into a book. The thickly described Gbaya ritual materials led her through the threat of defeat, but she would not give up and she would not look back, faithful to the dynamic of those rites themselves, until the transformation was completed.

To both of these friends I am deeply grateful.

Among the many Gbaya friends who have been so generous in their sharing of Gbaya ritual materials with me, extending now over more than twenty years, I single out especially the following: Haman Matthieu, Hamada Samuel, Yongoro Etienne, Yadji André, Djouldé Abel, Bouba Enoch, Ndoyama Enoch, Sambo André, Abbo Samuel, Zoyang Jean, Zama Bernard, Mbari Rémy, Barya Philemon, Adzia Dénis, Abbo Secrétaire, Darman Paul, Gbalaa Sorobana Rebecca, Azimi Pauline, Ndofé Nathaniel, Doko Illa, Saaré, Joseph and Naahii Abraham. The reader will learn from their experiences and insights throughout the entire book.

I would like to thank Drs. Philip Noss, Alliance Biblique du Cameroun, and Philip Burnham, Department of Anthropology, University College, London, for their long friendship and invaluable advice during the course of my research in Cameroon, and for the critique of interpretations of Gbaya language and culture presented here.

I wish to express my sincere gratitude to my adviser, Dr. James Scherer, Lutheran School of Theology at Chicago, and to Drs. Robert Schreiter,

xiii

Catholic Theological Union, Chicago; Lawrence Sullivan, Divinity School, University of Chicago; Carl Braaten and Philip Hefner, Lutheran School of Theology at Chicago, for their help, encouragement, and counsel in the preparation of my doctoral dissertation, "The Gbaya Naming of Jesus: An Inquiry into the Contextualization of Soteriological Themes among the Gbaya of Cameroon."

In 1984 Dr. C. Jack Eichhorst and colleagues and students at the Lutheran Bible Institute of Seattle granted me valuable time and reprieve from teaching duties to complete my dissertation. If they ever wearied of listening to Gbaya stories during my four years on the LBI faculty, they concealed it well, and even asked for more. The LBI community represents a strong branch of the tree of life I mentioned above.

I am grateful to colleagues of the Division for Global Mission, the Evangelical Lutheran Church in America, and particularly to Dr. Mark Thomsen, Executive Director, for their generous contribution toward the publication of this book. These friends have given exceptional testimony to their conviction that the contextualization of the gospel is a high priority in Christian mission.

Richard Caemmerer, Jr., has gifted this book with visual images. His images effectively convey, I believe, themes that emerge from the encounter of *soré* and Jesus. And they also reflect a love for Africa, which we share!

I am grateful to Dr. Gordon Lathrop, Lutheran Theological Seminary, Philadelphia, whose search for living images of the gospel has been a deep inspiration to me throughout my own search among the Gbaya and for years before that search began. He has significantly midwifed much that comes to theological expression in this book, and it is most appropriate that this friend and brother contributes the Foreword.

Finally, and most important to me, to my wife, Sharyn, and our children, Nyla, Matthew, and Mari, go my love and gratitude for their patience and understanding during these years when I have taken time from them for the sake of this study. We gladly share a calling, and we live hopefully forward by trust in Jesus, our *soré*-cool-thing, in whom all trees of life, everywhere, are fulfilled.

Thomas Christensen
École de Theologie
Meiganga, Cameroon

A Note on Orthography

The vowel and consonant systems of the Gbaya language, Yaayuwee dialect, have been analyzed by Philip A. Noss, who identifies seven vowels and twenty-eight consonants (Philip A. Noss, "Introductory Gbaya Lessons," mimeographed, Meiganga, Cameroon, 1967).

The author has simplified the transcription of Gbaya words for the uninitiated English-language reader. For the accurate transcription of Gbaya terms in this book the reader may consult Thomas G. Christensen, "The Gbaya Naming of Jesus" (unpublished Th.D. dissertation, Lutheran School of Theology, Chicago, 1984).

The reader may also note that the vowel rendered "é" (*soré*) is an upper-mid front unrounded vowel, as in English "bit." The consonant rendered "ḅ" (*laḅi*) is an implosive voiced bilabial stop, and "ḍ" (*ḍangmo*) is an implosive voiced alveolar stop. Nasalized vowels (as in *so*, et al.) are not indicated by the simplified transcription in this book, nor is the distinction between the "o" as in "sought" and "domain."

Foreword

And on the banks, on both sides of the river, there will grow all kinds of trees for food. Their leaves will not wither nor their fruit fail, but they will bear fresh fruit every month, because the water for them flows from the sanctuary. Their fruit will be for food, and their leaves for healing.

—Ezekiel 47:12

Here, in this book, are such leaves and such water. For there is a little tree growing on the West African savanna. It is a small bush, we might say; *anona senegalensis*, the botanists say. It is *soré*, say the Gbaya people of Cameroon and the Central African Republic, and its story fills the pages that follow in this book. In coming to this small bush, we have come on one of those trees growing beside the great river flowing from the depth of the meaning of things. When we come through the eyes and ears of the attentive interpreter who has written this book and through the astonishing wealth of stories and descriptions he has collected, it is as if leaves are applied to wounds we had forgotten we have and water is held out to a deep but ignored thirst. We find in the symbolic system that flows around this tree a full twelve months of fruits.

In some ways we ought not be surprised by this discovery both of our need and of the great attractiveness of the Gbaya symbol system. Many commentators have lamented the absence in Western technological culture of such robust, clear, trusted symbols as to hold and interpret our experience. Already in 1942, Susanne K. Langer (in *Philosophy in a New Key*) called for the kind of public symbolization that could orient us all in both "material and social realities" and thereby provide the space for the free and confident functioning of the individual mind. Such authentic public symbols must hold together personal interiority and social meaning, community and cosmos, death and life, real human limits and the transformation of limits.

Western culture is still looking for such symbols. The bookstores are filled with examples of the quest among Native Americans and Zen Buddhists for something the dominant culture has forgotten. Theorists of culture propose this age as a posttechnological time, perhaps the time of a

xvii

new "benedictinism," when small communities labor to find rituals and symbols that work. Some people have despaired of the quest and have turned to protected personal meanings.

Christians, of course, ought to believe that the biblical word and the sacramental symbols provide just such a public matrix of social and cosmic meaning. But when in practice the symbols have shriveled and the metaphors have ceased to surprise us, it is hard to see the application to the universe we currently know and to the aching and complex need of the late twentieth century.

It is not that the Gbaya give us the answers for Western society. But in the meeting with the Gbaya and with their use of the *soré* tree we suddenly know many things again. In encountering the life-giving meaning of these symbols in a new place we know again the importance of symbol and ritual. In meeting the attractiveness yet strangeness of these symbols we think again about how cultural boundaries may be crossed in a friendly way and how to attend with friendliness our own strange culture. In hearing how Gbaya Christians use ancient signs and names to confess the meaning of Jesus Christ we learn again the surprise of the universal gospel, also a gospel for us. Here is a book to help us read the Bible and receive the sacraments; and here is a book to help us think again and more deeply about mission—in our own culture and abroad.

Especially those who bear some responsibility for public symbolism—liturgists and pastors, but also teachers, counselors, artists, therapists, cross-cultural missionaries—will find here a rich resource and a hopeful reminder of their vocation. All of these readers might make their own lists of ways in which these vignettes and stories bear further reflection. But as I read, out of my own longing for communal sign and communal meaning, I would list at least these four proposals.

1. Among the Gbaya, traditional culture is ritually intense and lay-led. Strong symbols were present without the concomitant development of a priestly caste. Although something like this has very much been a goal of the Western Christian liturgical movement—"the participation of all the faithful in the mystery of Christ"—the realization of the goal has remained fragmentary. In fact, lay movements have often had an antiritual character, and liturgical movements have rarely escaped clericalism. An authentic public symbolism will be marked by pervasive intensity and participation. Meeting the Gbaya raises the question again for us.

2. Among the Gbaya one fragment of the symbolic world—a branch of *soré*, say, thrown across a path—can evoke a whole world of meaning. *Synecdoche*, the evocation of the whole by the part, is alive and well. Reading the Bible, especially reading the Bible in public assembly as the source of an authentic public symbolism, requires a recovery of the same skill. Reading about *soré* and *simbo* gives us fresh impetus for seeing the life-giving matrix evoked by the biblical *lamb* and *rock* and *city* and *anointed ruler*. Meeting the Gbaya makes that proposal to us.

3. Among the Gbaya, traditional symbols are part of symbolic processes, not static and isolated signs. To read about the "drowning," the hiddenness, the instruction, and the washing and anointing rituals that make up *labi*, the traditional initiation rite, reminds the literate Western Christian of the full processes of the third-century baptismal texts. Modern-day therapists and liturgists call for an unshrinking of our symbols and for their insertion into rich communal patterns of action. Marriages, births, and deaths need such gracious celebration. Much more so do the rituals of the assembly's identity, the washing and the meal, in the Christian community. Only as these symbols are full and participatory and processual will they be able to hold our experience and propose life. Meeting the Gbaya strengthens this call among us.

4. Among Gbaya Christians powerful symbols are remembered, even when no longer enacted, and turned to speak of Jesus Christ. Besides providing us with a remarkable example of profound Christian mission, this fact also calls those of us who are interested in renewed symbolism to see that ultimately all symbols of life open to and wait on God's grace. The most powerful symbols for us are *broken* symbols, for thereby all of our brokenness is gathered into the hope for healing.

If with the Gbaya our "*soré*-cool-thing" is Jesus crucified, then we learn again with joy how the tree of life is the cross and the ruler of the City is God dwelling in the midst of suffering humanity. When our strongest religious symbols are fulfilled in reference to the nonreligious event, to Jesus among historic human agonies, then we find the possibility of an authentic public symbolism for our time. Trying on Gbaya Christian language enhances that possibility.

Lay leadership and participation, *synecdoche* in biblical language, ritual process, symbolic intensity, a new kind of missiology, and the broken symbol — these are proposals I see as fruits for us from this tree of the savanna. And for that I am deeply grateful to many Gbaya people and to their faithful collaborator, Thomas Christensen. For now, I wish you the joy of your own reading and the joy of your own meeting with this small, life-filled tree.

Gordon W. Lathrop
Lutheran Theological Seminary
Philadelphia

An African Tree
of Life

1

Deep Symbols We Share

I have one self in the United States and another self in Cameroon among the Gbaya people. What I see, hear, and experience in one of my cultures often makes me look around in the other to see how the same kind of thing appears there. According to a Gbaya proverb, "Ban duk kpok zer ba zang na" ("The little antelope who keeps hiding in the same old clump of trees will never get pregnant"). The Gbaya are convinced it is no good sitting out one's life in a single spot.

The Gbaya also say, "A little trickle of water that goes alone goes crookedly." If we as individuals or as Christian churches keep hiding in separate clumps of trees, even if we think we are living, it is really more like dying. If our pluralism, especially as Christians, means our separateness, it is likely to kill us.

As a bicultural Christian I am always fascinated by the limiting but also limitless ethnic and cultural ways in which the one gospel of life and salvation in Jesus the Christ keeps coming to ever new expression among us and in the midst of all peoples. And these expressions are centered, not in the esoteric and exotic, but in the familiar symbols we have all been given, such as word and water, meal and people. In every place, a people becomes, thrives and opens itself to God through these earthy and ordinary elements. Walking and talking, bathing and sharing food together—these simple gestures and things express a people's deepest nature. They set the limits for what a culture can be, but they are also the elements for its transcendence; that is, they are the common thread that enables us to enter with rejoicing into a variety of cultural habits.

In all cultures, the most intimate and common experiences of community—marriage, family, friendship, and the relationships formed during daily work and play—contain these elements as symbols to lead us through

1

dissonance and the ever present threat of death to new life. Yet to an alarming extent we still have and hold these symbols separately and on the run, and thus use them to vitiate the meaning of life. The good news is that the way back to life has been given to us in the simple and ordinary gifts of word, water, meal, and people; and these simple things are worth sharing and worthy of our attention.

ON THE RUN

But do we really share our lives across cultures? In Hebrew the word for "blessing" and the word for "pool of water" are very similar. Both are rooted in the word for "kneeling." It is hard to share deeply or to kneel when we are on the run.

Gbaya people often remind one another, "Duk ka yi fé ne nding" ("There you sit right next to the water, but you may yet die in your own dirt"). It is not enough simply to emerge from our old clumps of trees and stare at one another from opposite sides of the water. We may and must practice kneeling together in the power of the Spirit; we must be washed together and take time to drink and eat together, if we are to receive a blessing from God and one another at the one pool of water. Gbaya friends who have undergone their initiation (laḅi), insist that they can know laḅi only "under the water," where they are thrust, not separately, but naked and together, to die under the water and rise again to new life.

Here in this culture among the Gbaya I have encountered symbols that mediate life, and I have learned that these symbols are given to everyone so that death may not be final. These symbols are full of hope because they enable us to kneel at the water, and even to go under the water, to die, in order to live again. Deep symbols for life are inherently ambiguous, and they are not easily penetrated. In the beginning, in Genesis, the symbol for life is a tree, the tree of life, and trees take time to grow, as God took time, a lifetime, to die for us on a tree.

The cross of Jesus is where we have the utterly strange condensation of what life means for us. The cross is the point of reference for whatever we may identify as a life-giving symbol in our midst. It breaks all symbols and transforms the most common stuff of our lives—word, water, meal, and people—and fills this common stuff, fills us, with new meaning. We cannot invent life-giving symbols for ourselves. Such symbols can only be given, and they have been given. But it takes time to receive and share them.

THE SORÉ TREE

Gbaya friends introduced me to a certain common, ordinary, little tree. They call it the soré (SOH-reh) tree, but they also call it soré-ga-mo-k'ee, "our soré-cool-thing." The name and metaphor make clear that soré is more than a tree, but the Gbaya do not worship this tree any more than we would worship, say, a glass of cold water.

The Gbaya say that the *soré* tree is for cooling murder. If a person from Adzia's family has killed someone from Abbo's family, a *soré* branch may be thrown between the two families to prevent revenge. That *soré* branch between them is at once a barrier to further fighting and a doorway opening up a new possibility for life with other people. To jump over the *soré* barrier is to do a *simbo*-thing, because it violates that which is inherently inviolable, the gift of life itself. But to step peacefully over the branch is to do a *soré*-thing; it affirms, serves, renews and preserves human life and society.

Simbo represents for the Gbaya that which limits human beings; for example, to kill a person or certain taboo animals is a *simbo*-thing, which leads to the sure threat of death. But *soré* serves *simbo* by giving human beings a way to cope with their limitations, their "sin." *Soré* is a tree of life among the Gbaya; like the cross, it appears at the center of a people's life to lead them through the threat of death and into new life. *Simbo* gives the Gbaya a way to see that violations of life entail the threat of death; *soré* lets them see that life and restored life are a gift.

A NEW NAMING OF JESUS

If you attend Catholic or Lutheran services in Cameroon, you may hear the preacher speak of Jesus as *soré-ga-mo-k'ee*, "Jesus our *soré*-cool-thing." A new naming of Jesus! But what does Jesus have to do with *soré* and what does *soré* have to do with Jesus?

Gbaya Christians tell us that *soré* leaves were for the making of a village, a new village, when witchcraft had broken the old village apart — *soré* leaves and the chief's nephew, who comes at the elders' call, alone before dawn, unnoticed in the dark. He leaves alone before dawn, for a new place, to make a new village. The chief's nephew finds the *soré* tree. He takes a leaf in his hand and ties the leaf into a loose knot. He speaks a blessing: "I bind up a new village right here, as my fathers entrusted to me this task. Let no harm come to the village. May death be taken away from this village. May sickness and quarrels and revenge pass away. Let the hearts of the people be soft *mborr* like the *soré*, who binds us here in his peace." Then the *okoo-pi-gangmo*, the woman peace-thrower, steps forward with her calabash of cool water, and with a branch from the *soré* tree she sprinkles the people and gives them a blessing that they may live, work and eat together again in peace. And the chief calls the people together, saying, "Now we may eat together again!" They wash their hands and faces and share a meal there by the *soré* tree.

Gbaya Christians tell us that Jesus is for making a new village. Jesus our *soré*-cool-thing makes peace by the blood of his cross to create a new community, a village of yet more enduring significance than our fragile communities of blood relation, idea relation, cause relation. Jesus ate with the outcasts and the ritually impure; his peace is a sword that cuts across all human structures to open a new world of unprecedented human relationships. We are all at peace in his village.

"I DON'T WANT YOU TO DIE!"

Two of my friends, Adamou and Bouba, went hunting one morning, taking about the same direction into the bush. Adamou soon came upon a bushbuck, released his arrow, then followed the traces of blood to the place where the animal lay dying. As he was about to butcher the animal and take food to his family, Bouba arrived, shouting, "Adamou! Get away from my animal!" So they fought over the animal, until Adamou said, "Let's not kill each other over this animal. Go ahead and take it, I give it to you!" And Adamou returned to his village, leaving his food to Bouba.

In the days and weeks that followed, Bouba was in poor health and had no luck whatsoever on the hunt. It was almost as though the animals were hunting him. Adamou knew what was happening and said to himself, "If I do not step in to help Bouba, he will surely die. He has done a *simbo*-thing by stealing food from me."

Early in the morning Adamou filled a new calabash with cool water and fresh leaves from the *soré* tree. He went and stood before Bouba's house and called out to him, "My brother, come see the cool water and leaves I've brought to you." Bouba came and stood on the threshold of his house as Adamou continued, "You are sick and dying because you stole from me. But I don't want you to die! Here, let me wash you, let me wash you all over!" Adamou washed Bouba with *soré* water and *soré* leaves and gave him a blessing, "Now go ahead and hunt and you'll be all right!" ... "Bouba," he added, "now we may eat together again!"

When villages fail to cooperate with the chief, the chief gets so angry he curses them, bringing sickness and death upon them all until, finally, at the urging of the elders, he calls them together in front of his house to put things right, to make things clear and clean again. He puts fresh water in a calabash, adds *soré* leaves, then pours the water and leaves on the ground. Representatives of the village families gather around this spot, grasp the same cassava stirring stick that the chief holds, and help him pound the *soré* leaves and mud. The chief confesses his sin for having cursed the villagers; he takes the mud and the leaves and anoints all the participants, blessing them for renewed life and health in the village. Then the chief invites the elders to eat together. They wash their hands and faces, eat cassava from a common bowl, and wash once more.

When the village gets messed up again, disrupted by witchcraft, curses, stealing, or jealousy, the chief's nephew is called back because everyone is quarreling, sick, and dying. He comes into the village very early one morning, shouting, "Hooo! This village is sick! Eeee! Everyone is dying!" And all the while he is dragging an enormous vine, cut from a tree in the forest.

As he drags it through the village everyone throws a little stick, like a tiny spear, on the vine. Old people and children, invalids and hunters — everyone throws his or her sins on the vine, and the chief's nephew drags the whole collection outside the village and puts it at the foot of a *soré* tree. He takes *soré* leaves and a new calabash filled with cool water and enters the village again to sprinkle the people and give them a blessing for health and well-being, a blessing they celebrate by eating together again.

WHERE OUR VILLAGES MEET

Jesus our *soré*-cool-thing, say Gbaya Christians, looks out from his cross to all of us, East and West, North and South, who put him there, and says, "Father, forgive them. . . . " He is in the middle, between our village in the East and our village in the West, saying to us, "Woman, behold your son! Son, behold your mother! Brother and sister, behold one another!"

Jesus our *soré*-cool-thing lives to make intercession for us, to save us who can draw near to God only through him. There are many villages, say Gbaya Christians, but only one *soré*-cool-thing, where our villages meet to be at one with one another, there to find each other as members, finally, of a single village called God's kingdom, where we may be ourselves and where we may be with and for one another because we are in Christ Jesus our Lord.

One major purpose of Christian mission is to invite and encourage people to tell their own stories. As we emerge from our individual clumps of trees, we may and must take time to kneel at the one pool of water to share our stories and to drink and eat together. Perhaps in the common human circumstances of our stories, God will give us ways to cope with our limitations and sin and lead us back to life. Perhaps we shall even be given a way to cope with God's silence. Surely there are among us many Adamous who need to say to many Boubas, "But I don't want you to die!"

Gbaya Christians offer to American Christians fresh and hope-filled images, rich metaphors, new and yet familiar to us. These images help to relieve our numbness and despair about the way things are and the way we live; they draw our attention to the one in whom all things really do hold together. Though we Christians are divided among ourselves, we yet long to have and hold true names, living water, trees of life, genuine community, the bread of life.

Gbaya symbols are a way back to biblical symbols. In trees of life we remember the tree of life. In the cool waters of a Gbaya calabash we remember the one who declares, "I am the living water." There are deep things in each culture and in each of the Christian churches that we are meant to share, for God has given them to us to have and to hold, not separately but together, as one body.

IDENTIFYING THE GBAYA

In 1951 it was estimated that 100,000 Gbaya live in east-central Came-roon and 400,000 in the Central African Republic. More recently, however, Philip Noss has written that the peoples who can legitimately be called Gbaya number closer to one million.[1] The Gbaya are part of a large lan-guage group, consisting also of the Mandja and the Ngbaka, that extends from central Cameroon through the Central African Republic and into northern Zaire. Joseph Greenberg has classified the Gbaya in the eastern branch of his Adamawa-Eastern subgroup of the Niger-Congo family, which also includes the Zande and the Sango.[2]

My interpretation of Gbaya ritual symbols is grounded in contemporary Gbaya language, especially as it is expressed in the Yaayuwee dialect.[3] The Gbaya who have contributed to my research, however, come from a great variety of Gbaya *zu duk*, "clan groups" and areas, and their experience spans three generations. Contacts with other ethnic groups and exposure to various religious, social, and cultural influences have certainly not been identical for all the Gbaya men and women I consulted. The people whose ritual traditions contribute to this description can nevertheless be said to share, in a broad way, the following characteristics: (1) a common language, despite variances of dialect; (2) a common social structure, with which significant values and mores are associated; (3) common social and religious institutions, beliefs and practices and the symbols that come to expression through them, such as the *to*, "tale," and the *yoya*, "dance" — symbols that are similar in type over an extensive area, although they permit a variety of expressions in local areas; (4) a similar political and economic history, which includes a reliance on manioc cultivation as the basis of their econ-omy, and a common love for, and considerable expertise at, hunting and fishing.

Today, the Gbaya peoples inhabit over 190,000 square kilometers (an area roughly the size of the state of Nevada) on a lightly populated central savanna area of Cameroon and the Central African Republic. Most of this area of rolling grassland hills varies from 900 to 1,500 meters above sea level, and the climate is rather cool although the entire area is only six degrees north of the equator. Five dry months, November through March, alternate with a seven-month rainy season. Bush fires, still linked to Gbaya hunting habits, blacken the landscape during the dry season, but dust and smoke give way to a rapid greening and lush vegetation when the rains return.

The Gbaya locate their maize fields in fertile stream valleys, whereas manioc, their staple crop, can be grown in most types of savanna soil. Philip Burnham describes the Gbaya way of manioc cultivation:

Normally manioc is planted without preparatory breaking up of the soil, although better yields result when the ground has been previously loosened with a hoe. Owing to the length of the planting season and the nature of planting and harvesting procedures, Gbaya may plant a manioc field little by little, fitting in the work between more pressing duties. To plant manioc, the Gbaya cut sections about 20 cm long from the woody stem of a mature plant and thrust these into a hole punched in the ground with a dibble. The piece of stem takes root and produces a new plant. After about eighteen months, during which approximately three weedings are the only attention the field receives, the roots are mature and ready for harvest.[4]

The Gbaya generally clear new fields rather than replant old fields, because land is abundantly available and the work is fairly light. The cultivation of maize is a far more arduous task, and since the maize farming period extends from January to September, it occupies the major portion of a Gbaya farmer's labor time. During the past forty years, maize has become the most important cash crop for the Gbaya, but it cannot compete with manioc as the preferred food of the Gbaya people.

A number of subsidiary crops—okra, squashes, various greens, groundnuts, sweet potatoes, sesame, and yams—contribute to the Gbaya diet and economy. Gbaya farmers also raise a few cattle, sheep, goats, and chickens. Dogs are valued hunting companions.

The Gbaya world is divided into two parts: the village, *saayé*, and the bush, *zangbee*. The savanna bush also consists of two parts: the heavily wooded stream valleys (*kozér*) and the wooded savanna (*zan*) between those valleys. Gbaya farmers set up their bush encampments on the fringe of a stream valley near their maize gardens, while the hunters locate their camps in or near a stream valley. Gbaya villages are clearly established out in the open between stream valleys. Danger lurks in the valleys, but "salvation" is also there—in the waters that provide physical nourishment and cleanliness as well as ritual and spiritual purification.

Hunting and to some extent fishing provide the natural contexts of activity for many (if not most) Gbaya rituals. The hunt may proceed on an organizational basis from individual or small family groups to large communal hunts involving several dozen men and representatives from two or more villages. Gbaya men kill animals with shotguns, bows, crossbows and traps. Crossbow hunting and animal trapping are typically undertaken by individuals during the rainy season. Whereas the crossbow is designed for hunting birds and monkeys, trapping and deadfall prey encompass virtually the entire range of wild game. Longbow hunting, on the other hand, is the practice on group hunts organized during the dry season.

Whenever I use the term "Gbaya" I refer to a group of people for whom the foregoing characteristics and experiences are sufficiently homogeneous to justify their being treated together. I avoid frequent use of the term "traditional," but when I do use it, I am referring to Gbaya culture, always bearing in mind local variations, as it appears to have existed before extensive contact with Muslims in the 1830s and Christians in the 1920s.

As we step into Gbaya living space and encounter the Gbaya way of seeing the world, Philip Noss provides us with four useful guidelines in his essay, "An Interpretation of Gbaya Religious Practice." He maintains that traditional Gbaya religion is "first of all a religion of society and family." Second, Gbaya religion is "pragmatic" in that it brings "the realm of spiritual reality down to the level of everyday need." Third, Gbaya religion is "a religion of the laity." This characteristic is exemplified in all Gbaya ritual activities and leads us to Noss's fourth and final point: "The essence of Gbaya religious practice," he writes, is "ritual and symbol."[5] Gbaya rituals help us to discover Gbaya meanings associated with specific places, creatures, objects, and times in the natural world; they also reveal, or at least suggest, understandings about the Gbaya spiritual world.

One matter at issue in this work is the sense in which it can be said that "traditional" Gbaya culture is still alive in the 1980s. It is true that "you cannot go home again," but continuities do persist and can be identified in the midst of and through the processes of change experienced by human cultures. High-rise apartments have not yet been planted in the spacious savanna grasslands where the Gbaya live. The trees and plants that have grown in that space for countless years still live and grow there. They are at the heart of the Gbaya symbolic world.

The same trees grow, but their meaning for each succeeding generation is indeed changing. The next generation of Gbaya may not live the same ritual stories that have been told to us. There is thus an urgency to listen now to the meaning of Gbaya rites and symbols, even while we acknowledge the tentative and provisional character of our reflections. Our attention is drawn especially to one among many Gbaya ritual symbols. I refer, of course, to the *soré* tree.

2

What We Bring, What We Discover

 The Gbaya preacher Mbari Rémy speaks about the meaning of Jesus' death for his parishioners by reminding them about what happens on a Gbaya hunt. Suppose Bouba invites Adamou's family to join Bouba's family on a hunt, in an area that belongs to Bouba's family. On that hunt, Adamou is gored by a buffalo and his blood is shed on Bouba's ground. Before anyone can hunt in that area again, the hunters must call an elder from Adamou's family to bless the land where blood was shed. Shed blood and spoken blessing effect a change; now that land and all the animals, birds, and fish therein no longer belong to Bouba, but to Adamou and his family.

Rémy explains to his congregation that "something like that" happened when God's only Son, Jesus, was sent to live on this earth with us. His blood was shed right here on this land where we walk, and God thereby blessed this earth and all who live here. All of us who live on this earth now belong to God and to God's Son, Jesus, says Rémy, because Jesus shed his blood here.

With a wave of tongue-clicking and other affirmative noises, the congregation indicates that it has understood the meaning of Rémy's analogy. The analogy relates a soteriological theme from the Christian Bible with a soteriological theme from traditional Gbaya ritual. It makes the ordinary experience of the hunt a parable for understanding the new ways of God in our midst.

Without having been trained or schooled to do so, Rémy has contextualized the Christian message—the good news of the word made flesh. He knows and sees in the light of the gospel that what Christians discover among the Gbaya is the spirit of God already present in the deep symbols of their culture to draw them to God's deed for them in Christ. His sermon illustrates with simplicity and strength how the Christian message can be communicated within Gbaya culture.

JESUS AND *SORÉ*

The shock of recognition that I feel every time I review Rémy's sermon underlies my own reflections on Gbaya ritual, which I began during my first years as a missionary of the American Lutheran Church in Cameroon and the Central African Republic, and which I have continued to pursue through many hours of conversation with individual Gbaya friends and colleagues and with the many people I serve as pastor and teacher. Some of these conversations take place in Gbaya homes, or around a fire, or on a path through the tall grass; many take place in my office or classroom at the Bible schools and seminaries where I teach courses on the Hebrew Bible and the New Testament. As our friendships deepen, so do our efforts to understand how the rites and symbols of Gbaya culture relate to the content of scripture and the new experience of Gbaya Christians.

Increasingly our search comes to focus on the *soré* tree, whose leaves, branches, bark, or roots are highly visible in a surprising variety of ritual contexts. Botanists label this tree the *Anona senegalensis*, according to its species, and *Anonaceae*, according to its family; but the Gbaya call it *soré-ga-mo*, their "*soré*-calm/pacify/cool-thing," and use it to express a wide range of cultural activities. For example, a *soré* branch thrown between two families puts peace in their midst and prevents revenge.

Other examples of how *soré* is used by the Gbaya enlarge our understanding of its significance for putting peace among them. But our concern about it reaches a deeper level when Gbaya preachers in Garoua Boulai call Jesus "*soré-ga-mo-k'ee*," our *soré*-cool-thing." Their reference to Jesus as *soré* is not an isolated case; it is part of a theological search for meaningful symbols that the gospel itself has evoked. It continues a process begun two thousand years ago when Jewish Christians called Jesus the "Lamb of God" and the "Son of man," and gave him many other names from their Jewish past.

Gbaya Christians are carrying on this search without the sophisticated tools of symbolic anthropology or even systematic theology. It is most notable in Gbaya teaching and preaching, for example, in sermons such as the one cited above by Mbari Rémy. The Gbaya have lived for generations with the reality of *soré* in their midst; now they are living with the reality of the Christian gospel, and their conviction that *soré* interprets and enriches the symbol of Jesus is a paradigm for understanding the principle of contextualization. Their proclamation that "Jesus is our *soré*-cool-thing" suggests that the recent proclamation of the gospel of Jesus and his kingdom has evoked in them an unprecedented reflection on *soré*. It also suggests—and this is more important—that *soré* may reveal dimensions of Jesus that we have not yet seen. The investigation that we undertake here is to answer these questions: What does Jesus have to do with *soré*? What does *soré* have to do with Jesus? Everything depends on the answers.

IN SEARCH OF A METHOD

Our first task is to describe and interpret *soré* and the root metaphor, *soré*-cool-thing, within their home in certain Gbaya ritual contexts. An ethnographic "thick description" of *soré* and the rituals associated with it will provide us with a complex of densely textured facts from which to draw the large conclusions necessary for the construction of a local theology. Thick description, as Clifford Geertz describes it, investigates cultural phenomena on their own terms; it looks for symbolic meanings to emerge from certain contexts or "micro-histories," which, understood from the Gbaya perspective, are small dramas or stories of people who follow a ritual way to cope with dissonance and the threat of death.

Thick description is anecdotal rather than sequential so that the data may speak for themselves. The risk of most ethnographic approaches is that we may be absorbed for long periods in interesting but, alas, dead symbols. Thick description, however, has the potential for generating an indigenous Christian theology as the micro-histories of the Gbaya are transformed by the word of God to evoke a new way of seeing salvation. This approach is concerned with the selfhood and identity of a particular people, and it shares this purpose with incarnational Christian theology.

The comparison of ethnographic data, thinly described, with similar-looking phenomena in Christian resources bears a heavy risk of linking false friends. Thick description cannot escape that risk, but the chances for discovering genuine semantic correspondences between Gbaya and Christian symbols are greater when Gbaya symbols are investigated on their own terms, in their natural ritual contexts.

A dialectical method complements description. For example, I consider some implications of the peace brought by *soré*-cool-thing, now reinterpreted by Gbaya Christians as Jesus our *soré*-cool-thing, where the peace at issue is peace by the blood of his cross. First, I interpret certain ritual contexts, each of which represents an episode of threat in the drama of ordinary Gbaya life. In each case salvation is sought and provided by *soré*. Next I describe how such life-threatening contexts are reinterpreted by Jesus. Here, the intention is not simply to baptize meanings of *soré*; its ritual contexts stand, but now with their various meanings of *soré* reinterpreted by Jesus and his cross.

In the cross of Jesus we have the utterly strange condensation of what Jesus "means" for us. The cross as a symbol that stands for all that God has done for us in and through Jesus of Nazareth is the crucial point of reference; it links Jesus with *soré*, and it also distinguishes Jesus from *soré*. The ultimate critique of *soré* is the cross of Jesus, in which *soré* as symbol is broken. Yet it is also the cross that saves and transforms *soré* and even fills it with new meaning.

INTERPRETING THE DATA

As we discover the integrity of symbolic relationships in Gbaya ritual, we can compare this ritual to the material of Christian scripture and tradition. Ethnographic thick description is still a tentative approach. It is a matter of making guesses about meanings, then arranging and assessing the better guesses in ways that not only help us to converse meaningfully in a particular culture, but also open us to the possibility of "contextualizing" Christian theology.

If it had never occurred to Gbaya Christians to say, "Jesus is our *soré*-cool-thing," or if that metaphor did not resound as it does among Gbaya Christians, this book would never have been written. But in the power and meaning of the metaphor's occurrence the thick description of *soré* becomes a theological, Christological, and missiological task, not merely a prolegomenon to a biblical or theological discussion. Thick description of *soré* is correlated to the biblical description of Jesus, just as the biblical doctrine of creation is correlated to the redemption.

In view of the current debate about the Lordship of Jesus Christ in an age of religious pluralism, the Gbaya metaphor is an important Christological issue as well as a reflection on the Gbaya attempt to name the name that is above every name. Gbaya Christian stories about God are new stories, but they have Jesus at their center — and the reign of God that he proclaimed.

The micro-histories of the Gbaya people are bound up and fulfilled by the one God in Jesus Christ. Consequently, we must presume a missiology and a theology of mission that is consciously oriented to and expressed in the eschatological reign of God. That reign is grounded in the Bible, but it is actively focused on peoples, nations, cultures, societies, and religions. Knowing that each particular people is already related to God in its own history is the beginning; understanding that their relationship is not yet all that God has promised is the middle; and God's eschatological promise in Christ, historically oriented to the real history and micro-histories of the people, is the endpoint of a biblically grounded missiology and theology of mission.

The metaphor "threshold," which is encountered in the study of Gbaya ritual symbols, also helps to describe the meaning of the eschatological reign of God. As people who are consciously alive to God's reign, Christians are citizens on the threshold of two worlds, in a betwixt-and-between place of eschatological tension. On this threshold, Christians are oriented to God by way of their neighbor. The church may be seen as an eschatological community characterized by its power as a "sign": it exists in and for the world, and it works for the renewal of the world's structures and against their hardening into demonic forms. The church, as body of Christ, stands unambiguously for life. A person or a church can be in two worlds like this, or live on a threshold like this, only by grace through faith.

THE POWER OF THE GOSPEL

My first years of ministry in Cameroon and the Central African Republic extended from 1967 through 1981. In 1985 I was invited by the Lutheran churches in those two countries to conduct five week-long seminars on contextualizing the gospel. I called the seminars, "The Power of the Gospel in Our Village," and focused them on the realities of life in the "modern" African village. We considered various ways that life is threatened and how Christians can cope with the threat of death. We worked with local African symbols and resources, seeking to discover what help was already present in the village.

When we focus like this on local resources, we can do so straightforwardly from a preparation-fulfillment perspective because a dialectical continuity exists between old and new ways of life. For example, the early Christians retained valuable ideas and images from the Hebrew Bible. These images were not present in the scripture accidentally but intentionally, and yet they were broken apart by the gospel of salvation in Jesus and transformed to speak that gospel in particular historical and cultural circumstances. The Hebrew Bible's images of the "lamb" and the "tree of life" reappeared in the New Testament, having undergone the same kind of transformation now happening to the New Testament in relation to African images. They are, therefore, a helpful paradigm for reflecting on the African churches' transformations of the New Testament.

In the 1985 workshops we explored areas of village life in which traditional African ways still flourish. For example, the ancient purification rites continue to be practiced among Gbaya Christians, and the power of witchcraft and sorcery continues to disrupt and threaten the life of the church. These problems will not disappear by simply forbidding people to believe in their traditional practices. As long as our missionary attitude and approach is dominated by the idea that all aspects of indigenous African traditions are pagan and worthless, if not evil, these traditional practices will persist behind the village.

This dual or parallel practice of religion is certainly not unique to Africa, but we North American and other observers can learn from the African churches how best to deal with this problem. Only if we are entirely honest about what is happening in and behind the Christian village can we work at discovering together what we as Christians bring to the village, and what we can expect to find there that is honorable, just, pure, lovely, gracious, excellent, and worthy of praise (Philippians 4:8). What we bring to the village is the message of salvation in Jesus Christ and his way of life as proclaimed in the New Testament; what we discover in the village are the indigenous symbols and ritual traditions that will draw our attention to the new deed of God in the life, death, and resurrection of Jesus.

Concrete examples from Gbaya ritual tradition, which has a peace-bringing tree at its center, are encouraging and powerful reminders to African Christians that there are indeed praiseworthy and God-given ritual symbols in their past. In light of the gospel, which they know, these ancient gifts draw their attention to God's new deed in Jesus Christ. We must learn to think of Gbaya rituals in a way not unlike the way the author of Hebrews thought about ritual symbols from the traditions of Israel.

Traditional African rites are for something; that is, they address a people's particular needs when its life in community has been threatened. If they persist among African Christians, then we must ask whether the church is responsive to those needs or whether there are empty places or areas of life that do not experience the power of the gospel. In our workshops we identified some of these problems and explored the possibility of transforming certain traditional rites into explicitly Christ-centered liturgies. Many such transformations are intended to help Gbaya Christians remember Christian baptism, the once-for-all washing that is the renewal of their covenant with Christ Jesus.

The discovery and careful description of traditional African rites and symbols offers great potential to the Christian missionary task of communicating the power of the gospel in the African village. That power centers in the cross, in its manifestation of strength and hope in apparent weakness and vulnerability. The communication of the gospel message occurs at various levels or dimensions of village life. It includes, but is not limited to, the verbal proclamation of the gospel in preaching and teaching. Beyond that, we iconoclastic Protestant Christians have been reluctant to go, but we need to spend far more time on matters of worship and liturgy, on rites that address particular needs in the community. Nothing less will truly draw attention to the one in whom all things hold together.

3

You Cannot Build on Rafters: Common Gbaya Meals

A Gbaya proverb asserts that "a house is not built on rafters," that is, from the top down. That obvious but often neglected wisdom applies to Gbaya rites and symbols, which begin with water, word, meals, people, and trees—the most common and fundamental elements of experience in every culture. The sharing and offering of food is a communal event among the Gbaya; their meal rituals build from the most basic, ordinary domestic forms to explicitly symbolic practices.

Gbaya religious experience involves common family activities—not only meals, but also hunting, field work, the rituals that accompany these activities, and storytelling. Gbaya rituals and tales share the same concerns: the quest for food on the hunt or in the fields, and the need to maintain the peace and well-being of family and society. A major character in Gbaya tales is Wanto, who is both a trickster and a culture hero. Wanto's three children are named Papolo, manioc stick; Tikin, manioc stirring stick; and Gong (or Gondo), manioc scoop. As Wanto's character displays an overpowering love of food, he expresses in a lively and unique way a universal concern, yet Wanto also stands for far more than the quest for food among the Gbaya.

The significance of food is illustrated, though not exhausted, by a discussion of common meals, kinship and friendship meals, and meals in offerings and sacrifices. These rituals occur in the process and flow of daily Gbaya living; if they are separated from this context, their symbolic meanings—always difficult for outside observers to discover—may be distorted. Therefore our discussion will avoid being arbitrary and artificial only if we search for and attend to apparently related networks of meaning. The

15

Gbaya who gave these examples to me are certainly the best help in this process, and my use of the "ethnographic present" reflects their own personal experience of the rituals they describe. Their words reveal that sacrifices and washing or purifications are dynamically interrelated and provide in turn the context for understanding initiatory and conciliatory rites.

MEANING AND PROCESS

In common Gbaya meals residential group principles of reciprocity and exchange, in addition to principles that involve collective, cooperating groups of family members, comprise the structural and symbolic axis for the way Gbaya people eat together. Common Gbaya meals consist of a three-part process: washing hands together, eating together, washing hands together. Further, the meanings of many Gbaya symbols are rooted in common meals; such symbols are often associated with preferred foods and the physical properties of these foods.

Kinship and friendship meals are more overtly ritualistic. In them the spoken word is united with gesture and object to disclose "consecrated behavior." The characteristics of common meals are played out and expanded symbolically in kinship and friendship meals—and each time for a specific purpose. The focus in common, everyday meals and in kinship and friendship meals is on the maintenance or restoration of peaceful relationships with living persons in the local community. Kinship and friendship meals, however, suggest that this Gbaya concern for peace is not limited to the safekeeping of interpersonal relationships, but extends to the living-dead, whose continued presence in the community is assumed.

For the Gbaya, to "be" is to "belong" in specific relationships. The three-part common meal (washing, eating, washing) is extended ritually into confession; sharing and offering food; thanking and anointing. Certain components of the common meal (slippery sauce, white manioc flour, water, salt) reappear symbolically in ritual performances; and prized, highly valued objects from everyday life (chickens, eggs, blood) function to cool or propitiate the spirits, and thus to protect life itself. The meals discussed in this chapter will make a significant contribution to our understanding of symbolic meanings associated with *soré*.

DOING THINGS TOGETHER

The Gbaya clearly do not like to eat alone. A Gbaya proverb explains their preference: "If a member of your own family is at the mouth of the honeycomb, you're not going to eat wax!" There is security and well-being in doing things together: "A trickle of water that goes alone goes crookedly!"

Common meals represent the most familiar patterns of reciprocity and exchange in Gbaya society. Adult men and adolescent boys generally eat together during the seasons of the year when they live in the village rather than in the field camp. Married women prepare these meals in loose rotation, helped by their unmarried daughters, and each wife contributes food she has produced with her husband. Women generally eat with their own small children, although small groups of women often share meals together.

One of my students, Ndoyama Enoch, explains that Gbaya do not usually eat *kpasa kam*, a genuine (manioc-centered) meal, at noon. They prefer manioc paste in the morning and especially in the evening, when they gather outside one of their homes. Meal times, however, are not rigidly fixed. The meal groups squat together around common bowls: one bowl for the manioc paste, another for meat or meat sauce, and also a finger bowl. There is a simple, three-part structure to the meal: hands are carefully washed before the meal, the food is eaten together "by hand," and hands are again washed after the meal.

The meat sauce that accompanies manioc paste is often of a strongly seasoned, glutinous, and "slippery" nature, called *woo*, made from the leaves of plants that produce a mucilaginous substance, *gbolo*. This particular kind of sauce facilitates the Gbaya way of eating *kam*: a mouthful of manioc paste dipped in the meat sauce is not chewed but swallowed whole. The Gbaya tend to measure their well-being in terms of the amount of *kam* they eat each day, and a recent study has determined that *kam* contributes 69 percent of the Gbaya's daily caloric consumption. Manioc paste is not very nutritious, but manioc leaves are rich in vitamins and are used in many sauces.

The Gbaya offset the lack of protein in manioc by eating meat as often as possible, which they obtain by trading their surplus manioc supplies to neighboring Fulani pastoralists. Gbaya craving for meat is manifested in an "affliction" they call *bala*: a disgust for all food except meat—especially wild meat—as a suitable accompaniment for the ever present *kam*! A *wi-bali-mo*, a "person hungry for meat," is never content to stay in one place and is never happy to eat mere leaves. Wanto is the Gbaya prototype in this regard. Such a person is always on the move because "the little red duiker who always stays in the same forest will never succeed in getting pregnant!"

"Success" is measured especially in terms of the satisfaction experienced at daily collective meals, which require the regular effort and contributions of all participants. Thus the principle of cooperation is crucial to the production and consumption of Gbaya meals and also contributes to the sense of well-being experienced in the maintenance of successful interpersonal relationships.

The Gbaya way of eating together and their principal foods play a symbolic role in determining their ethnic identity. What is at issue here is the maintenance and ordering of the most basic network of human relationships and interaction. Common Gbaya meals serve to confirm, re-create, and perpetuate life in the community, without which there is no "life," as Gbaya understand it. Nor can there be any sharing of this life if *ḍangséé*, "bad liver" or anger, occurs among participants in the meal group. The common meals that Gbaya eat together are an effective symbol of the reality they call "being with one liver together," that is, being at peace with one another.

THE GIVER DOES NOT EAT THE GIFT

When my wife and I lived in the village of Bounou in 1967, a Gbaya friend from Meiganga brought us a gift of chicken. While our friend visited with me, my wife prepared the chicken and invited him to dinner. But when the meal was ready, he excused himself, saying that he does not eat chicken. Later we learned that it would have been discourteous for a Gbaya to eat the chicken he had offered to friends. Each Gbaya clan has an animal *zim*, or "taboo," which is firmly linked to the Gbaya sense of both personal and clan identity, but chicken is not *zim*. Our friend refused to eat the chicken because the gift of a chicken is a significant sign of Gbaya love and respect. The Gbaya say that if someone gives you a chicken, you will never forget that person.

Another Gbaya proverb relates that "children do not eat chicken with old men." This proverb illustrates the need to distinguish between the various members of society and their relative importance, but it is also rooted in the social and religious symbolism associated with the chicken itself. Ndoyama notes that children in any case do not eat from the same bowl with genuinely important or elderly men, nor may a young married woman eat with her mother-in-law until the proper ritual has been performed to open the way for them to eat together. A Gbaya man may give a chicken to his in-laws or, if they come to visit him, he may kill a chicken and have it prepared for them. But he must not eat that chicken with his in-laws. If they give a chicken to his child (their grandchild), his wife and child eat it, but he may not eat it—at least not in their presence.

Barya Philemon explains that if a woman is sick, or fails to give birth to a child, her father takes a chicken and prepares it for a ritual offering to his own *so-daa*, his deceased fathers. During the sacrificial meal he prays that his daughter's health may be restored. If that woman's husband had eaten his father-in-law's chicken, explains Barya, he would have closed the way for his wife's health to be restored; the chicken has to be available for the *so-daa*. According to Barya, this is why a man refuses to eat with his father-in-law.

As we shall discover in a later chapter, chicken is also the principal food offered to *so-kao* and *so-daa*, that is, to the territorial spirits and the father spirits, the male ancestors. Chicken blood is sprinkled on weapons in preparation for hunting or battle, and chicken is the sacrificial victim in various rites performed by *bé-noko*, the "little uncle/little nephew," whose ritual role is so important among the Gbaya. The chicken itself is not important; that is, it is not set apart as sacred or untouchable. Nevertheless, as a living being and the most common of Gbaya domestic animals, it is a suitable sacrifice.

Our discussion of common meals has already led from their matrix in Gbaya society to their wider symbolic implications in social and religious life. In this process, the significance of manioc paste and chicken has been emphasized both as food and as symbol. There are, however, several other common Gbaya foods and objects that play significant roles in Gbaya rituals.

USES OF WATER

Water is so common that it might easily be overlooked, but the Gbaya know its material and spiritual significance. Water, whether alone or accompanying food, nourishes, cleans, and cools—or it kills. Gbaya women, for example, soak the manioc root in water for three days as part of their preparation for eating it. Later, when the root is chopped up, dried, and pounded into flour, water is added to make paste (or porridge): *kam*.

A traveler through Gbaya villages can usually find a clay water pot resting in the fork of a tree beside the path, from which he or she is welcome to drink. A calabash is close at hand to dip the water.

The village chief keeps a *kpana-zora*, clay water pot (or calabash), designated for various ablutions, on the floor of his house under his bed. The leaves of several trees are kept in this ritual pot, especially *soré* leaves. The water in this pot is never allowed to evaporate, nor must this pot ever come into the light or heat of day. A *kpana-zora* may be used by an *okoo-pi-gangmo* (woman [who] throws peace) for many ablutions, including one in which she washes her vagina over the pot. The water is then used in the preparation of a special meal offered by the chief to his elders, the purpose of which is to assure peace and well-being.

CHICKENS ARE ON THEIR OWN

Chicken is the most common and most important domestic animal kept by the Gbaya, but its own quest for food goes virtually unaided by its keepers! Eggs, either cooked or raw, may be given to guests, but usually they are left in the nest for the purpose of raising more chickens.

During the annual village rite, eggs will be offered to *so-kao*, territorial spirits, and from tales in the oral tradition we learn that when eggs are thrown at a deep river, the river will separate to provide the Gbaya "hero" a passageway to the other side! The Gbaya describe eggs as an excellent, clean food that contains a substance similar to "pure water." That substance is also slippery, like *woo*, the sauce that accompanies *kam*. Eggs resemble smooth, white stones, which are associated with oracular or divinatory powers.

Salt is a highly prized condiment in virtually all Gbaya foods. Whereas chickens or eggs may be given to guests and important authorities, they in turn may offer a bag of salt to the women who prepare their meals. Lutheran church conferences do not conclude successfully until bags of salt have been offered to the village women. Some Gbaya women still make salt and soap from the ashes of bush plants, and salt still plays a role in their noncash barter transactions. Salt may seal a covenant between Gbaya and Fulani pastoralists who enter a special friendship relationship, and it is also an important offering to *so-kao*. Hot pepper is a popular condiment in Gbaya foods, but it is not a common gift among the Gbaya, and it is never used to season food offered to *so-kao*; the territorial spirit "doesn't eat hot pepper"!

Oil (butter or fat) is another Gbaya favorite. The quality of meat is measured in terms of its fat content. Oil is typically made from groundnuts, sesame seeds, or cucumber seeds, and the "butter" produced from these foods is a popular ingredient in meat or vegetable sauces. Oil is another "clean food" in Gbaya eyes, and appears regularly in purification rituals for unctions.

SLIPPERY IS GOOD

Woo, a mucilaginous substance obtained from a variety of cultivated and bush plants, is used consistently in Gbaya meat and vegetable sauces. There is a symbolic link between *woo* and *soré*, the wood of which is soft, moist, and fibrous. An elderly Gbaya, Mbélé Ninga, makes this connection. Referring to the mucilaginous substance between the thin bark (or thick skin) of a *soré* branch and the wood of the tree, Ninga says that bad or dangerous things slip right off the *soré*. This reflection may be a genuine insight of indigenous exegesis, or it may be one of several illusive reasons for the variety of symbolic meanings manifested by *soré* in Gbaya ritual tradition. In any case, *soré* produces one of the most popular edible fruits among common savanna bushes. Its leaves are also used to wrap fresh meat or boiled manioc, because *soré* leaves, say the Gbaya, are strong, clean, and have no odor. Finally, *soré* roots are used by the Gbaya as a medicine for diarrhea and elephantiasis, and I have been told by many Gbaya that *soré* roots are useful medicine for stomach worms.

TOOLS MEAN MUCH

Tools and utensils used by the Gbaya in the production and consumption of food are also important ritual objects. All tools made by a blacksmith for use in the fields or on the hunt—for example, hoes, knives, spears, and arrows—are associated materially and symbolically with *dono*, the blacksmith's anvil and hammers. *Dono* is an object of strength, power, and truth. For example, if an oath is uttered with *dono* in hand (that is, with any of the tools mentioned above), the oath is particularly heavy and the guilty party shall surely suffer hard consequences. If the person uttering the oath is lying, that person will die, say the Gbaya, if he or she does not request a blacksmith to perform the washing, the *dono* purification rite or *zuia-dono*. All tools made by the blacksmith are essential in one way or another for procuring food and the physical and spiritual well-being of persons in the Gbaya community. *Dono* appears to be both a "male" and a "hot" tool and symbol in Gbaya culture.

The *tikin*, manioc stirring stick, plays a role no less fascinating than *dono*, and may be symbolically related to *dono*. The *tikin*, a light bamboo stick about four feet long, is the principal Gbaya kitchen utensil. It is thus a distinctly "female" tool and symbol that can be used symbolically to "cool" people or situations. As it is "strong" and "truthful" like the *dono*, speaking an oath while holding a *tikin* is risky. A respected law in Gbaya society holds that husband and wife must never beat each other with a *tikin* because the victim will be rendered sterile. The Gbaya claim that both *dono* and *tikin* possess a kind of electrical charge — but with a difference: if *dono* is waved aggressively in someone's direction, that person will die, whereas if the same is done with *tikin*, the adversary is merely immobilized or "cooled."

Finally, we can note the significance of the *ḍélé* calabash and the *kpana*, or clay pot, both of which contain food and water. Their importance, unlike *dono* or *tikin*, is not in themselves but in the food or water contained in them and the specific use to which they are put. There are, for example, many types of *kpana*, including *kpana-yi*, in which water is conserved for family washing and cooking purposes; *kpana-kam*, to cook manioc; *kpana-kpoo*, to cook meat; *kpana-nyina*, to prepare and conserve various herbal medicines; and *kpana-goḍo*, to cook the food (reptiles and felines, for example) that is reserved for male members of the family.

The *kpana-zora* can be either a calabash or a clay pot. It is used for ritual baths or ablutions, in which medicinal leaves accompany the water. *Nyina*, medicine, is an inclusive and potentially ambiguous term; it includes traditional Gbaya and modern Western medications for specific illnesses as well as medicines believed to have "spiritual" efficacy — medicines used to protect or to destroy others.

We have seen three aspects of common meals in Gbaya society that have critical implications for Gbaya rituals. First, residential group principles of reciprocity and exchange, as well as principles involving collective, cooperating groups of family members, comprise the structural and symbolic axis for the way Gbaya people eat together. Second, common Gbaya meals consist of a simple three-part process: washing together, eating together, washing together. Third, for the Gbaya, symbolic meanings are usually though not always associated with eating ordinary, preferred foods or using the physical properties of these foods or both. Among the Gbaya, the meaning of many key symbols is rooted in common meals, as is the structure of many key rituals.

KINSHIP AND FRIENDSHIP MEALS

Our reflection on common Gbaya meals must be enlarged to include meals that are set apart for special occasions. Kinship and friendship meals reveal "consecrated behavior"; that is, they unite words with gestures and actions. These meals enable the Gbaya to establish new households, to cover fires, to end quarrels and to make covenants. I am indebted to many Gbaya friends for these and other descriptions of kinship and friendship meals, but especially to my student Haman Matthieu and his friends.

A. Nyongmo-ke-tua, *Meals to Set Apart a House*

When a young man takes a wife, the couple often resides with his parents until he has completed the construction of their new house. When that house is ready for occupancy, the father *ke tua ha wa*, sets apart a separate house for them. A younger brother of the groom is sent early one morning to the bush to break three termite nests and bring them into his elder brother's new house, to whom he explains, "Here are the termitaries for your hearth!"

The bride is not immediately informed of the proceedings, but soon thereafter the young man's mother sets about preparing a feast. When the meal is ready, she carries it to the new house and informs the couple, "Here's your *nyongmo-ke-tua* that I've prepared for you! This is your own house! From now on you no longer stay with me!"

This meal is shared with other members of the residential group, and invitations are also extended to a wider family circle; only the young couple does not eat any of this meal. After the guests have eaten, they offer gifts to the bride and groom: calabashes, various types of clay pots and other kitchen utensils for the bride; spears, machetes, knives, arrows and hoes for the groom. These gifts bear a meaning; from now on, this young man and his wife must no longer depend on their parents for all these needs; now they must contribute their part to the well-being of the family. The groom's father reminds him of their new responsibilities by quoting a Gbaya proverb, "The little bush cow who is separated from his mother no longer runs around playing as before!"

B. Nyongmo-kpé-wéé, *Meals to Cover the Fire*

In the evening of the same day that *nyongmo-ke-tua* is celebrated, the young wife prepares a meal over her new hearth for the first time and brings it to her in-laws. They gather the family together once again to share in *nyongmo-kpé-wéé*, the meal (that) covers the fire. This meal represents the consecration of the new hearth, which is accomplished by offering the "first fruits" of the hearth to other members of the family. It is another sign of family union and well-being.

C. Nyongmo-yi, *Meals in Each Other's Eyes*

The young married woman may not eat together with her mother-in-law until she has prepared *nyongmo-yi*, a meal that opens the way for them to eat together. This meal does not occur until after the young woman has given birth to her first child. Then she goes to her own father and tells him, "I want to eat together with my mother-in-law!" He procures all that is needed for a fine meal, and she prepares it with great care.

When the meal is ready, the young woman takes it to her mother-in-law and offers it to her, together with the pots and bowls containing the food. The young woman says, "Here's *nyongmo-yi* that I've prepared for you! I'd like to eat together with you from now on!" Although she does not eat any of this particular meal with her mother-in-law, the way is now open to share their future meals together. Her mother-in-law invites her family to eat this meal with her. *Nyongmo-yi* establishes a firmer bond between the two families united in marriage.

D. Nyongmo-kpé-wén, *Meals to End Words*

When a young bride prepares the family meal, it may happen one day that she fails to pay sufficient attention to the pot in which the meat is cooking, and the meat burns to a crisp! She must then go to her own father and tell him, "I'm in trouble with my in-laws about food! My father-in-law's meat burned up as I was cooking it! Please help me to end the quarrel!"

Her family then procures a fine portion of meat, for example, cane rat, red duiker, or fish. Sometimes they may even buy beef! The young woman takes this meat back to her house and prepares a feast. She garnishes the meat with cucumber seeds, pours oil over the seeds, and puts the dish on hot coals. She then prepares an enormous ball of *kam*, and carries the food to her father-in-law, saying to him, "I angered you when I burned your meat! I hereby offer you this food to end the quarrel between us!" Her father-in-law assembles the children, adults and old women to share the meal together. This meal restores peace in the family.

E. Nyongmo-hii, *Communal Labor Bee*

Once in every season, when a Gbaya has much work to do in his field, he is entitled to organize a *nyongmo-hii*, a communal work bee. First he prepares for the *hii* by procuring large quantities of meat, while his wife prepares manioc flour and beer. Then, when they have sufficient food supplies, the man goes around the village inviting his friends and their families, including adolescent girls: "Early in the morning, come help me in my fields!"

In the morning the group leaves together for his fields, carrying the supplies for the meal. On the way they sing, "Let's work eeeee! Then we'll eat eeeee!" The Gbaya say that singing together as they work improves their health and good spirits. They sing, "Foods do not refuse each other!" One must not refuse aid to another or fail to share within the community.

When the sun is high and everyone is exhausted, the owner of the field halts the work and tells everyone to get ready to eat, saying: "Many thanks for all the work you've done for me! Now we're all hungry! Let's replace work with food and then go home! The food we've prepared for you is really nothing compared to your work and the love you've demonstrated for us! Isn't it great to work together like this! As our fathers say, 'It takes more than a single blade of grass to sweep the house!' "

No one is obliged to help with a communal labor bee, but if a man's closest family members (agnates) do not attend, their relationships will suffer. The *hii* illustrates that Gbaya principles of collective activity are arranged on an ad hoc basis. The principles are loose, contingent and fluid, yet certain to be applied within commonly acknowledged boundaries. In the *hii* and in the following two meals, participants extend beyond residential group limits.

F. Nyongmo-kendao, *the Last or Farewell Meal*

The Gbaya term *kendao* refers to the activities of a person who is about to undertake a final journey, or before a person's imminent death. In the case of someone leaving the village, a man will request his friends and family to prepare *nyongmo-kendao* for him with no hard feelings about his departure. If there is no time to prepare a feast, his friends may give him clothes, money, or some personal "treasure."

Nyongmo-kendao is associated particularly with the approaching death of an old man. He calls his children together, saying, "I've lost all my strength! Let me eat my last meal with you, because I'm just waiting to die now!" His children look for something good to eat, prepare it for him, and all eat together from one bowl. The old man then greets each of his children and gives them his blessing, "When you eat together again, remember me!" Before he dies, he gives them some medicines he has found useful, or entrusts certain purification rites to them, explaining their meaning and all the interdictions involved in their practice, so that they will preside over these rites in the appropriate way.

Gbaya colleagues explain *nyongmo-kendao* as a touching and sorrowful occasion and as a meal of gladness, unity, and love. The meal witnesses that quarrels have not separated the participants; it serves to strengthen the relationships between the survivors and also marks their continued consciousness of the deceased, who remains "spiritually" in their midst.

G. Noa-tok, *Drinking Blood, or Covenant Meals*

"Covenant meals" are shared in a context of social conflict and resolution. Their purpose is not to fill one's stomach but to effect reconciliation. Among the Gbaya, for example, the act of splitting a hooked stick apart at the joint symbolizes the restoration of peace between enemies because the hook can no longer function. An elder from each warring faction grasps the hook handle, one of whom may say, "An end to fighting and revenge between us! Let's eat together again! Let's change our ways!" The two men then rip apart the hook and exchange greetings, and *noa-tok*, drink blood, together. They cut their forearms so that blood flows, then dip a piece of manioc root into each other's blood and eat it as a covenant meal together.

In another rite of reconciliation, an elder of a neutral village calls together representatives from two warring villages. He throws a *soré* branch on the ground between them, exhorting them not to "jump over *soré*," that is, not to ignore the covenant of peace thereby established. This covenant, also referred to as *noa-tok*, although blood is not directly involved, is then sealed by a common meal together.

In the *laḅi* rites of initiation for adolescent boys, each boy is marked by a cut on his stomach, into which the boys dip a piece of manioc root and each eats his own blood in covenant with fellow initiates (two close friends may also eat each other's blood). This "meal" symbolizes that *laḅi* secrets will never be revealed to the uninitiated. Further examples of the *noa-tok*, the drinking of blood in covenant agreement, will appear in subsequent chapters.

H. Nyonga-zoḅo, *Eating Zoḅo Leaves*

Zoḅo leaves are *gbolo*, a term applied to any plant leaves that serve as a vegetable or produce *woo*. *Zoḅo* leaves are a fundamental component of the network of symbolism associated with *soré*. For example, *zoḅo* is cooked "ritually," out in the open, not over a hearth inside a house; and the pot in which *zoḅo* is cooked is supported on three *soré* sticks under which a fire is kindled. *Zoḅo* is not eaten "to fill the stomach," says Haman Matthieu, but is a matter of *do-mo*. It is a symbolic or "consecrated" gesture that has a deeper, ritual meaning than the consumption of ordinary food.

The eating of *zoḅo* in the course of purification and initiation rites symbolizes covenant unity between the participants. As Haman explains, "It means that all sins have died," and that the problems threatening the well-being of the community have been cooled. Its meaning, however, is not limited to the safekeeping of interpersonal relationships; *zoḅo* can also be used to improve relationships with the spirits.

With the exception of some covenant meals, the meals described thus far consist of *kam*, manioc paste (even the exceptions involve manioc root), and meat in a slippery sauce, *woo*. The meals, especially kinship and friendship meals, are symbolic, but they also satisfy physical hunger and nutritional needs. Gbaya spiritual relationships are, however, closely linked to the practical Gbaya concerns for a full stomach and full peace with family and friends in community.

To put this matter another way: our study of Gbaya meals reveals that the material concerns of their everyday life have an inherently spiritual or transcendent dimension. The Gbaya spiritual realm is transcendent, that is, invisible; but it is not unrelated to life. In the next chapter we shall discover whether or not the spiritual realm can be said to contain a practical or "earthly" dimension of meaning.

4

Meal-Oriented Rituals and Sacrifices

RITUAL BEHAVIOR AND DAILY EXPERIENCE

The interpretation of ritual symbols requires an understanding of the daily experience that underlies ritual behavior. In the following paragraphs I shall continue my investigation of meals as communal events among the Gbaya. Only now I shall attempt to integrate a variety of ritually oriented Gbaya experiences, all of which involve the quest for food, and most of which involve a concern about the role of *so*, or "spirits," in that quest. That is, the meals related in this chapter are not daily occurrences but occasional or seasonal rituals oriented to offerings and sacrifice. They are a way to make the extraordinary or highly charged experiences of life nonthreatening.

The person who officiates in the performance of a Gbaya rite is first an initiate of the rite who is then specifically entrusted with its performance. Hunters, for example, regularly consult a *wan-ngala*, a diviner or seer, in order to determine how best to proceed in a given situation. Whenever possible, I shall use the Gbaya term to designate these ritual specialists because no single English term is adequate for all cases. Though I shall also use the words "priest" and "priestess" in this connection, the Gbaya have no such elaborate institutions. Indeed they have no traditional clergy, though the persons I so designate do serve as representatives of the community in ritual functions.

We should not underestimate the symbolic complexities of Gbaya ritual, but in keeping with the Gbaya way of life, their ritual "travels light"—that is, with a minimum of paraphernalia, and whatever paraphernalia we do find is part of the ordinary "stuff of life." Nevertheless, some general observations can be made concerning the Gbaya worldview.

As we have already discovered, the Gbaya live within two distinct areas, in the village and in the bush. In fact, there is no "neutral" or "meaningless" space for the Gbaya, nor are there meaningless plants, animals, or people. Gbaya ritual practices are associated with specific places, creatures, plants, objects, and times in the natural world and, in many cases, Gbaya rites also reveal, or at least suggest, the world of *so*, or spirits, and the relations between the Gbaya and the spirits.

So, the Gbaya term for "spirit," is ambiguous. The verbal distinctions common in the English language—for example, we distinguish "God" from "the gods" and both of these from other kinds of "spirits"—are not always made by the Gbaya. Not only is the term *so* itself conceptually unclear, indeed mysterious; it is also true that my Gbaya informants live in a Christian milieu. Their ideas about the spiritual world must inevitably bear a Christian character or influence.

Experience is the best guide to the interpretation of the Gbaya spiritual world, but the identity of the *so* is easier to determine when the term itself is qualified; that is, when it appears as part of a compound word, as in the following examples: *so-daa*, soul or spirit of the father (ancestor); *so-naa*, soul or spirit of the mother; *so-dan*, spirit of twins; *so-fio*, spirit of death or of the dead (again, a term for ancestors); *so-labi*, spirit of the male initiation rite; *so-doo-yi*, spirit in (or under) the water; *so-gun-té*, spirit at the foot of a tree; *so-kao*, territorial spirit; *so-salala*, *so-sirta*, *so-gia*, spirit of the hunt (again, a reference to territorial spirits); and *so-é-wi*, creator god.

The term *so-é-wi* is more positive today than it formerly was, influenced, perhaps, by the Christian message. To this list can be added the term *Gba-so*, which refers to a great spirit or creator god, a mythical character who appears in contemporary Gbaya tales as Wanto's adversary, but who may have merged in oral tradition with *Gba-nyong-wi*, the great man-eater.

Finally, we may note the term *dan-te-wi*, which means literally the "friend of a person's body," or the "soul" of a living person. When a person dies, the *dan-te-wi* becomes the *so-te-wi*, the "soul or spirit of a person's body," which is later transformed into the *so-daa* or *so-naa*, the spirit of one's father or mother.

A. Dafa-so-daa/Wora-so-daa, *Sacrificing to or Speaking with the Ancestors*

The Gbaya quest for food involves the sharing of ritual foods within several levels of human and spiritual relationships. Ordinary, everyday concerns of the Gbaya community are traditionally expressed in rites of communication with the ancestors, with the "dead who are not dead." Whereas *so-kao*, the territorial spirits, are thought to be present in the savanna bush, the most recent generations of the ancestral spirits are thought to be present in, or explicitly associated with, the other main part of the natural world, the *saayé*, or village. In terms of simple visibility and everyday accessibility, the *so-daa* are closer to the Gbaya community than the *so-kao*, and consequently their rites are more frequently practiced.

The *so-daa* shrine is located at the right side of a Gbaya house, that is, if the owner of that house is a man whose father has died. The shrine is on the right side, say the Gbaya, because "the ancestors are not wicked or unprincipled." The right side is "proper" and "strong"; the left side is "improper" and "weak." The ancestors are, literally, not "left-sided."

The *so-daa* shrine is surrounded by a grass or bamboo-leaf enclosure to keep it clean and free of debris. The entry to it is never closed, since there is nothing secret here. The *so-daa* are not at all like *ginaazi*, the demons or devils who do evil things to people. Inside the enclosures three termitaries form the fireplace in which sacrificial food is cooked. After food is cooked, a part of it is offered to *so-daa*; another part is consumed by the priest, and the remaining food is stored in the sacrificial pot in which it was cooked. This pot is used only for *so-daa* sacrifices. It is placed in a forked branch that has been planted in the ground beside the termitaries. A water pot is brought from the house for washing hands before and after the meal, but there are no interdictions regarding its use.

The man's wife and children may freely enter this area to sweep it, but they may not touch any food prepared for *so-daa*. During the actual performance of the rite, women and children remain in the house or at a distance outside. The priest is usually alone, but if he has a younger brother whose importance is equal to his own, that brother may also eat the sacrificial meal with him.

The sacrifice itself proceeds in the following manner. A man whose father has died may hear his father speaking to him in a dream, or a particular family need may occasion this communication with the ancestors. The man chooses a chicken, preferably a large, white rooster, although the color is of secondary importance. Above all, the rooster must be strong and healthy.

The priest ties its legs together and approaches the termitaries, where he kindles a fire. Then he washes the sacrificial pot, fills it with water, and places it on the fire. Next he unties the rooster's feet; he spits, *"touffee!"* (ideophone for a blessing via spittle) on the chicken as a sign of blessing, then prays or speaks to his fathers: *"So-daa*, spirit of [my] father, *so-zom-daa*, spirit of [my] grandfather, I kill this rooster for you in order that you may give us food! Take away our problems! Give me strength and health, give strength to my children and wives! Help us find food, and chase away all hardships!"

Holding the rooster's feet, the man hits its head on the termitaries to kill it and drips its blood over the termitaries, the wood, and the ground around the fireplace. He proceeds deliberately; it would be inappropriate to rush through this ritual. He removes the rooster's feathers and separates its carcass into pieces, but he is careful not to break any bones. The bones are never broken in the *so-daa* rite, as a protective measure to assure sound bodies in the priest's family.

When he puts the rooster in the pot, the priest adds salt and sesame oil or butter, but no hot pepper. No vegetables or leaves are ever cooked for the *so-daa* sacrifice. No other objects are presented to the *so-daa*, such as hunting weapons or sticks symbolizing spears, nor are raw eggs offered. The priest's wife brings a bowl of *kam*, over which she has poured fine sesame oil. When the food is ready to eat, the priest takes *kam*, dips it once into the meat sauce to find the gizzard for *so-daa*, then throws the meat and manioc on the ground, praying:

> "Father, Grandfather, the offering others have made before me, I make my own offering after them! Bless us and keep sickness away from us! Protect me on the hunt! Bless my wives, my children and my fields!"

Then he eats the rest of the chicken, washes his hands and the pot beside the territaries, and the sacrifice is over. If food remains in the pot, he places it in the forked branch and returns to eat it later in the day.

Occasionally fish, goat, or wild meat is used for the *so-daa* sacrifice, but very rarely are sheep or cattle used. Eggs are sometimes cooked and eaten as part of this rite; honey and beer may also be offered. Some informants say that if a portion of the meal remains, it may be poured out over the territaries, but it must not be carried away from the shrine to be eaten or disposed of elsewhere.

As we shall discover shortly, rituals celebrated explicitly to ensure success on hunting or fishing expeditions solicit help primarily from the *so-kao*, the spirits into whose territory the hunters and fishers will venture on their quest for food. The following example illustrates, however, that adequate communication with the *so-daa* is also essential to assure a successful hunt.

If a man has been setting traps in vain for several days, he might return to his village one evening and find an old dried-out animal skin from which he cuts a small piece. He then goes to the back of his house to kindle a fire. (This is not done at the *so-daa* shrine, nor does the hunter require territaries, because no meal is prepared in this rite.) He kneels down by the fire and burns the animal skin, calling out the names of his deceased father and grandfather:

> "Bouba, Adamou, here I am before you this evening! I don't have anything to eat! I've hunted and killed no animals! The only thing I have left to eat with my *kam* is this dried-out old animal skin, so I

burn it here before you as a witness! Grant me an animal! Grant me success on the hunt!"

As he blows on the fire, the smoke from that skin blows all over the back of the house, until at last it reaches the spirits of his fathers. My students explain that if the hunter has performed this rite happily, with no hard feelings and with the honorable intentions of a pure heart, his fathers are sure to grant his request!

The importance of maintaining a wholesome relationship with *so-daa* is more clearly documented in Gbaya ritual than is the relationship with *so-naa*, spirits of the mothers. My students observe, however, that a *so-naa* ritual does exist. It involves the offering of a small animal (for example, a field mouse), which the woman catches and offers to her *so-naa*. (We may note that mice are often hunted by women and children and roasted for food. Thus the offering of a mouse to *so-naa* does not constitute a comic offering!) The prominence of the *so-daa* rite is probably associated with the patrilocality of Gbaya residence patterns. Because a woman follows her husband, her "space" and that of her ancestors is less clearly defined than her husband's. On the other hand, ancestors evidently participate in Gbaya mobility, because wherever a man moves and builds a house, there he may communicate with his ancestors. We must presume the same for his wife.

Gbaya ancestral sacrifices participate in the quest for food, again within the context of peaceful family and community relations. The Gbaya live in an extended community that includes the ancestors, the "dead who are not dead." The sheer possibility and condition for finding food and sharing it together rest on the maintenance of peace within the community. No part of the interpersonal nexus of relationships, whether "visible" or "invisible," may be violated or neglected. Ancestral sacrifice is a crucial part of peace-keeping in traditional Gbaya villages.

The following ritual offerings and sacrifices acknowledge the importance of the spirits' role in such daily activities as hunting, farming and fishing. These rites refer less to ancestors than to territorial spirits, though the former are not forgotten.

B. Bura War Gia, *Opening up the Way to Hunt*

When Gbaya men go hunting, they must be sure that family relationships are in order, that everyone is at peace with everyone else. If, for example, a bad quarrel has caused anger among family members, the father will kill a chicken so that its blood can cool things between the family and *so*. He kills the chicken in the house, spilling its blood on the floor and adding sesame oil to the blood. Then he takes a *soré* branch, dips it in the blood and oil, and anoints all the angry members of the family. My informants refer to this rite as a "peace offering."

Immediately before a hunt, a hunter from each family will kill a chicken and spill its blood over all the weapons. The blood cools the danger that threatens the hunters, thus clearing the way for the hunt. Chicken blood on the weapons is a guard against the animals' horns, lest a hunter be gored.

After some days on an unsuccessful hunt, the hunters may choose one of their party as a *wan gia,* or chief of the hunt. This one must be calm, easygoing, and not quick to anger. He is asked to take charge of a new hunt. Early in the morning the hunters bundle up their belongings, as though to return home. But just as they are about to leave the camp, the *wan gia* cuts them off, saying, "Come on back! I've found a new hunt!" Then he collects a blade of grass from each bush hut and dirt from a little hole that he digs in the midst of the camp. He takes the grass and dirt to the back of the camp and throws them away in the bush; next, he cuts new grass and digs a new hole to replace the old one, declaring, "Here's my new village that I'm making right here!"

That same evening the *wan gia* looks for a place to address the territorial spirit in the *so-kao* rite. He finds a *kolo* or *gété* tree and places all their weapons at the foot of the tree before *so-kao.* Then he invokes the spirits, offering them salt, dried manioc, and tobacco. He says, "I offer you all these things one hundred times over! Grant us something to eat! Grant us good luck on the hunt!"

Then all the hunters gather with the *wan gia* to perform the *zanga-nu* rite before the *so-kao.* In this purification rite, they wash their "hearts" (literally, their "livers") before the *so-kao;* that is, they confess their sins. The *wan gia* fills a small calabash with water and adds manioc flour to make it white. This mixture, called *zeze,* is a reminder to *so-kao,* as if to tell the spirit, "I need this, and there is no sin separating me from you!" The mixture witnesses to the peace already existing between the people and *so-kao.* The hunters stand in a circle together, holding the calabash of *zeze* and speaking these words: "We wash away our anger—the anger we expressed when we said we would abandon this hunt and return home! We wash it away right here before you! Grant us animals on the hunt!" The *wan gia* then pours the *zeze* on the ground before the *so-kao.*

Early the following morning the hunt begins and, if it is successful, the *wan gia* takes the raw liver of their prey to *so-kao,* saying: "Here is your part! Eat your part first, then we'll eat ours! Now grant us another animal, still bigger than this one!" When the Gbaya offer the first portion of an animal or the first fruits of harvest to *so-kao,* or to the ancestral spirits, they call this rite *ngmara-zu-mo,* offering the first part, but they also call it the *koya-saḍi.* The term *koya* may refer to rites performed especially to obtain a favor from the spirits; when *saḍi,* the word for "animal," is joined to *koya,* the rite is a thank-offering for present success and a petition for future successful hunts.

C. Dee Baza, *Building a Fishing Dam*

The Gbaya prepare seriously not only for the hunt but also for fishing, for example, when they build a *baza,* or fishing dam, across a stream. In the evening before construction of the dam, offerings are made to *so-kao*. Early the next morning, the "priest" (the person in charge of the *baza* preparations) fells a tree that was tall enough to extend across the stream. He removes the bark from the tree and stores it in a safe place. He also cuts a small hook from the *ḍéré* tree and a branch from the *soré*, and places these together on the bank, declaring, "I've got my own *baza* today, and I put this hook right here as witness! This is my father's water where we're building our dam! I put *soré* here to cool us as we build the dam and to cool things under the water as well."

The villagers work all day to build the dam. In the evening, the priest places an egg next to the dam for *so-ḍoo-yi*, the spirits in the water. The egg is food for *so-ḍoo-yi*: it requests them not to become angry and break the dam. In the morning the dam is checked and all fish killed that day are prepared and eaten next to the dam. Not one fish bone is allowed to fall to the ground. The priest carefully collects all the bones and puts them with the bark of the tall tree. Next he cuts a *nyak-bé-deme*, a tough little vine, and gathers *ganaguna* and *yekele* leaves. He puts all of these things together as his medicine, goes to the opposite bank, and begins to wash the medicine in the water all along the dam, declaring as he moves along, "This is our own real *baza* that we built, and I hereby wash it!" He also names several kinds of fish, saying, "May these fish be trapped by our dam!" Each participant in the construction of the dam has an area of several meters width, and all fish caught by a fisherman in his own area belong to him. After the priest washes his medicine in each place, including his own, each person is free to collect the fish in his place, the fruits of his labor.

D. Ngmara-zu-nyono, *Offering First Fruits of the Harvest*

When Gbaya farmers are ready to gather the harvest from a new corn or manioc field that has never before yielded food, they take special care with the first fruits. For example, a farmer might fill a big basket with corn and bring it to his father, saying, "Father, here are the first fruits of my cornfield, which I've brought for you to eat! Give *so-daa*, the spirit of [your] father, his part so that I may eat mine, too!"

The farmer's father takes a little corn and water and pounds it into flour. He stirs this *zeze* and takes it out to the right side of his house, which, as we have seen, is the usual place for sacrifices to *so-daa*. As he pours *zeze* over the *so-daa* shrine of three termite nests, he prays:

"Father, look at my child's corn, which he was able to produce because you gave him health and strength. The corn grew well, and he brought your part to me so I can offer it to you! I hereby give you your part! Here it is!"

When he is again inside the house, his family roasts an ear of corn for him. Since the ancestors have received their part, the father can now eat his, and the way is also clear for the young farmer to eat his.

If the harvest in question is not the product of a new field, the farmer waits until the corn is ripe, then he gathers and cooks *soya* leaves and prepares *kam*, manioc porridge, which he takes to his elder brother, asking him to offer it to *so-kao* on his behalf. If he has no elder brother, he may take it himself to the *so-kao* shrine, sit on the ground there and pray: "Here are the first fruits of my harvest which I bring to you!" He dips *kam* into the sauce twice, each time offering it to *so-kao*, but the third time, he eats it himself.

E. Ḍafa-so-kao/Wora-so-kao, *Sacrificing to or Speaking with Territorial Spirits*

Rituals performed to clear the way for the hunt have already shown the importance of *so-kao* for the Gbaya. Such rites are performed from time to time as the need arises—chiefly for the benefit of individuals or small groups of hunters engaging in the quest for food. The final series of rites in this chapter clusters around the annual *so-kao* rite and involves the participation of an entire village. The annual *so-kao* rite is an important Gbaya sacrifice for two reasons. First, it pulls all the residential groupings together in the closest example of village-wide "corporate activity" observable in "traditional" Gbaya society. Second, Gbaya mobility is related to the maintenance of peaceful relationships with the *so-kao*.

Wan-wor-kao, the priest of *kao*, is always a senior man of the founding clan, ideally the eldest son of a revered founder of the village. In addition to the kinship qualification, the priest must also be a *ga-wi*, a "cool," peaceful fellow not easily inclined to anger or disruptive behavior, and he must be capable of expressing his thoughts clearly. As the eldest son of a village founder-ancestor, the *wan-wor-kao* also communicates with that founder-ancestor in the *so-daa* rite. Indeed his prayer to *so-kao* may include reference to the founder through an address not unlike the biblical formula, "O God of Abraham, Isaac and Jacob. . . ." For example, a *so-kao* priest in the village of Illa begins his prayer, "Kao of Doofuu," Doofuu having been a founder of that village.

The Gbaya preference for a close kinship tie between the *so-kao* priest and the village's most revered *so-daa* implies a hierarchical chain of relationships, which Gbaya ritual tradition functions to protect. The living, the living-dead, and the territorial spirits are "actors" in the hierarchy; a "creator god" is absent from it.

We have no examples of Gbaya rituals involving a specific sacrificial relationship with a "creator god," though the "existence" of such a god is assumed by the Gbaya. Some Gbaya may see such a god as the ultimate hearer of their prayers, and ideas associated with the annual *so-kao* rite may be larger than the term "territorial spirit" would suggest. Indeed the *so-kao* rite is important precisely because of the prominence of these spirits in the Gbaya spiritual hierarchy. The territorial spirits have many names and are intimately related to many Gbaya activities.

The annual *so-kao* rite is performed at the beginning of the dry season, usually in December. The choice of this particular time corresponds to the preparation of the savanna grasslands for hunting: the Gbaya burn off the grasslands, a procedure that is itself a kind of annual ritual.

My informants emphasize that the *so-kao* rite cannot take place until the need is revealed to the priest in a dream by *so-kao*. Or the *okoo-pi-gangmo*, the woman who throws peace, may dream about it and reveal the dream's message to the priest, who in turn informs the other villagers. The phenomenon of Gbaya dreams relates to both the *so-daa* and the *so-kao* rites as a possible precondition for their performance, and thus leads us still closer to the "spiritual realm" and Gbaya "spirituality." My Gbaya students and friends witness to *mbanga-te-mo*, reminders mediated in dreams to Gbaya priests (or other important old people in the community), telling them to perform ritual actions. These "reminders" represent the initial step in a ritual process of relationships involving living persons and self-communicating spirits. Thus the Gbaya suggest that the process of some rituals begins, not with the performers of the rites, but with the initiative taken by the spirits to whom the rites are addressed.

Peaceful relationships among the villagers must be assured before the *so-kao* rite can be performed. To assure that no hard words are disrupting village harmony, the *wanyé*, or chief, may be asked to lead representatives of the village in the *zanga-nu* rite, one example of which was described above in connection with preparations for a hunting expedition. *Too-zanga-nu*, literally, "speaking the quarrel," means confessing the hard words expressed during a quarrel, including the utterance of a curse. In Gbaya tradition confession is basic for the maintenance of peace and a sense of well-being in human and spiritual relationships. Verbal confession is typically accompanied by key ritual gestures and objects, including in this case the *soré* leaves.

The chief assembles representatives from village residential groups early in the morning. When all have arrived, the chief pours water on the ground in front of his house. Leaves of the *bun* and *soré* trees are thrown on the water, and everyone takes hold together of a single *tikin*, that is, a manioc stirring stick. As they pound the stick on the mud and leaves, the chief and others confess any hard words they may have said and so express their desire to reestablish peaceful relationships. Each one is anointed with mud from the *tikin*, and the chief spits *"toufee"* (ideophone for a blessing received via spittle) in the direction of the company. (The "spitting" is more a ritual gesture than an actual sending of spittle.) All make the gesture of washing their mouths before pouring the remainder of the water over the pounded leaves and mud. Thus ends *too-zanga-nu*, as peace is reestablished in the community.

When the preliminary measures have been accomplished, the *so-kao* rite itself may be performed. This may occur in the late afternoon, but first the sacrificial "shrine" must be cleared of debris. The same site, usually at the foot of a large tree, rock, or hill several hundred meters from the village, is chosen year after year. My informants emphasize that the *so-kao* rite is always performed in the open savanna, never in the gallery forest. The path leading to the shrine is swept clean and the tall grasses around it are cut down. No instances of shouting, disturbing, or aggressive behavior are permitted near the shrine. In contrast to the *so-daa* shrine, the site is not enclosed and there is no fireplace because meals are not cooked here.

The villagers "fix themselves up" for the rite, and a silent procession is formed; the priest leads, followed by the drummers, the chief, and all the villagers, including women and children. They bear offerings consisting of sticks (representing hunters' spears), corn and especially manioc flour, one or two raw or boiled eggs, sesame and peanut oil or butter, tobacco, salt, and a large, healthy rooster. Someone also carries wood for the sacrifice. This must be a hard, dry wood such as *ngo-gbakua*; it must produce a good, clean fire, because only the best objects are sacrificed. When the procession arrives at the site, the priest removes his clothes, receives the people's gifts, and places them carefully on the ground before *so-kao*.

The people sit silently on the ground, some twenty meters behind the priest, as he prepares the sacrifice. He places three short *gbakua* sticks on the ground in the form of a triangle. The bark has been removed from these sticks, and each stick is tricolored: red, made with oil mixed in powder from the *kui* tree; black, from charcoal; and white, from kaolin powder. The hunters' "spears" are laid across these sticks. The priest makes *zeze* with manioc flour and sprinkles it liberally over the foot of the tree and over the shrine area. He may prepare a fire to cook eggs and *kam* before spreading this food on large leaves found at the shrine.

Or, the priest may select a large rooster as the most appropriate offering for the annual *so-kao* rite. He kills the rooster by hitting its head with a piece of firewood and spills its blood on the firewood and over the shrine area. The rooster's feathers are not removed, but its viscera are, and it is thoroughly cleaned. The priest then kindles a fire and roasts the whole rooster over the fire until it has a pleasing odor. The priest does not eat any of this meat, however, or any other part of the offering; the roasted chicken is placed on the ground with the other offerings, all for *so-kao*.

Doko Kela explains that if the offering consists of an egg instead of a chicken, the egg may first be passed from hand to hand so that every man present may touch it. The chief is the last to take the egg in his hand, and he declares, "This village was my father's before me, and I came to live here too! Now we need food, so I bring this gift to you, *Kao* of Doofuu!" The priest carefully places the egg on the ground with the other gifts.

Whether the offering consists of eggs or a sacrificial chicken, the climax of the *so-kao* rite is the priest's prayer. The priest lies on the ground and softly "claps" his hands in supplication as he prays:

Gba-wan, Great One! I come before you on behalf of my village! *Kao* of Doofuu, we are just termites of the earth! Your children collected their spears so that I could *si-ne-mo-h'ene-oi-nu-wa*, "honor you in their place"! I offer all their gifts to you and implore you to listen to our requests! Send peace to our village! Take away death and sickness! Give us food and bless our crops! Let our wives give birth to many children! Protect us on the hunt! Accept these spears and this food one hundred times over! Here are your eggs which we offer you, because your food is clean food! Tobacco, salt, corn, and manioc — here they are for you! Grant us all these things in return, one hundred times over! I implore you, give us peace! *So-kao*, if you are really here listening to us, then agree to our prayer!

The priest blows three times on a whistle made from the horn of an antelope, to which the people respond, *"Tiiiii!,"* "Yes, yes!" He blows it as loudly as possible, because if it fails to produce a loud blast, it is thought that *so-kao* has refused to accept the sacrifice. But when it resonates loud and clear, the people respond happily and compliment the priest, "He's a real child of *so*[-*kao*]!" The priest puts on his clothes, the drums beat, and the people return to the village. Women lead the procession home, ululating and dancing. No one looks back toward the shrine.

When they have arrived at their homes and all fires have been extinguished throughout the village, the priest kindles a new fire in front of the chief's house, and people from each household come to take fire from his hand, as new light fills the village. The priest may also pull up fresh shoots of grass from the nearby bush, and insert them over the threshold of every home in the village. There is no immediate feasting, and the remainder of the day is set aside for rest. People are advised not to work in their fields.

The food left at the *so-kao* shrine is not touched by anyone once it has been offered. The priest may return to the shrine later in the day, or the next morning, to discover that no food remains there. He knows, explain my informants, that *so-kao* has "eaten" the food. On his way back to the village he may then find a dead animal on the path, which he takes as a gift from *so-kao*, and as confirmation that *so-kao* has accepted the village's sacrifice. As regards maintenance of the *so-kao* shrine itself in the weeks and months that follow, anyone may walk freely by the place at any time, but no one should shout or speak loudly there, nor should any trees be cut down in that immediate area.

After the *so-kao* rite, the villagers wait, making sure that everything in the village is peaceful and that no one is sick or quarreling. Then, if all is well, a week or two later the communal hunt is prepared. A chicken is killed in each family and its blood sprinkled on the weapons. The chicken is cooked, and the man who killed it eats it in the company of his own blood brothers in the same maternal line. No one else — not their own sons or their hunting friends — may eat with them, as each family prepares for the hunt in the same way. The heads of each family also perform the *so-daa* rite at this time, since the ancestors can also grant strength and success to the hunters and their families.

We may compare the basic structure of the hunt to the structure of a Gbaya meal, which begins by washing hands, continues through the sharing of food, and concludes with another handwashing. The Gbaya hunt cannot proceed until the way has been made "clear" or "clean" by means of water (washing) or blood (sacrifice). Just so, the appropriate way to conclude the hunt also involves water and blood. For example, whoever kills an animal on the communal hunt following the *so-kao* rite must bring a portion of that animal (e.g., liver or heart) to the priest, who takes it to the *so-kao* shrine. He thanks *so-kao*, leaves the meat and returns home. My students refer to this second offering as an offering of the first fruits of the hunt, a thank-offering to *so-kao* that opens the way for further success in the ongoing quest for food.

CONCLUSION

The meal-oriented rituals described in this chapter illustrate (but by no means exhaust) the wide range of Gbaya symbols, which I was privileged to discover inductively in conversation with Gbaya interpreters and through experience. I have presented them here with somewhat more order than they had in my experience, if only to show that a knowledge of the Gbaya people and their symbolic world depends on the simple acts of finding food and eating. As the physical elements of ordinary Gbaya meals reappear at the heart of their sacrificial rites, so we can also identify direct correlations between the physical properties of the *soré* tree and its symbolic manifestations.

Soré wood is tender and flexible, too fibrous and soft to serve as firewood, yet strips of *soré* bark may be wrapped around a person's head to cool a fever or tied around a person's neck to heal an inflamed throat. Mature *soré* leaves are large, strong, and odorless, useful for wrapping meat and medicine; young *soré* leaves are clean and absorbent, useful as "toilet paper," or to bear the brunt of angry words in the *zanga-nu* rite. *Soré* leaves are the foremost ingredient in the peace-thrower's water pot, from which water is thrown on people for health and well-being—to "cool" them and to bless them with a medicine that has the power to deflect danger. For this purpose, too, a *soré* branch is placed on the bank of a stream next to a fishing dam.

The mild-tasting *soré* fruit is full of seeds and a bit messy to eat, but appreciated especially by children. Its roots may be cooked to serve as medicine for strength-sapping diarrhea or to kill stomach worms. Between the thin bark (or thick skin) and the white wood is a slippery, mucilaginous substance, a quality that appears to be of great symbolic importance. For example, there is a correlation here between *soré* and *woo*, the preferred meat sauce or vegetable sauce made from *gbolo*. This slippery quality may be associated with oil or mud, either of which may be used with *soré* in anointing rites. Lightning is said to "slip right off" the *soré* tree, leaving it unharmed. Since the Gbaya often think of lightning as a witch in disguise, we encounter yet another field of symbolic implications issuing from *soré*. *Soré*'s slipperiness is a blessing; it deflects evil and transforms dangerous situations into peaceful ones. The peace-thrower's use of *soré* may be related not only to "cooling" but also to its slipperiness; when she washes her vagina over the water pot in which *soré* leaves are the principal ingredient, she implies that *soré* is related to the sexual act and new birth.

Blood is also involved in this network of interrelated meanings associated with *soré*. Blood is shed *ha war mo me sa*, that the way to fresh possibilities of existence may be clear, clean, and open. Blood and *soré* cool and reconcile when used separately or with oil or when a *soré* branch is thrown between adversaries, after which they "drink blood" together in a covenant meal. The slippery contents of an egg offering may also be related to *soré*. Because Gbaya meal rituals recapitulate these characteristics of *soré*, they are sufficient grounding for an eventual encounter between the two symbolic systems represented in the metaphor, "Jesus is our *soré*-cool-thing."

5

Making Things Clear and Clean: Purification Rites

Duk-ka-yi-fé-ne nding is the Gbaya name for a dirty little fish that lives in the rocks beside streams. It is also a proverb expressing deep reproach: "There you sit next to the water, yet you are sure to die in your dirt!" As people who are capable of accomplishing their assigned tasks but fail to do so must suffer the consequences, so failure to make use of traditional ways to be or to become clean is like sitting next to the water. The nonaction attracts both dirt and death, whereas the use of washing and water makes the way to fresh possibilities clear and clean.

Although we first encountered the importance of water and washing in relation to blood sacrifice, water is one of the deep symbols in Gbaya culture and its use is no more optional than blood. In fact, purification rites and blood sacrifice are complementary; together they open the way from dirt and death to life and health. Together they express the community's need for propitiation and the individual's need for penitence.

Purification rites are *ha war mo me sa*; that is, they make the way clear and clean. *Nding*, or dirt, is closely related to *simbo*, and its washing by *soré* symbolizes the Gbaya struggle with danger, fear, sin, evil, and death. In this chapter we shall focus on the complex details of Gbaya purification rites in order to distinguish more clearly the role of *soré* in this struggle. Especially in relation to *simbo*, *soré* is not only a symbol for an underlying structure of justice; it also symbolizes a nonstructural or liminal source of transformation. The depth of these symbols in the Gbaya system offers valuable clues, if not definitive answers, to questions about life and health that confound the whole world.

For purposes of this discussion, I have divided the purification rituals into two groups. The first group, the subject of this chapter, contains rites that primarily concern the quest for food, especially on the hunt. This group includes rituals related to the ordinary structures of village life, but it culminates in *zuia-simbo*, a complex and paradigmatic ritual that protects the hunter or warrior against the impurity or curse of shedding blood.

The second group deals with the need for purity through various life crises. It contains several rites associated with childbirth, ceremonies involving the Gbaya blacksmith and funerary rites. We shall discuss these rites in chapter 6. This division is not clear-cut; life situations of surpassing danger are certainly addressed by washing *simbo*, and the blacksmith's products are often indispensable on the quest for food. Such overlap, however, only underscores the dynamic interrelationship of purpose and focus that we have already discovered in the deep structures of Gbaya ritual.

The various *zuia-simbo* and *zuia-gera* rites are important ritual contexts for the thick description of *soré*. In particular, they reveal its deep relationship with *simbo*, a relationship wherein the ambiguities and contradictions of Gbaya life are revealed as subtle and inseparable companions: fear and celebration, solemnity and play, hot and cool, male and female. *Soré* lets the contradictions stand, and even permits them to emerge as complementary. In a word, *soré* manifests a transformative power in the most critical circumstances of Gbaya social life. It effects what no violence can achieve: the restoration and renewal of human lives. A husband's penis violates his wife, but cooled by *soré*, this act issues in fresh human life; a farmer's hoe digs into the earth, but cooled by *soré*, the violation becomes cultivation, and the earth yields a fresh harvest; a hunter's spear kills a magnificent animal, but cooled and blessed by *soré*, that animal nourishes a community of human beings; the death of a great man spears peoples' hearts, but cooled and blessed by *soré*, the pain of his death is washed away, and a new way is opened for those who follow him. *Soré* neither banishes nor destroys life's violators; as a person-reconciling-thing, it provides safe passage through violence and transforms potential evil into good.

Simbo surrounds whatever one cannot disturb, violate or touch without consequences. It represents whatever is "sacred" and "holy"—whatever is set apart, whatever is "life." As such, *simbo* is neither *ḍang-mo*, a bad thing, nor *nding-mo*, a dirty thing, but *simbo* "takes" a person, when the gift of life is violated (when blood is spilled badly, or when someone ignores or jumps over *soré*). In such cases, if death occurs, that is precisely what ought to happen. *Simbo* is just; it takes the one whose life is forfeit, no matter why.

The mystery of *simbo* is expressed in a rite of anointing. While oil is being heated for anointing a person, the priest places a woven basket of tiny sesame seeds over the oil, saying, "All the bad things of *simbo* and all the malicious thoughts of people who heard about your *simbo* and wanted you to die, that's why I'm placing this basket here today! If those people can count all these sesame seeds and all the holes in this basket, may *simbo* take you! If they can't count these seeds and holes, may *simbo* leave you!" No one can explain the mystery and secrets of God, but to acknowledge *simbo* is to show obedience, because it is God's decree; human beings who encounter it know that they are in the presence of mystery.

Gbaya Christians interpret *simbo* by pointing to its presence in scripture: the Israelites' fear of seeing God's face was *simbo* (Exodus 3:6); Uzzah's death when he touched the ark was *simbo* (2 Samuel 6:7); and the sins of Achan and Judas Iscariot were *simbo* (Joshua 7 and Matthew 27:5). This tradition enables the Gbaya to experience God as "a consuming fire" (Hebrews 12:29), and to know that "the fear of the Lord is the beginning of wisdom" (Psalm 111:10). Such fear is something to dance about, say the Gbaya, and an occasion to celebrate. The washing and anointing of *simbo* embraces the fear of death and the celebration of life. There is always a way back from *simbo* to life. *Soré* is a tree of life.

The cares of old women who throw peace and blessing and the concerns of village blacksmiths about the consequences of the metal they handle every day are cares and concerns addressed by *soré*. "There you sit next to the water, yet you are sure to die in your own dirt," say the Gbaya, unless your way is washed clear and clean; unless you place your cares at the foot of the *soré* tree.

PURIFICATION AND THE QUEST FOR FOOD

A. Washing with Zora

Helen Laka, a Gbaya woman about sixty years old when I interviewed her in 1979, served her village as an *okoo-pi-gangmo*, a woman who throws peace. The chief's mother in Laka-Kombo had been the peace-thrower before Helen, but when she died, the people entrusted the *zora-gangmo*, the village's ritual pot of peace and blessing, to Helen because she was the chief's wife. The pot and the peace-keeping tasks that revolve around it were given to her.

Her *zora* was in the chief's house, in a little hole beneath his bed. To prepare the *zora* for ritual use, Helen drew water from the stream and completely filled the pot. Then several elder, well-respected women put a variety of leaves into the water, but especially *soré* leaves. After this preparation, the *zora-gangmo* was never brought into the light or heat of day. If a village site was abandoned, it was transported to the new site in the evening because its purpose was to keep peace, or coolness, among the people. So long as it remained in the cool recesses of the earth, its water would never evaporate.

Helen explains how the villagers gathered in the chief's compound before any hunt. In a new calabash, she dipped water from her *zora-gangmo* and poured it over their hands, then over their spears and other weapons, saying, "Go in peace! May nothing harm you! Kill many animals and bring them back to me!" As she blessed them, they dipped water from her calabash and washed their hands and their faces. Helen blessed them again, "May your weapons see clearly, may they hit the mark!"

After the hunt, when they had killed many animals and brought them home to the village, the hunters took blood from one of the animals and brought it to the *zora*. They poured the blood into the pot, covered it, and went home happy. Their wives then prepared a great feast, which everyone ate together at the chief's place. When they had eaten, the women ululated their joy and thanks to the men who had brought them meat.

Before the older women went home, they again gathered around the *zora*. They brought the water that had been used at the feast for washing hands, poured it into the pot, and invoked a blessing: "May peace reign in our village! May nothing harm us! May there be no quarreling among our young men! May they speak softly and peacefully to each other! May food be abundant in our village!"

When the women had returned to their homes, Helen called the chief over to her *zora*. He rolled up the robes covering his shins, and Helen the peace-thrower took water from her clay pot to wash him, saying, "Walk in peace and in health! May nothing harm you!" Helen explains that "everything we did with the *zora*, we did for peace and for joy!"

The Woman of Peace

Other *gangmo* rites like the washings described by Helen Laka are celebrated in the chief's compound to ensure peace and prosperity for the village. The *okoo-pi-gangmo*, or *ko-gangmo*, the woman of peace, is the person who presides over these rites, and *soré* is *té-gangmo*, the tree of peace. The *ko-gangmo* is one of the principal custodians of *soré*, if not the most important one; because *soré* is a sine qua non for the accomplishment of her tasks, she may herself be called "*soré*," or "*soré*-cool-thing" in her village.

When I inquired into the relative importance of the ritual specialists in Gbaya society, Ndoyama Enoch and several other students described the woman of peace as second only to the priest of *so-kao*, whose ritual activities are primarily sacrificial. The priest focuses on propitiatory and prophylactic measures to assure peace and well-being between the community and local spirits; he is one of the principal stewards or custodians of life in the Gbaya community, and the central symbol of his activities is blood. The woman peace-thrower's ritual activities are primarily for purification and blessing; they focus on prophylactic, conciliatory, and restorative measures to assure peace and well-being within the community and within the rest of the world. She is also a guardian of life, and the central symbol of her activities is water.

The Right Thing To Do

Adzia Dénis and Abbo Secrétaire agree with Helen Laka that the *ko-gangmo*'s pot is fixed in the earth directly under the chief's bed, and that the *ko-gangmo* herself is ideally one of the wives of the chief. The *ko-gangmo* washes her vagina over the *zora*, saying, "May this village prosper for my husband!"

Occasionally, the village chief will invite members from each residential group to share in a special meal. The cooking water for this meal is also drawn from his wife's *zora*. Adzia explains that of course all men are attracted by a woman's sexual parts, but this washing with the cool medicine of *soré* is symbolic of birth, not sex. It is a cooling of the birth canal through which all human beings must pass. The birthing path must be blessed, and it must become a blessing, because everything in life depends on being born well. Whoever is born badly (that is, in bad health, "in sin," or illegitimately) cannot succeed in this world.

Adzia explains that the Gbaya prepare food from the same pot that is used to sprinkle people with blessing, and over which a woman's genitals have been washed because "it's the right thing to do." To have a clear, clean way in life and to accomplish everything necessary for peace and well-being begin when the *ko-gangmo* washes her vagina over the *zora*. A peaceful, successful life is conceived and born in her action.

Settling a New Village

Another *zora* to which the chief and the *ko-gangmo* are both related is the *zora-dengimo*, or amaryllis pot. Adzia and Abbo explain that when a new village site is desired, but for reasons not sufficiently critical to ask the chief's nephew for ritual assistance, the chief himself will seek a *soré* tree at the new site. He takes a *soré* leaf in his hand, knots it, and invokes a blessing: "I bind up a new village right here! May peace and health reign in our village! May we find abundant food in this place!" Then he builds a new house next to the *soré* tree.

The morning following the first night spent in his new house, the chief rises very early. He unties the knotted *soré* leaf, saying, "My village that I bound up right here, I now open it up! May no danger come to us here! May death stay away! May our village grow, and may our wives give birth to many children!"

Adzia explains that knotting the *soré* leaf symbolically draws the villagers together in one place under the peace established by *soré* and prevents them from scattering into various other settlements. Untying the *soré* leaf indicates that the villagers have indeed settled in the new place. Their new village is now visible; henceforth, they are free to lead a new life here.

When the *zora-gangmo* has been installed in its place under the chief's bed in his new house, he plants an amaryllis next to the *soré* tree and places another *zora* in the ground beside them. Adzia says that the leaves in the chief's *zora* are the same as those in the *zora-gangmo*, because they are "leaves of peace for both men and women." The chief is the custodian of the amaryllis pot, however, because its purpose is to protect the village.

Averting Danger

If danger threatens the village in the dark of night, the chief gives pieces of amaryllis to the *ko-gangmo* and the elderly women who assist her. She removes her clothes (or "skirt" of leaves, as the case may be), holds a piece of amaryllis leaf in the small of her back, and turns first in the direction from which the danger is anticipated, then back to her ritual pot. Her gesture, explains Adzia, is a supplication to avert the danger. When she is again dressed, she takes a new calabash of water from her pot and adds this water to the chief's pot.

The women take water from their pot and sprinkle it on the path, invoking a blessing on the village as they work. Next they take water from the chief's pot and carry it back to the house. The *ko-gangmo* is again naked; she approaches her pot with water from the chief's pot, turns her back on it, then bends her knees. Reaching backward with her right hand through her legs, she pours water from the chief's pot into hers. *Gangmo* water that has been mixed with the *dengimo* water thus returns to its source, and the two work together for peace and well-being in the village. The backhanded gesture of the woman peace-thrower suggests that water from the "male" pot is returned to the source from which it comes, the "female" pot, as she faces away from her pot toward the chief's pot.

The Chief's Bath

The chief stands on a white stone, which is on the floor next to the woman's ritual pot, and washes himself with water from the pot. The stone is white, says Adzia, because white stones are stronger than red stones. The color white represents a clean heart; the color red would indicate that quarrels, hard words, and hot tempers are troubling the village. The chief washes himself over the white stone because whatever disrupts peace, success, and health is *nding*, or dirty.

The importance of washing from *zora* for traditional Gbaya purification rites corresponds in its expressive ordinariness and foundational symbolism to the significance of meals for Gbaya offerings and sacrificial rites. Female labor and female symbolism appear to function at the very source of both types of ritual, but the fact that the peace-thrower keeps her most important source of blessing under the chief's bed suggests that Gbaya notions of peace and well-being on the quest for food or in life-threatening situations are linked to the blessing of fertility. Male and female must collaborate; a woman is custodian of this pot, but it remains in the space of her husband.

B. Dance for the Hunt

The Gbaya term *yoya* (or *yee*) can be translated either as "dance" or as "festival and celebration," and the *baminga*, or dance to prepare for hunting, is closely related to the rites of washing *simbo*. Yadji André, a man widely known among contemporary Gbaya not only as a Lutheran pastor but also as an enthusiastic hunter and performer of folktales, describes this dance in the following paragraphs.

The dance, or *yoya*, to prepare for hunting is always celebrated at the beginning of the dry season. Its participants must abstain from eating three foods before and during the rites: *gbere*, a savanna plant that yields a red fruit at its root in the dry season; *mboḍomo-gala*, an oily paste made from cucumber seeds; and all kinds of *woo*, the slippery vegetable sauce favored in Gbaya cuisine.

Only alert young men who already possess a certain experience in hunting qualify for this dance, which is celebrated to help the hunters perform more effectively. The *ḅaminga* also teaches them how to find and kill various kinds of animals. The leader of *ḅaminga* is called *Dua*, or goat, which is also a Gbaya symbol for witchcraft. (The "evil principle" or "substance" that resides in the intestines of extraordinary persons, according to the Gbaya, is *dua*; it gives them occult powers for hunting, divining the future, or destroying other people.)

When *Dua* has set the day for the rites to begin, he calls the young men together, and gives a name to each one: *Godanga* is a man of superior courage; *Sananga* knows how to be especially alert and energetic; *Gonwaka* can run faster than any of his comrades; *Mboro* is a sturdy fellow who must carry the heaviest loads, whether manioc flour on the way to the camp or meat on the way home. If a large number of men participate, *Dua* divides them into several groups; then these names are shared and designate each group and its responsibilities. There is only one *Dua*, however, and his wife is called *Ngorongo*. She is like the *ko-gangmo*, woman peace-thrower.

The men go together to the gallery forest to find a tall *ngekere* tree, which is cut down and carried back to the village, to the ground before *Dua*'s house. This tree is used as a drum and for making poles and bows. The first *ḅaminga* dances are performed in the village at this house. Later, during the hunt, another *ngekere* tree will be cut as a drum for use in the bush encampment.

When the men have danced the night through, they leave for the stream, where they will wash. On their way they circle several trees, scraping each tree and carefully guarding the scrapings as *mbutu*, or medicine, to wash themselves. Before leaving the open savanna they break a fresh termitary (one that has not yet assumed the shape of a mushroom), and put it with the scrapings they have collected. In the gallery forest, they circle and scrape more trees, including the *zee*, a thick grass plant with wide leaves that are used in many purification rites. They also cut three long, flexible stems from the *zee* plant. One stem is planted in the soft earth on the far side of the stream; another, on the near side. The stream is dammed up with dry leaves, and the termitary is placed on the dam. Two *zee* leaves are bent down to touch the termitary.

Dua gathers all the scrapings and puts them in the pool of water created by the dam. One by one the men remove their clothes and squat naked on the termitary and *zee* leaves in the middle of the stream. As they wash themselves, they speak an invocation, saying, "I wash away the dirt that closed my eyes and the dirt that made my arm flabby and weak! May this water save and heal me so I can see the animals clearly and track them well!"

When they have washed themselves, they climb up the bank to the place where the third *zee* stem is planted. That stem has been split down the middle, and the men pass through it. *Dua* breaks the dam with his heel, saying, "May all the dirt that passed from these men into the water now be carried away! As this water flows far away where we can't see the end of it, so may this dirt be carried far away from these men!"

Dua steps out of the water and passes through the *zee* leaf, breaking it with his heel as he goes. As the men leave the water and pass through the *zee* leaf, no one looks back. Then they put on the same clothes they had discarded before washing and prepare to return to the village. On the path leading to the village, *Dua* has kindled a little grass fire. They all jump over this fire, which *Dua* then extinguishes with his heel, and they proceed to the village, no one looking back.

When they arrive at *Dua*'s house, a ritual pot awaits them, placed there by *Ngorongo*, *Dua*'s wife. This pot contains *soré* and many other leaves to bring health and assure a safe hunt. All the men wash their faces with water from this pot. *Ngorongo* has also prepared *zoḅo* leaves for the hunt.

After the men have eaten the *zoḅo* leaves, they gather the potsherd, the charred wood, and the three *soré* sticks that had been the fireplace, and wait for a bird to fly overhead in the direction of the setting sun. When the bird appears, they throw all these things after it, crying, "May all the dirt remaining on our bodies be carried away with this bird! Hooooo!" Then they prepare weapons for the hunt, because their way is already clear and clean. They have no fear, they are all in good health! Next year, says Yadji, they will return to celebrate *ḅaminga* once again.

According to Yadji's account, *soré* is not a primary symbol in the *ḅaminga* rite, as it appears explicitly only at the end of the rite, in *Ngorongo*'s ritual pot. Several other symbols related to *soré* by virtue of their slipperiness, namely, *woo* sauce and cucumber butter, are also forbidden to participants of *ḅaminga*. The reason for this may be related to the cooling properties of *soré*, which are also shared by *woo* and cucumber butter. Thus, for example, *soré* leaves are never used to wrap the poison that will be used on arrow tips, and *soré* leaves may never be put in a hunter's quiver, because *soré* would cool the potency of the poison. *Soré* cools, *soré* repudiates any kind of violence, and hunting is intrinsically violent: there can be no successful hunting without killing. The prominence of *soré*, *woo*, and cucumber butter could inhibit or constrain the hunters' desire and ability to kill, either of which would abort the hunt. Since *ḅaminga* is performed for success on the hunt, its ritual objects, gestures, and words are all measures to assure that success.

The prohibition of *gbere* fruit relates in a polar way to these same ambiguous dynamics: *gbere* cooperates with *soré* as its opposite. The *gbere* stem is used by a diviner, for example, to designate a person accused of witchcraft, whereas in the same rite *soré* is thrown to innocent parties. Thus, its prohibition from *baminga*: *gbere*'s bright red fruit is associated with quarrels, contentiousness, jealousy—with any hard words that could ruin the hunt. Peaceful relationships, physical and spiritual health, must prevail before and during the hunt.

Zora-gangmo, the ritual pot, and *zobo* protect the hunters by their inherent capacity to deflect danger. The *gangmo* water, in which *soré* is the first medicine, symbolizes that the hunters engage in their inevitable quest for food with clear and clean hearts, with all the right intentions. *Zobo* symbolizes the hunters' unity and also anticipates their encounter with the dangers of *simbo*.

Every hunter risks the violation of life. For example, each one is in danger of being mauled by a leopard or gored by a buffalo; or he may kill or be killed by a fellow hunter or a taboo animal. The quest for food on the hunt poses a dilemma: the hunter has to take a life in order to keep a life. *Soré* does not resolve the dilemma or wash away the ambiguity, but it does provide safe passage through this unavoidable predicament.

Baminga may be interpreted as a foreshadowing of *zuia-simbo*. It is not only that, however, for participants in *baminga* are justifiably concerned to wash away the dirt that can prevent successful hunting. As a purification rite, *baminga* is concerned with penitence. To give up choice foods, *woo* and cucumber butter before and during *baminga* is a kind of penance or spiritual discipline, and to give up the *gbere* fruit can symbolize leaving behind all those things that make for dirt: quarreling, jealousy, sexual promiscuity, theft, and deceit.

The dirt washed by *baminga* is not yet a violation of life, but it does clear away the weaknesses and blindness that accrue to anyone who participates in the activities of everyday life. When this dirt is washed, newness is restored; there is regeneration, a new birth. The hunters pass through the *zee* leaf immediately after they have washed. This leaf is another slippery symbol among the Gbaya; here it symbolizes—like the passing through *ko-gangmo*'s legs—a passage from the womb through the birth canal into a world that is completely new. After this birth, no one looks back.

C. Zuia-simbo, *Washing* Simbo

Haman Matthieu and several other students collaborated with me on the following ritual story, although some details and reflections have been added to their description. Ritual performances are never identical, even when the actors are the same from one time to the next. Nevertheless, reports from widely separated areas of Cameroon and the Central African Republic indicate a striking consistency in the form and symbolic substance of the rituals for washing *simbo*.

Haman Kills a Taboo Leopard

Haman set a snare to catch a gray duiker, and the snare caught a leopard. After the leopard was snared, Haman arrived and saw what had happened. His father was right behind him; his older brother, nearby in the stream; and his brother-in-law, not far away in the bush. When they heard the leopard's scream, they came running to help. Haman was afraid, but he threw his spear at the leopard and it died! Haman's father was an experienced *wi-zui-simbo* (a person who knows how to wash *simbo*). When he had looked at the leopard, he bound its right paw in the leaves of the *zee* plant.

Haman explains that whenever someone kills a *simbo* animal or a human being, one does not call out to anyone by name lest *simbo* take that person whose name is called. The Gbaya expression is *ba*, "to take," rather than "to pollute" or "to contaminate," and a *simbo* or taboo animal is any beast that is magnificent: for example, the leopard, the eland, and the bongo. When this happens on the hunt, Haman says, no one's name is spoken, and when the hunter enters his village, he does not speak to any member of his family, but only to those who have themselves killed—and been washed for killing—the same *simbo* animal.

Haman and the other men with him called out to each other, "Come here, come over here!" When the others arrived, Haman's father untied the snare from the leopard's foot and bound the leopard to a carrying pole. He also bound the leopard's mouth. According to Haman, "A human being should not really kill a leopard, but this leopard had already been taken in the snare and wounded. Therefore, I was able to kill it. As the right hand is a sign of strength, so strength and danger reside especially in the leopard's right foot and mouth. That is why they are bound—so that the leopard is no longer dangerous, so that it can no longer kill a person. The *zee* leaves are the medicine that breaks the leopard's strength and cools *simbo*."

If a hunter is alone and kills a leopard that is too heavy for one man to carry, he must leave the leopard and go to his friends for help, and he must carry a *soré* branch along the way so that everyone he meets will be alert to the danger he has encountered. In some cases, says Haman, if the hunters are many, they must all remain on the path outside their village until a *wi-zui-simbo* has washed their shins and weapons with water and *mbutu*, or medicine, from the *soré* tree. The washing cools *simbo* and allows the hunters who were not directly involved in the kill to return home without further precautions. For those who killed the animal, however, the ritual process is just beginning.

Returning to Camp

When the leopard was firmly attached to the carrying pole, Haman and his brothers picked it up and carried it to their camp. Haman's father said,

"We must not walk silently into camp lest our wives be surprised and taken by *simbo*!" So he began to sing in a loud voice. "Grandchild of Mambere," he sang, "let them bring their battle-shields, let's have a fight! Today's the day for a fight!" When their wives heard this song they fled in fear, and the men carried the leopard into the camp. Some friends camping nearby also heard the song and knew that a *simbo* animal had been killed. They took *soré* branches in hand and came to see the leopard.

The four hunters went directly to the open shelter at the center of the camp, as *wi-simbo* are not permitted to enter their own huts. Had they gone to the village, they would have entered an unused or abandoned house rather than bring *simbo* into their own houses. They took their hunting gear and all their clothes into the shelter because nothing they had taken on the hunt was to be touched, even inadvertently, by other people. Although Haman's father could wash *simbo*, he told them that it would be best to call a *wi-zui-simbo* who had not been on the hunt and participated in the kill. So they stayed under the shelter all night, and in the morning the priest arrived, cut *soré* branches, and placed them on the ground at the shelter's threshold.

The *simbo* priest untied the *zee* leaves from the leopard's mouth in order to pull out its whiskers, which are very dangerous. Concealed in food, a leopard's whiskers can be used to poison people. The priest plucked out thirteen short whiskers (six from each side of the leopard's face and one from below its mouth) and burned them, calling on the hunters as witnesses and saying to the leopard, "May your *simbo* go back with you, as I cut you up today!" Haman explains that this *simbo* was not the priest's own; his words were meant to contain or limit the danger, lest *simbo* take a person not responsible for the leopard's death.

When the leopard was no longer dangerous, the priest turned it over to the hunters to be butchered. It was just like any other animal once its *simbo* had returned to the killer and become entirely the killer's responsibility. Since Haman had killed this leopard, the skin belonged to him, but he gave it to his father. The priest took the vines and leaves, the carrying stick and everything that had been used to bind the animal and carried them to a *soré* tree, saying, "*Soré*, take all this *simbo*!"

The older men divided up the meat to be cooked, and when it was ready to eat, Haman's father stuck a needle into it, then put the needle in Haman's mouth once, twice, three times. Each time Haman spit on the ground, not because he had killed the animal, but because he had never before eaten leopard meat. This gesture, called *do-mo*, occurs in many Gbaya rites: three times for men, four times for women. Gbaya Christians relate this action to sin and the forgiveness of sins. They say, for example, that a man could be forgiven three times for committing a serious sin, a woman, four times, but after that "they would die!" *Do-mo* characterizes particular activities as extraordinary or dangerous events, as something "real" or "genuine" that is not to be taken lightly. In my opinion, *do-mo* is an act of consecration; that is, its occurrence indicates that the Gbaya believe that life is sacred.

Haman notes that women must not eat leopard meat, but once a man has eaten it observing *do-mo*, he may eat it again at any time without *do-mo*. The amount of time the *wi-simbo* spend in the shelter or in some other cold abandoned house often extends to three days — another *do-mo*. During this time, the hunters' family members and other villagers keep their distance from the men. Haman's group, however, spent only one night in the shelter.

Invoking the Good Trees

The day after they had eaten the leopard, the priest told the hunters to undress, except for their loincloths, and prepare to leave for the stream. He put their clothes, weapons, personal belongings, and eating utensils at the foot of a *soré* tree. Then he took a *soré* branch in his hand, extended it to Haman, and they set out for the stream, holding *soré* between them. Haman's father followed, then his brother and brother-in-law, all holding a *soré* branch between them. (The priest may also give them bits of amaryllis to chew and swallow as they leave the village.)

On their way to the forest, they circled several trees, scraped them, and put the scrapings into a *soré* leaf. The priest spoke to each tree as they circled it: "You, tree, that I am circling, there are no words between us! What we are doing here is because of the one who killed a leopard! May the leopard's *simbo* return with you!"

Haman also spoke as he walked around the trees, saying: "I set a snare to catch a gray duiker. I had no intention of killing a leopard with that snare! You, leopard, you came along and got caught in my snare. May your *simbo* return with this tree, may your *simbo* leave me alone!" Many informants also say that the priest and the *wi-simbo* tap their heads gently or rub their foreheads on the trees as they speak.

Haman's group circled many trees, speaking the same words to each one. At last, they came to a termitary that was still oozing fresh mud. Here, the priest pulled out a bit of Haman's hair and stuck it into the termitary, saying, "May this termitary cover over Haman's sin [just as the oozing mud will eventually cover the termitary]; may it cover over the *simbo* of the leopard he killed!" Some priests remove the top of the termitary with a knife, and pass it through the legs and under the crotch of each *wi-simbo*, speaking an invocation as they work.

All trees circled and scraped for medicine are "good trees," says Haman. Some of my informants call them "God's trees" because they help people. Good trees seek no vengeance and offer only healing; when they are addressed as in the *zuia-simbo* rites, they hear our requests. The Gbaya, however, do not worship trees or think of them as having souls.

Words and Water

The priest led the men down to the water, but before anyone entered it, he cut *soré* and *gbedila* or *zee* leaves and used them to fashion a little dam. When a pool had formed behind it, the medicine from all the trees was put into it. Then the priest split the tops of three *soré* sticks and placed a *ɓui-so* stem in the slit of each one, in the form of a cross. He fixed the three crosses in the dam so that the *wi-simbo* sat on them, breaking them apart. The reason for this intriguing practice lies in the name of the grass used to make the crosses: *ɓui-so*. The verb *ɓui* means to carry something in one's arms, as one carries a small baby; and the verb *so* means "to ooze" or "to anoint." The same word, used as a substantive, however means "God," "the gods," or "spirit."

The priest entered the water first and pulled Haman along with him. He made Haman sit on the *zee* leaf, facing downstream, and began to wash him. Three times he dipped water from the pool, poured it over Haman, and said, "The leopard that you killed, may its *simbo* go away with this water; may this stream carry away the dangerous *simbo*. I am not deceiving you with this washing! This task was entrusted to me and I'm doing it exactly as it should be done! *Simbo*-eland, *simbo*-bongo, *simbo*-leopard, I hereby wash away *simbo* once-for-all! May this water carry *simbo* away! If I had not been given this task, I would not do this today! As I wash away this *simbo* today, may it leave you, your wife, and your children, too! May you stay well! May no harm come to you!"

The power of *simbo* is in the words, Haman says, as healing is in the words that Jesus spoke when, for example, he anointed the blind man's eyes with clay and told him to wash in the pool of Siloam (John 9). Not the mud, nor the water, but the spoken word is important. Not just any medicine will cure *simbo*, but words must accompany the medicine and the water, because words can reveal the heart's intentions.

The priest also washed Haman's father and brother, saying, "You did not kill this leopard! May its *simbo* leave you alone!" In the rite presided over by Mbele Ninga, which I attended, after washing all the *wi-simbo*, he stood for a few moments next to the dam, trembling as if in a kind of ecstasy, saying again and again, "Everything depends on God! Only God! Only God! Blessing! Blessing!" He did this, the Gbaya say, to communicate with his ancestors without whose "approval" he would not presume to wash *simbo*.

In Haman's account, the men discarded their loincloths in the water as the priest broke the dam with his heel, saying, "May this water carry *simbo* far, far away! May it never return to hurt you!" When the hunters climbed out of the water, they passed through a long *zee* leaf (split down the middle), which the priest ripped apart with his heel when the last one had passed through it. The men left the stream without looking back. Haman says, "We came up out of the grave that would have held us. We left the hole of death!"

The priest kindled a fire on the path, saying, "May this fire burn up *simbo*. May its danger be burned up in this fire!" When the hunters had jumped over this fire, he extinguished it with his feet and everyone left that place. The men put on new loincloths brought along by the priest and headed back to camp.

No one looked back. We did this, Haman said, to end *simbo* right there.

Eating Zoḅo

The men went directly to Haman's hut, behind which the priest had kindled a fire using three *soré* sticks as a fireplace. He put a potsherd of sesame seed oil and *soré* scrapings on the sticks. This was to prepare for *kpaia-mo a te-wi*, a Gbaya rite of anointing and purification. He stirred the oil with a "spear" made from the stem of the *gbere* plant, and said, "May *simbo* leave you! *Simbo* of the leopard, *simbo* of the eland, *simbo* of the bongo, may *simbo* leave you!" Then he dipped the *gbere* stem into the oil and anointed each man on the forehead, breast, hands and feet. The hunters held their hands over the fire, and the priest poured water over them extinguishing the fire. He said, "May all sin and danger end right here!" Smoke from the fire surrounded the hunters; it was a sign of peace and healing.

Haman explains that a *gbere* stem was used for this anointing because the leopard had been killed by a spear. Only the weapon used in the kill can cool or bring peace to the killer. All of the characteristics of this anointing are contradictory and ambiguous; that is, *simbo* is simultaneously burned up and cooled down. Oil mixed with *soré* scrapings is heated in order to cool people, and fire is kindled (between the legs, as it were) of the three *soré* sticks to symbolize and bring under control the heat of violent actions.

The men were anointed at strategic places on their bodies: on the forehead because one receives good things on (or with) the forehead. The expression, *sonti-me déa kaḍi*, "your forehead [is] made already," means "you've got it made," "you're really lucky!" Anointing on the breast, *yi-séé-wi*, at the heart of a person, cools the heart that has been upset by danger; anointing on the "fork" of the hand and foot heals and restores a person's strength. A person's grip, for example, is strongest when the object is held between the thumb and forefinger. Haman compares these gestures with Christian baptismal gestures, especially the sign of the cross made on the forehead and on the breast, and the great commandment: "You shall love the Lord your God with all your heart, with all your soul, with all your mind, and with all your strength" (Mark 12:30).

When the priest had anointed the hunters and extinguished the fire, they gathered the leftover *soré* sticks, the potsherd and oil, the charred wood, and the *gbere* stem, and as soon as a bird appeared flying west, they threw all these things after it, shouting, "May all *simbo* go away with that bird! Hooooo!"

Haman's family brought new clothes for all who had been washed. The priest prepared *zoḅo* leaves with sesame butter for the hunters, their friends, and members of their family. Three times, he took *zoḅo* and put it carefully into the mouth of each hunter, then the whole gathering ate *zoḅo* together. After this meal, they washed their hands in the clay pot from which they had eaten, and the priest poured the water on the ground, saying, "It is finished! Go home satisfied and happy! Don't worry anymore! Nothing will happen to you! If something does happen to you, something else has caused it, not this *simbo*, because I have washed you the right way!"

Whenever the *zuia-simbo* rites occur in or near a village, the villagers participate in the celebration. The hunters paint red and white spots on their faces and engage their friends in mock warfare. When they have made the rounds of this war game three times, the villagers bring small gifts to them; the drum used at funerary celebrations is brought out, and the entire village begins to dance. Dance is a sign of good health among the Gbaya; whenever Gbaya men hear the drum, says Haman, they rejoice to remember and to tell the story of the brave deeds they have done and the times of personal danger they have survived.

If a person gets sick without cause after *zuia-simbo*, it must be assumed that something was not right about the washing. Perhaps the killer's intentions were not clear, or perhaps the priest did not perform the rite correctly. In such cases the priest may be asked to perform a sacrifice for the ancestors. He kills a chicken, spills its blood on the ground, then roasts it whole over a fire until it is completely consumed. Then he washes the killer next to the place of sacrifice, saying, "Now it's done! Nothing more will trouble you! Go home and be well!"

Gbaya Justice

According to Haman, the Gbaya associate several offenses with *simbo* in addition to the killing of people or animals. For example, a young person's disobedience and lack of respect for an elder, especially if it involves hard words, can cause *simbo* to "take" that person; so can hurting a small or domestic animal; deliberate and habitual stealing, lying, or spreading false accusations; adultery, especially if a man commits adultery with a pregnant woman, and her child dies. Only the shedding of blood, however, requires the full ritual for washing *simbo*.

The result of being taken by *simbo* is death, because justice must be served. When a life that was freely given is violently taken, then—if one does not confess, if one is not washed in the right way—that one will die. *Simbo* takes the killer's life in a way that is closely related to the life that was violated. Thus the hunter who kills a leopard and is not washed will get sick with a terrible cough; the noise leopards make is not a roar, but a cough. If a hunter kills the long-necked eland and is not washed, his throat will swell until he dies. If he kills the reddish-brown bongo, he will vomit blood until he dies. If anyone kills a human being and is not washed, his or her body will waste away.

One who is taken by *simbo* has "jumped over *soré*"; that is, he or she has ignored *soré* or held it in contempt, either verbally or in ritual activities. One avoids being taken by *simbo* by respect for *soré*. *Soré* is the root metaphor that not only carries and extends the principle of *simbo* into areas of everyday living, but also keeps it firmly linked to the fundamental danger of violating life, which is inherently inviolable. If someone is taken by *simbo* for whatever reason, *soré* provides safe passage through the danger; once the person is washed in *soré* water and anointed with oil from a *soré* stick, that person is ready to be received back into the community. The *soré*-cool words spoken by the priest and joined to right intentions protect the one who seeks refuge under the *soré* tree.

6

Cleanliness in the Midst of Life

PURIFICATION RITES

This chapter continues our discussion of the purification rituals begun in chapter 5. The rites in this case are related to life-crisis situations: childbirth; the tasks of village blacksmiths; funerary rites. These ritual uses of *soré* mark its presence at the beginning and end of life and deepen our understanding of its purpose, meaning, and service among the Gbaya.

PURIFICATION AND LIFE CRISES

A. Zuia-soka-zang-ko-bem, *Washing a "Ready Stomach"*

When a pregnant woman is about ready to give birth, that is, when her stomach is "ready," "old," "ripe," or "mature," the Gbaya seek an old woman to wash her. Early in the morning, the old woman leads the pregnant woman into the gallery forest, directly to a fork in the stream. She tells the younger woman to undress and to sit with her legs spread over the place where the waters meet. Using dry leaves to dip the water, the old woman washes the girl with water and many words.

"I brought you to this fork in the stream to wash you!" she says. "On the day when your labor pains begin, may your birth canal open wide just like the fork in this stream. So may you give birth quickly! May your child not stop on the way! May nothing afflict you! If anyone has treated you maliciously, or if you or your husband has committed adultery or other sins, may these things not close the way for the child to be born safely! If a witch is trying to kill your child, may that witch open the way for the child! May

God give you strength and help you to give birth without any problems!"

After her speech, the two women return to the village, but they visit the stream again on the following three mornings, until the woman has been washed four times. After the fourth washing, the old woman prepares sesame oil to anoint the girl's stomach. Azimi Pauline says that the priestess dips a *gbere* stick, or "spear," into sesame oil four times, but anoints only the girl's navel. According to Azimi, *soré* is not used in this anointing, and no objects used in this rite are thrown after a bird, because *simbo* is not specifically involved.

Azimi does not explain why the *gbere* stem is used for this anointing. In Haman's interpretation of washing *simbo*, the *gbere* was used because it represented the weapon used to kill the leopard. In this ritual it may represent the husband's penis, which had penetrated the woman, literally, violating her, to make her pregnant. If so, the "weapon" is here "cleansed" in the cool act of anointing; the man and his wife are purged of the dirt that could kill their child.

Other interpretations are possible: perhaps the *gbere* spear represents witchcraft as a threat to the baby's life or merely the heat generated by the misdeeds of the woman or man. In all of these interpretations, the common element is heat; penitence is expected for deeds that need cooling.

B. Zuia féé-kui, *Washing (Away) "Lost" Egg*

Féé-kui is a religious rite performed the first time two people lose a child. It marks their acceptance of the child's death as a sacrifice to God so that a new child may be granted. This acceptance or sacrifice is not, however, a *ḍafa-so/wora-so*. The Gbaya do not sacrifice their children or any human being to God. The shape of Gbaya sacrifice is quite different from the ritual event called "washing away lost egg."

The first time a family loses a child, its parents do not weep or express their grief as the custom is at most deaths. Nor do couples who have never lost a child embrace the affected parents, explains Hamada, lest one of their own children die. The Gbaya fathers say that when a couple's first child dies, "A drop of oil from the top of the bottle spilled on the ground." That is, one child among many has died, but many more will be born. As the child has simply returned to God, this is not a "hard death"; its cause (though it may be witchcraft) should not unduly preoccupy the family.

The family breaks branches of the *ndoya* tree and puts a stick at the pit of the child's stomach. The child is wrapped in a white cloth and laid on the ground next to the *ndoya*, while a shallow grave (about 50 cm) is dug. The gravedigger is a father who has also lost a child for the first time and been washed in the *féé-kui* rite. When the grave is ready, the cloth and *ndoya* are removed, and the naked corpse is buried in the earth. No protective framework of sticks covers the corpse as in most burials; nor is any gravestone or marker provided.

If a male child dies, the period of fasting will last three days; if a female child, four days. During this time the parents eat sparingly from the same utensils, which no one else touches. They are also careful to refrain from walking; should they stub their foot on a rock or a tree root, the accident would "put lost egg to them." They would become infertile, with no more hope of bearing children. The fasting precautions are taken, says Hamada, in order to bear more children. From start to finish, that is the purpose of this rite.

When the fasting period has expired, before the break of dawn, a priest or a priestess arrives to wash the parents. This person may be either a widow or a man who has been washed in *féé-kui* and to whom the task of washing others has been entrusted. The priest throws a *soré* branch on the threshold of the parents' house and summons them to pass over it on their way out. Next, he gathers several items: a bit of charcoal from the parents' hearth; their old sleeping mat; the clothes worn by the child when it died; the clothes worn by the parents, if the child died in their arms; and the utensils they used during the fast. The priest places all these items except the charcoal at the foot of a *soré* tree, to cool them, and later claims them as his payment or inheritance.

He takes the charcoal, a calabash of water, and a branch of *ndoya* and leads the parents away from the village to the first fork in the path. The parents undress and sit while the priest washes them. "I'm washing you," the priest says, "lest you be afflicted by lost egg! May you give birth to children again! May you be strong and healthy!" After the mother and father have been washed, they put on clean clothes and go home, leaving the charcoal and *ndoya* there on the path.

Since the charcoal is taken from the couples' hearth and left on the path, it may symbolize that these parents are on a path or at a "crossroads" through which many human beings will pass. If so, then the gesture is a visible prayer for many children to flow through their loins. A more plausible interpretation, however, is that the charcoal represents the sinners' place in the fire. Then the ritual is a gesture of confession, and the abandoned charcoal symbolizes the parents' misdeeds, which may be responsible for the child's death.

Hamada comments that the Gbaya fathers call washing *féé-kui* a kind of *sadaka*. This Fulfulde/Arabic term means "sacrifice," but the Gbaya use it to denote a gift or "offering": for example, a gift given in memory of someone. When we use the English or French word for sacrifice in references to *zuia féé-kui*, we should keep in mind its association with *sadaka* — more so, I think, than its link with *ḍafa-so/wora-so*. Although the gift that is offered does appear to be a "giving up," it is their claim to the child, not the child itself, that the parents relinquish — unless the dead child's blood is construed as propitiatory.

The *féé-kui* rite is a washing, which implies a recognition of "dirt." Although the "sin" may not be identified, the rite is an implicit acknowledgment that some act requiring penitence has been committed by one or both of the parents. When they step over *soré* on their threshold, they are "turning over a new leaf." By passing over the boundary from dirt to cleanliness, they arrive at hope for the blessing of more children. The charcoal symbolizes the penitential character of their passage.

Two additional uses of *ndoya* may be noted. First, if a woman discovers that children have stolen from her garden, she may curse those children by taking a *ndoya* branch in hand and saying, "You children who ruined my garden, *yaa-o, yaa-o, yaa-o,* may your own children die! May your own children suffer for this!" Years later a diviner may diagnose a person's loss of children to be the result of this curse, *oo-yaa-bém,* and prescribe an anointing rite. Though none of my informants refers to *zuia féé-kui* as the specific "cure" for *oo-yaa-bém,* there does appear to be a relationship.

Second, *ndoya* leaves are used to hasten the ripening process of bananas, for example, by putting bananas and *ndoya* leaves together in a large covered pot. I have not been able to establish any clear relationship between this use of *ndoya* and *zuia féé-kui,* but it may be that this physical property of the *ndoya* — its ability to hasten the ripeness of things — is symbolically extended in these rites to refer to a couple's fertility.

C. Zora Koo Bém, *the Children's Ablution Pot*

If a pregnant woman feels threatened by the *oo-yaa-mo* curse, she will look for an older woman to anoint her stomach. She may seek this anointing, even if she has already lost a child and been washed in the *féé-kui* rite. After she gives birth, her family may suggest that the *zora* rite be performed for the child. One month after the birth, when it is time to shave the baby's head, the older woman takes a new calabash and fills it with water and the leaves from many trees and plants, including *soré, gbere,* and several types of amaryllis. When the child has been shaved, its head is washed from this calabash to prevent fever and sickness. The priestess performs this washing the first time, then gives the calabash to the child's mother, who uses it to wash the child during the next two years, or until the child can walk with confidence. Fresh water is added to the calabash from time to time, to keep it from drying up, but the leaves are never replenished. As soon as the child can walk and its health is assured, the father takes the calabash back to the priestess and pays her, with thanks for her help. She then places the calabash at the foot of a *soré* tree and leaves it there.

D. Ea-tom-dono Er Ngma Bii, *"Consecrating" a Blacksmith*

Doko Illa's father wanted to entrust to him the work of a blacksmith; that is, he wanted to put the work of the blacksmith into Doko's hands. Early one morning he led Doko, his wife, and their children down to a stream to be washed. They did not circle trees, nor did Doko's father construct a dam, but he did cut a *zee* plant and fix it in the soft earth. After splitting open the long leaf of the *zee*, he led Doko and his family into the water and washed them, saying, "I'm washing you today for the work of a blacksmith! May you enjoy good health; may your bodies be strong and alert!"

Doko led his family through the *zee* leaf. His father did not make this passage, but he did break the *zee* with his heel before leaving the stream. On the way back to the village, he cut a *soré* branch and carried it to the blacksmith shelter where he worked. When they arrived at the shelter, Doko's father entered first, then extended the *soré* branch to Doko, to draw him into the shelter, where another blacksmith was already heating metal to make a hoe. When the metal was red-hot, Doko held his father's hand while his father struck the metal and fashioned the hoe. "It was as though I myself had made that hoe," Doko said. "This is how my father initiated me into the work."

Then Doko took the hoe and a new grass mat, one that did not yet have a border-piece, and offered (*si*) these gifts to his father. Hamada interprets Doko's gifts as a way for him to pay homage, respect, and honor to his father, to thank him for entrusting the blacksmith's work to him. Doko's father accepted these gifts and made *soré* scrapings to anoint Doko, his wife, and his children, so that *soré*'s slipperiness could cool them.

After that, Doko worked with his father as blacksmith. *Soré* is the dominant symbol in the process of purification and initiation that "gives birth" to a blacksmith. It also keeps the blacksmith and his family well during all the time he works with metal.

E. Zuia-zee-dono, *Washing Blacksmith Sickness*

Zee-dono, a sickness associated with the work and tools of the blacksmith, afflicts or "takes" a person who steals from a blacksmith or disturbs anything in the blacksmith's workshop. Only the blacksmith's washing can cure this sickness, which consists of a violent diarrhea. The blacksmith takes medicine from several trees, especially *soré*, and mixes it with water in a new calabash. He leads the offender to the *zukupaa*, or garbage pit, behind his house, and washes him, saying, "I wash you today for *zee-dono*! May that sickness stop right now!"

Next, the blacksmith plants three young *soré* sticks in the ground as a small fireplace. In a dish made from an old clay pot, he mixes *soré* scrapings, sesame butter, and amaryllis leaf with a little water, heats it and anoints the offender, using the stem of a *gbere* plant. *Soré* medicine not only cools the offender and restores health; it also reconciles him with the blacksmith. The *gbere* stem represents the violation that needs cooling. The rite is ended when the blacksmith extinguishes the fire.

F. Zuia-simbo-dono Te-wi Wén Zu Baa-dono, *When a Person Has Taken an Oath on* Dono

My source for the ritual description that follows is Appollinaire Yaya, a young Gbaya Christian. Yaya, a blacksmith and an assistant catechist in a Lutheran parish, was born of a long line of blacksmiths and regularly performs the rite he describes, interpreting it as a matter of *simbo*. It is dangerous to take an oath while holding any metal object made by a blacksmith, because *dono* is both powerful and truthful.

When a man asks Yaya to wash him for having taken an oath by *dono*, Yaya goes alone into the bush to collect what he needs. He goes first to the gallery forest, scrapes the bark of the *gbaradua* tree, and collects small amounts of *ḅui-so* and *gbedila* grass. Then he returns to his village, cutting a single, young *soré* stick on the way. When he arrives home, he cuts the *soré* into four pieces, each of which represents one of his blacksmith tools: the hammer, the anvil, the tongs, and a round piece used to fashion the hole of a spearhead. Yaya calls these four *soré* pieces *té-zui-bii*, tree-wash-person, for those who have taken an oath by *dono*.

He puts these things on the ground behind his house and digs two holes to form a tunnel about twenty centimeters deep and twenty centimeters long. Yaya places *ḅui-so*, *gbedila*, and the *gbaradua* scrapings in one hole; the four pieces of *soré* and his blacksmith tongs, in the other.

The two men involved in the argument that occasioned the oath wait beside this tunnel while Yaya goes to the stream to fetch water in a new calabash. When he returns, he leads both men to the hole with the *soré* in it and washes them, saying, "As I wash you of *dono*, let it be clear; if I'm deceiving you, this washing will not succeed! But if this is the washing my father showed me, then may it succeed for you!"

Then Yaya lights a straw fire and tells the men to jump over it, because when they pass over the fire, their "way" will become clear and clean. Yaya then leads them into his house and bids them sit on his bed. This position reminds one of the *zora-gangmo*, which is placed under the chief's bed; ideas of fertility associated with the *zora-gangmo* are here extended to the realm of covenant relationships. The two men feed each other with raw manioc, Yaya says, so that the *simbo-dono* that had taken them will leave them alone.

According to Yaya, the tunnel represents the blacksmith's workshop. The one hole and four pieces of *soré* are there to represent the smith's hearth and tools, literally, "to replace the fire." The other hole and medicine represent the smith's bellows. The men who had quarreled must be washed beside the "fire," near the hole that symbolizes the metals or "violent" tools of *dono*; it is the *simbo* of these tools that must be cooled by *soré*. When Yaya has overseen the men's reconciliation on his bed, he takes the objects from the tunnel and the new calabash to the foot of the *soré* tree.

"This year [1980] I've washed people three times," Yaya told me. "They were all Gbaya, either Christian or Muslim. Each of them gave me five hundred francs [about two dollars]. I didn't fix the price because I washed them to help them, not to earn money. If I had fixed the price myself, it would have been more, but that's what they gave me!

"I'm an assistant catechist, and my brother is a leader of our Lutheran youth group. I went to primary school through the fourth grade. The reason I washed those men was to prevent their suffering. When you take metal in your hand and swear by it falsely, if you are not washed, *simbo* takes you and you die. First you'll get sick with diarrhea; and probably you won't last more than two days before you die. But I don't want people to die, so I wash their *simbo* and heal them.

"*Simbo* is a terrible sickness because the *dokta*, the white doctors, can't do anything about it. Whenever it takes you, it kills you quickly. It's a sickness related to metal because metal works to help us find food on the hunt or in the fields. No one should say an oath when they're angry, because no one can play around with metal. *Zee-simbo-boi*, sickness-*simbo*-metal, takes you. Swearing a false oath by metal is like breaking God's law; you'll inevitably suffer the consequences of your law breaking!"

The blacksmith is one of the most important Gbaya "priests." He often performs the *zuia-simbo* rites for his villagers or plays a leading role in the rites of initiation, and he is another principal custodian of *soré*. His workshop is said to be "hot," and his tools and products are inherently "violent," since they are used as instruments of death in everyday life. *Soré*, however, transforms the smith's workshop into a cool place and his tools into instruments that bear life-giving fruits for the community. These tools are always potentially dangerous, but cooled by *soré*, their ultimate intention is to protect life.

G. Zuia-gera, *Washing (Away) Mourning*

Death in traditional Gbaya society is a complex drama. The washings of the widow or widower at the beginning and end of the mourning period constitute the crucial denouement of the entire drama. From a religious perspective, these washings represent the core of the traditional liturgy; that is, they reveal the intensity of the drama at its highest points. As rites of purification, the mourning rites focus on the removal of dirt from the widow or widower. Again the Gbaya reference to dirt in this ritual context indicates that life is sacred and death is an impurity that "curses" or destroys all who come in contact with it.

I shall describe the Gbaya death drama by focusing on the death of a Gbaya elder. As the central elements of this ritual process unfold, the importance of *zuia-simbo* as the paradigm of purification becomes more conspicuous. The *zuia-gera* rites consist of five acts: (1) the death of a Gbaya elder and preparations for his burial; (2) the elder's burial; (3) making mourning and washing away mourning; (4) celebrating the end of mourning; and (5) the nephew's sacrifice and washing the tears away.

The Death of a Gbaya Elder

A respected Gbaya elder has died. It is Monday morning, and the body is prepared immediately for burial. Fellow elders, members of his family, and close friends wash the body with a soap made from animal fat and ashes. It looks like the excrement of wild pig or donkey and is so named. They cut his fingernails and toenails, and shave the hair under his arms and around his genitals. His wife or sister collects the nails and shavings and places them behind the village at the foot of a *soré* tree. The body, wrapped in white cloth, is placed on a new *bu-déré*, a grass mat, which is a Gbaya symbol for death.

The grieving widow, her family, and her husband's family cover their heads and entire bodies with ashes and kaolin. The widow sits naked on the ground and does not eat any food. After the first day, she will eat something at her family's insistence; they remind her that unless she eats, she will follow her husband to the grave. Because she is associated with the dirt of death for a year she will eat alone at a friend's house, serving herself from an old calabash.

The mourners throw themselves violently on the ground and cry out in anguish. Some mourners are injured, either from throwing themselves on the ground or by cutting themselves with knives. The death of a great elder and leader is a painful loss for the community; the more highly respected the elder was for his contribution to Gbaya society, the more agitated the mourning behavior is likely to be. His peers in the village tell each other "A great *gera* tree has fallen!" The *gera* is a kapok tree of the gallery forest, highly valued for its strength, its fruit, and its fine shade. The departed elder resembles the great *gera* tree.

When the warriors' or hunters' drum has been heated beside the fire to draw the skin tight, it is beaten three times to signal the death of a leader. Then the dead man's friends stage a mock battle in front of the village public shelter, where the elder's body has been tied into a large chair. The elder's friend shouts, "The lion is dead!" and honors the dead man by raising and shaking his arms before the body.

The wrapped-and-bound, propped-up body may be adorned with a handsome robe; the face is visible, and a cord of *yoyongo* vine binds the elder's right hand in *zee* leaves as a symbol that either this person killed many *simbo* animals in his lifetime or an enemy in battle. The *zee* suggests that the elder was a strong, knowledgeable, and respected leader who did great, dangerous, and new deeds for his people; he was "a real man"!

Kua bird or chicken feathers have also been fastened to the man's right hand. The chicken feathers indicate that he has killed a woman; they are a propitiatory gesture. The *kua* is a magnificent black bird with red tail and red wings. Its striking red feathers symbolize blood, and the *kua* itself is associated with *simbo* animals. The *kua*'s call is like the call of a person who responds to a friend in distress.

The Gbaya fathers tell this story about a Gbaya captured in the bush. His captors asked him, "Are you alone or are some of your friends nearby?" The prisoner answered, "My friends are close by, and if I call out to them, they'll answer me!" "Go ahead and call your friends," they taunted him, "we'd like to see what happens!" So he cried out, "Huuuk! Huuuk!" They all listened, and soon came the answer, "Huuuk! Huuuk! Huuuk!" The man was freed as his captors fled—but in fact only the *kua* bird had responded to his call!

The red *kua* feathers in the elder's right hand indicate his brave deeds; he risked shedding the blood of enemies to protect the community, and he killed *simbo* animals to nourish it. In the past, say my informants, if the Gbaya received the red *kua* feathers, one could be sure that he had killed a *simbo* animal.

The Elder's Burial

The burial takes place on the day of death. Close friends and brothers carry the body to the grave, accompanied by the beating of the great drum and by mock battles and hunts, the latter staged by the elder's sons to honor him. The grave is dug to the depth of a meter, with a "room" on one side to accommodate the body, which is placed there, still wrapped in the new, clean mat. Then the elder's children are summoned to the grave. Each child throws a piece of charcoal on the body of the elder, after which the gravediggers collect one piece of charcoal from each child to count how many children the dead man had brought into the world.

Immediately after the elder's death, his children had rubbed charcoal on their faces to prevent his spirit from recognizing and cursing them for the hard words that had come between them. The Gbaya throw charcoal on the body and blacken their faces to erect a black wall between them and their father's spirit. It prevents the spirit from taking them into the realm of the dead or from returning to bother them.

The Gbaya also say that the charcoal represents the confession of sins. According to this more significant interpretation, if one does not confess, he or she will die. The charcoal is a symbol; it takes the sinner's place in the fire.

Hamada Samuel says that the charcoal also symbolizes the heart or liver of an animal. For example, if a hunter's child eats bits of charcoal as he crawls about the hearth, his father will bring back many animals. When the hunt is finished, the hunter will give choice raw liver to his child. Thus the charcoal symbolizes the contents of a person's heart, and its presence in the burial rites symbolizes what the heart ought to confess.

We have already noted this interpretation of charcoal in connection with washing away lost egg. In that ritual, charcoal from the parents' hearth is left at the fork in a path. In a washing performed for a young girl giving birth to her first child, if she has slept with someone other than her own husband, she may give pieces of charcoal to the midwife. The number of pieces represents the number of her illicit relationships. At the burial of a childless man or woman, charcoal is placed between their toes to indicate that their failure to give birth is associated with some sin on their part.

After he has thrown charcoal at his father, the eldest son grasps a shield and gestures toward his father, saying "I will take over from you! Go well!" When the grave has been filled by the elder's friends, they take the stick that had been used to measure the body, break it into three pieces and bury it. The stick represents the dead person and must be buried with him: "the stick used to dispatch the centipede goes right along with the centipede!" The gravediggers wash themselves beside the grave.

Following the burial, the mourners gather in front of the eldest son's house for the wake, while the dead man's younger brother collects their spears and sticks them in the ground. Each spear represents a brave deed performed by the elder in battle or on the hunt. His brother tells the assembly, "All of you who are doing *nana-goré*, pull out these spears and let's see what happens!" *Nana-goré* refers to recriminations that the deceased person's family (especially his sisters and nieces) direct at the widow and members of her family. The in-laws may be suspected of having caused the elder's death; if so, his widow is beaten, even by her own daughters, and accused of mistreating or killing her husband. The term *goré* referred in times past, explain my informants, to the dead, especially the abode of those whose earthly life had been evil; it refers in a more general way, in current usage, to the practice of speaking hard words to someone because of that person's unacceptable behavior, whether or not death is involved.

Those who respond to the call for spears to be pulled out of the ground are witnessing to their friendship and solidarity with the dead man's family. These mourners are his peers who participated in the same battles and hunts. The person who pulls out two spears is honored as having participated in two brave deeds with the departed elder. The whole village recognizes that the peers of the deceased are to be seriously reckoned with in the community; they must be respected on the same level as the man who just died.

Déa-gera *and* Zuia-gera, *Making and Washing Mourning*

The elder died on Monday. His widow eats little or nothing the first day following his death and does not wash in this initial mourning period. For three days she shuns all personal and social habits. Mourning is a rite of passage, and the widow's behavior clearly exhibits Victor Turner's three stages in the ritual process: (1) rites of separation; (2) rites of liminality, the "threshold," "betwixt-and-between" stage; and (3) rites of reintegration.[1]

The initial mourning period of three days is associated with the Gbaya belief that a man's *so-te*, spirit or soul, leaves the grave and goes "into the bush," there to become a *wi-zo*, a person of the grass. In the case of a woman's death, this passage occurs on the fourth day. During the initial and continued mourning period, leaves of the *ndende* tree are placed over the threshold of the widow's house, and under her head while she sleeps, in order to keep her husband's spirit at a distance, lest it trouble her.

Early morning on the third day (Wednesday), the *gera* priest cuts *soré* branches and places one in the doorway of the widow's house. The *gera* priest must fulfill two principal conditions before he is qualified to conduct these rites. He must be a widower who has himself undergone all the *gera* rites; and the person who washed him must have charged him specifically with the task of washing others. The priest waits until dawn breaks, then takes the *soré* branch into the house and summons the widow to follow him. Holding the *soré* branch between them, they proceed into the bush, accompanied by several members of her family and some of her husband's relations. In the bush, several savanna trees, including *soré*, are circled, scrapings are taken and an invocation is spoken: "May the *simbo* of [the elder's] death return with this tree!"

They circle a fresh termitary, depositing in it some of the widow's hair, then proceed into the gallery forest until they reach a place where two streams converge. Near the water they first circle a *gee* tree and a *gbanyak* vine, collect the scrapings, and go down into the water. At last, the priest washes the widow; he dips water from the stream three times, saying, "You were a good wife to your husband! Now he has left you. He has died! I therefore wash away all the dirt of your marriage! Your husband is no longer yours! Don't be preoccupied with his death! You may eat well again. Remain in good health! May the spirit of your husband leave you alone! Keep leaves of the *ndende* tree in your hand and under your head while you sleep!"

The widow then washes herself and invokes a blessing on herself. Family members are present, but they are not washed. When the washing and invocations are completed, the priest and the widow step out of the stream. The widow steps over, not through, a *zee* plant that has been placed on the path. The Gbaya interpret stepping through *zee* as a "new birth," but the widow's "new birth" is not accomplished until one year later when the mourning time is over. For similar reasons, she does not jump over a fire on the way back to her village.

The widow is led to the door of her own house, where she sits down on a new, clean mat. This mat may have been provided by the elder's younger brother, who will have the right to take this widow as wife once the mourning period has passed. The widow is counseled about fasting and abstinence during the mourning period. The most important instruction is that she refrain from sexual relations with anyone. No one other than a nursing child is to share her sleeping mat during this period, lest the dirt of death afflict that person. She also does not share her eating utensils with anyone, nor does she eat catfish (*yoo*), because that fish "slips" or makes mistakes! The catfish shares the physical properties of *soré*, and it can also be used in a sacrifice performed for the ancestors. In this case, it reminds the widow to be on guard against "losing her balance" or slipping into any temptation to unworthy behavior during her mourning period.

While the widow is receiving these instructions, she cuts her fingernails and toenails, and her husband's sister shaves her head. Her hair and nails and the clothes she has worn since her husband's death are carefully collected and carried away to be placed at the foot of a *soré* tree. The priest anoints her with *soré* scrapings. She will not trim her nails or cut her hair again for a year, and she will wear a white string or thread around her neck. Roots from three different trees are attached to this string to protect her from the elder's spirit. Batoure Ruben notes that after this washing, the widow's children may jump over a fire, but not the widow. Bobo Pierre explains that the family may also circle a chicken coop following the *déagera* washing. These gestures are related to the danger and dirt of death; the second one — the circling of the chicken coop — appears to have propitiatory implications.

The actions that comprise the widow's washing are described as *déagera*, "making" or "fixing" the state of mourning. As rites of separation they affect her entry into the betwixt-and-between liminal period of one year. Mourning is a sober time for the widow. She is in passage during this year from one state of existence to another. She is not physically separated from Gbaya society, but she is ritually and symbolically separated. The dirt of her husband's death threatens her and those whom she contacts; caution must be exercised in her regard, lest she "give dirt" to other people. The rules of abstinence and ritual separation must not be broken by the widow or by those who live with her, for such a disregard for her state would endanger their health and put their lives at risk.

At the end of a year, the priest is summoned by the widow's family and told, "Tomorrow morning you will wash the widow!" He arrives before dawn, places a *soré* branch in the widow's doorway, and returns at the break of day to lead the widow once again into the gallery forest to be washed: *zuia-gera*. This time they do not circle trees and collect scrapings but go directly to the stream. The priest washes the widow with invocations similar to those spoken a year earlier; and, after that, she washes herself. But this year, when they come up from the water, the widow passes through a *zee* leaf and jumps over a little fire on the path.

On their way to the village, the priest cuts stems from a young *soré* tree, which he will use to anoint the widow, members of her two families, and other villagers. He may also collect *zoǫo* leaves for a ritual meal. The anointing rite, or *kpaia-mo*, takes place in front of the widow's house. Again, sesame seed oil is mixed with *soré* scrapings and heated in a broken piece of pottery over a fire kindled between three *soré* sticks. The priest dips a *gbere* stem or a *soré* stick in the oil and anoints each person on the forehead and breast; between the thumb and forefinger; and between the toes— invoking blessings of health and well-being on everyone he touches. After the anointing, family and friends collect the broken pottery and charcoal and throw these in the direction of a bird flying west toward the setting sun. "Hooooo!" they shout. "May *simbo* return with this bird! May this *simbo* be over and done with!"

At last the anointing rite is finished, and the widow sits before her house on a new, clean mat. She trims her fingernails and toenails, and someone does her hair. Her nails and hair, old clothes, utensils, and sleeping mat are deposited at the foot of a *soré* tree. The widow is praised for her good behavior during the preceding year; then she is anointed with *kui* mixed with oil, given new clothes to wear, and adorned with necklaces and brace- lets. Her family and friends greet her as she is reintegrated, or received back, into everyday Gbaya society. They also join her in a meal of *zobo* leaves mixed with peanut butter. Eating together is a sign that unity has been reestablished and that the danger of dirt is over.

On the day of her reentry, the elder's younger brother may claim the widow as his wife, thereby sealing her reintegration and renewing the cov- enant between the two families. The elder's inheritance is also distributed and shared by his family. As *déa-gera* effected entry into the betwixt-and- between year of abstinence, so the *zuia-gera* effects reentry into the ordinary activities of Gbaya society.

(Gbanga-fio) *Celebrating the End of Mourning*

The widow's second washing, the anointing of her family and friends, the *zobo* meal, her remarriage, and the distribution of the elder's goods reestablish the widow's position in the normal flow of daily life. For impor- tant elders, however, the drama of death continues until the *gbanga* has been celebrated. *Gbanga-fio* is not celebrated for any and every death, but only for a man who has killed many *simbo* animals. The elder's family makes extensive preparations for this community celebration; his oldest son under- takes the planning to coincide with the *zuia-gera* rites. The celebration often occurs, however, several years later.

When the family has decided that the time has come to celebrate, that is, when the family is ready to provide food and drink for many people, the elder's daughters prepare a prodigious amount of manioc, and the family pools their resources to procure great quantities of meat from both domes- tic and bush animals. The women also exert themselves to produce corn beer, without which the *gbanga-fio* cannot succeed.

When a preliminary amount of food and drink is ready, the elder's son sends baskets of meat and manioc flour and a pot of beer to members of his own family, important in-laws, and head chiefs in the area as a gift and reminder that the *gbanga* is in serious preparation. Some time later, perhaps as long as two years later, the elder's son again sends gifts to these people, with the message that the *gbanga* will begin in a few days.

On the appointed day, family, friends, and government authorities arrive from everywhere, animals are slaughtered, beer is distributed and the feast begins in the afternoon or evening. The elder's son exhorts the "village crier" to invite the guests to celebrate the feast with this warning: "Drink lots of beer! Have fun eating and dancing, but let there be no fighting! Don't be jealous of your wives—let there be no fighting between husbands and wives, or there will be fines to pay!" This proclamation has the force of law; sexual license reigns throughout the night of drinking, eating and dancing. As everyone is urged to have a playful time, recriminations between husbands and wives cannot be tolerated during the *gbanga-fio*.

The dancing continues until the next morning, when the elder's son again summons the town crier to "tell everyone to clean up!" The guests wash and put on clean clothes. The elder's son also gets the village shelter ready, where the important guests will eat another meal. He asks for the drummers, who enter his house with him, carrying a new, clean mat. In a few moments the drummers lead the elder's son, who is hidden under the mat, out among the guests. They raise their arms to greet him, the women ululate to show their joy, and he emerges from this symbol of death to lead the crowd in another round of dancing.

After a few hours, the dancing stops and the elder's son sits down in a chair by the village shelter. Everyone approaches to give him money in thanks for the feast! Someone is appointed to announce the name of each contributor and the amount of money he brings. When all the gifts have been collected, the elder's family retires to count the money. Then the elder's son summons the town crier to thank everyone for coming, and to thank them for their gifts. He says that he and his father and their family have been honored. May everyone go home well and happy.

The Nephew's Sacrifice and Washing the Tears Away

When the *gbanga-fio* celebrations are drawing to a close, the departed elder's nephew is summoned: this nephew is the son of the elder's sister, and resides in another village, his father's village. The *bé-noko*, or nephew (the term can also designate a niece), fulfills a number of important ritual roles in Gbaya society, especially those having to do with sacrifice or rites of reconciliation.

The nephew arrives on the last evening of the *gbanga-fio*, just as the guests are leaving. Early the next morning, the great drum is again heard three times in the village, and a goat or a chicken is attached to it, to await the nephew's arrival. The elder's younger brother stands next to the animal and invokes a blessing, addressed to his departed brother, "I am doing this *sadaka*, sacrifice, in your memory, and have called our nephew to do it in your honor!" He names his great-grandfather, his grandfather, his father, and his departed brother, and continues while the drum beats: "I called our nephew to do this sacrifice in your honor in order to protect our village, to assure good health for us all! Don't be angry with us! Don't let any sickness fall upon us! Help us to get what we need to eat!"

After this invocation, the nephew runs up with a pestle in his hand, which he uses to kill the goat or chicken. The drum stops beating; the nephew butchers the goat or chicken and roasts it over the fire, still standing in that same place next to the drum.

When the meat is ready to eat, he cuts off a piece and throws it to the ground, saying, "Here I am, your nephew! I have come to do this sacrifice in your honor! Take sickness away from our families! Grant good health to my uncles! If I am not really your nephew, may sickness fall on our families! In that case, let them have no food! But since I really am your nephew, give them good health! Let them have all they need to eat!"

The nephew invokes this blessing from the departed elder. As he had been a great man and a blessing to the community during his lifetime, so he is the one to receive the nephew's prayer. He is addressed as one who is expected to continue to bless the village.

The nephew does not leave for his own village the same day. About noon some of the villagers leave for a brief hunt and, in the evening, return with food. The nephew congratulates and thanks them, saying, "The purpose for which I came has been accomplished! God accepts our sacrifice! I'm going home now! Take good care of your village!" The grateful villagers collect cloth, arrows, hoes, spears, and knives and give them to the nephew.

When the nephew arrives in his own village, he tells his mother what has happened. She in turn goes to the village of her departed elder brother, and thanks the brother who had summoned her son for the sacrifice. Then, in the evening she goes to the gallery forest to find a small *kanga* plant, which she will carry back to her brother's village. Early the next morning she pounds the *kanga* plant in a mortar and puts the pulp in an old pot filled with water.

The elder's sister then summons all the villagers—men, women, and children—and washes their faces from the water in her pot; she washes the rest of their tears away, and she tells them, "I came to wash away all your tears, tears from the hard times that fell on your village! May your joy return! May you eat well and enjoy good health!"

When she has washed everyone's face, she takes the old pot to the foot of a *soré* tree—and it's all over. She greets everyone and returns to her own village. The nephew's sacrifice and his mother's rite of purification have brought the great Gbaya death drama to a close.

7

Growing Up in Gbaya Society:
Tales and Dances

In the Gbaya family, children are "initiated" at an early age. Through the performance of elementary tasks they begin to assimilate the fundamental values of their culture. Many of these values revolve around the development of appropriate kinship relationships and preparation for marriage. Play, dance and oral tradition contribute significantly to this development, as they communicate and reflect the words and deeds that are "for life"; that is, these dances and storytelling transmit the values that make Gbaya life worth living. They culminate in *labi*, the major initiation rite for boys, which will be described in the next chapter. Gbaya initiation is an integral part of the wider Gbaya symbolic world; its ritual dances are related to sacrificial and purification rites, on the one hand, and *to*, the oral or narrative expression of Gbaya values, on the other. Symbolic connections between *simbo* rites and initiation rites prompt difficult questions about the complex values expressed in Gbaya ritual and myth. Connecting these values in one symbolic whole is difficult because they are about life and death. In Gbaya initiation the fear of death and the celebration of life are inseparable.

GROWING UP IN A GBAYA COMMUNITY

Any person's socialization is a long and complex process that occurs in the course of everyday family life and in the familiar relationships developed within the local neighborhood and surrounding community. A Gbaya child—male or female—first participates in the rhythm of life from a position on its mother's back or breast; the mother maintains close physical contact with the child until it begins to walk and talk. A small girl carries a calabash of water or a piece of wood to assist her mother and by the age of five or six already helps to look after her younger siblings. In the evening by the kitchen fire, a Gbaya mother counsels her daughter how to prepare for marriage. She must learn to care not only for her husband's daily needs of food and bath water, but also for the needs of her in-laws.

A small boy eats with the men and sits by the fire in front of his father's house where he, too, receives his first instructions about marriage. He must learn to respect his elders and take his part in family work routines, especially as he goes to the fields with his father, helping to carry tools and hunting weapons. Gbaya children are given specific responsibilities toward younger siblings, parents, and grandparents at an early age. The extended family is a microcosm of the larger Gbaya world; therefore, it is among family that the child learns to establish relationships that will be at the center of adult life.

Young boys participate with their friends in a variety of games involving competition and skill: sports and hunting games. War games, pantomime, toy-making (blowguns are made from *soré* sticks; animal or human figures, from bamboo) and games of chance are all in the Gbaya repertoire. Boys especially enjoy the competition between two teams of spear-throwers; each boy tries to cast his spear through a rolling grass hoop, which represents an animal. A favorite game of young girls is the organization of picnics in the bush; they collect everything needed for the preparation of a Gbaya meal, and play house, cooking, and sharing manioc paste or mud imitations of it.

The Gbaya personality finds its freest expression in dance, however, which is, so to speak, the most frequently played game in all Gbaya villages. In Philip A. Noss's classification: "There are dances for hunting expeditions, for harvest celebrations, for drinking parties and for nighttime games. There are dance festivals to mark each major event in life, birth, initiation, marriage and death."[1]

Festival celebration and education of Gbaya youth merge in their dances, which are dramatic representation of Gbaya folktales, or *to*. Gbaya narrative, song, and dance as well as many Gbaya games are important rituals and myth. The Gbaya do not transmit their values by lecturing and didacticism; instead, they wrap the lesson in enjoyable media, and learning is a by-product of fun. The rites of passage are occasions for dance, but so is almost every event in Gbaya life.

Concerning men, women, and marriage, the concept of authority in Gbaya society is consistent with principles of patrilineal descent. Wives in a domestic group represent the interdependence of the clans; they do not belong to their husbands' clans. Although they eat their meals apart from their husbands, and are often largely responsible (with the children) for the upkeep of the family garden, their role in Gbaya society is far from "domestic servanthood." Girls' initiation rites are an effective witness to the importance of the female in Gbaya tradition.

THE SUITOR AND HIS IN-LAWS

Gbaya tradition has focused much attention on the role of the *wi-kofe*, or suitor, including the metaphorical designation of that role in terms of the *soré* tree: a suitor is a *soré*-cool-thing. In April 1981 I drove an old Gbaya friend, Garba André, to the village of his in-laws; on the way, we discussed his relationship with his in-laws. "I'm a *wi-kofe* among them," he said. "I'm *soré* among them!" That is, in addition to bringing members from two clans together in a covenant agreement, the *wi-kofe* also carries out peace-keeping responsibilities toward his in-laws, not only prior to the marriage (for example, by working in the in-laws' fields), but also after the marriage, for as long as they live.

The *wi-kofe* is a "man who begs" for his wife; marriage sets up a relationship of economic obligation between a husband and his in-laws. Thus the bride-price is an essential feature of the marriage arrangement. It is promised during *hara-koo*, the period of betrothal, and completed at the time of the marriage, the *baa koo*, the "taking (of) a wife." A Gbaya man may avoid living near his father-in-law, however, if he is under constant pressure to perform services or provide more money.

As to the criteria for choosing a marriage partner, we are instructed by a *lizang*, a parable about the toad and the frog. The toad represents the Gbaya, who are blacker and considered by some less beautiful than the Fulbe, who are represented by the frog. In the parable, a girl is given in marriage to a Fulbe because he is better looking. When the Gbaya candidate proves himself to be more resourceful, however, the narrator concludes:

> Goodness isn't in the skin. If you have *hakkilo*, carefulness and wisdom, then you are good. If you are good-looking, but your conduct is bad, then you are bad. So we Gbaya say, "If you show respect for me, I will give my daughter to you. But if you don't show respect for me, I won't give my daughter to you. I don't care about good looks."[2]

Gbaya narrative also provides clues to "ideal" marriage relationships. For example:

> In contrast with Wanto stands Laaiso, his wife. . . . Laaiso is everything that Wanto is not; where he is happy-go-lucky, she is serious. Where he loves to dance, she concentrates on her household duties. When he thinks only of his own enjoyment, she thinks of him and goes to

his rescue. If he sometimes plays tricks and fails to live up to his responsibilities, she corrects him.[3]

A premium is placed on the brother-sister relationship in Gbaya society, which is seen as a model for friendship, respect and mutual aid. A long tale about "the brother's quest" describes a young man who was mocked by his friends because he has no sister. When he learns that his sister had been carried off while still a baby by the villain, *Gba-so*—who, in Gbaya tales, is not a great god at all, but a devilish person—he sets out to find her. After the narrator has finished this tale, he comments to his audience:

Now that is the reason why a young man and a young woman should not make love. Because if you, a young girl, are with a fellow somewhere, the place where the girl is, no matter what happens, her brother must go to that place even if it means his death.[4]

Another narrator tells how a wife helped her husband when his brother tried to kill him and take away his inheritance: "And the reason why Ngeesi lived was thanks to his wife. Because ... some wives look after their husbands as though they were brother and sister, and that's how he was saved."[5]

GBAYA BIRTH AND NAMING RITES

Ndoyama Enoch explains that a generation ago when he was a child, a pregnant woman usually went to her father's village for the birth of her children, so that her own mother could assist with the birth. The Gbaya have not altogether abandoned this practice, but today the mother is assisted by a midwife, and children are ordinarily born in their parents' home. Modesty prevents the father from being present at the birth, says Ndoyama, but he is called inside soon after the birth. The midwife carefully disposes of the afterbirth by burying it next to the house. Ndoyama explains that the afterbirth must never be simply "thrown away" because that would prevent the woman from ever bearing another child.

When the umbilical cord has dried up and dropped off, perhaps several days after the birth, the child's mother takes it out to the foot of a *soré* tree, or at least to the foot of a thick grass that does not easily burn. Ndoyama claims that it is still very common to dispose of the umbilical cord at the foot of a *soré* tree in order to assure the health of the newborn child. Naming the child does not occur until after the umbilical cord has dropped off and been cooled by *soré*.

Hamada Samuel says that a person's name is that person: *Nin-wi ne kiite-wi*. The Gbaya respect and fear a person's name; thus, if they give the father's name to a child, they do not address the child by that name. Gbaya never address their parents by name, as this would be to ridicule or despise them. At the very least, it would be disobedient, as one should be of one mind and spirit with one's parents. Hamada's assertion that a person's name *is* the person indicates that names are metaphorical: a person's name participates in the bodily reality of the living being. It is a symbol that points to or opens one to a dimension of reality that would not otherwise be perceived. Names constitute persons; therefore, naming ceremonies are accompanied by dramatic performance (dance) and appropriate symbol-bearing media to celebrate the new life that arises from the grip of death.

CIRCUMCISION RITES

Circumcision is not part of a Gbaya initiation rite, although it is an important step for a boy's integration into society. On the day of circumcision, the lad wears no clothes and must carefully observe certain food taboos. He must not eat slippery vegetable sauces or catfish; nor does he eat raw or salted meat until the wound has healed. He should, however, eat *kpasa*, fresh-water shrimp, and *gaa*, little white fish with a silvery belly; meat smoked over a fire and sesame butter are also recommended.

Not just anyone may circumcise; only a man who has been consecrated, that is, entrusted to it with *do-mo* may perform this task. When this "priest" arrives at the boy's home, he digs a little hole by the house. The child sits on a rock above the hole, held in place by two men, and the priest ties a thin cord around the boy's penis. His knife is a special instrument used only for circumcision, and it is cooled by *soré* before and after the operation. He holds up the cord and the knife approaches once, twice, three times, then with a single cut he removes the foreskin and drops it into the hole. No words accompany the operation, according to my informants.

The boy's old loincloth is thrown into the hole with the foreskin and burned with it. Smoke from the fire rises to heal the wound. The boy remains over the hole until the blood stops flowing, at which time his penis may be wrapped in a *domo* leaf, in which medicine from the *dere* tree is contained. The hole is then covered over and the rite is finished.

Some days later when the wound is completely healed, the priest informs the boy's parents that they should procure a new loincloth for their son. He arrives at the boy's house, removes the cloth worn since the circumcision, and brings the new cloth to the boy's crotch three times, saying, "I hereby consecrate this cloth for you!" The boy puts on his new loincloth, and the priest lays the "interim" cloth at the foot of a *soré* tree to cool the period of abstinence and fasting.

Hamada explains that among his Gbaya clans, on the day the boy receives his new loincloth, his family prepares a generous skewer of dried and smoked catfish, which the boy presents to the priest. The priest takes the smallest fish from the spit, breaks it and puts a piece into the boy's mouth, saying, "I hereby consecrate this fish for you today!" This is done three times, and each time the boy spits the fish on the ground, after which the priest gives him his new loincloth. The skewer of fish is a gift for the priest.

Gbaya circumcision is not a simple surgical operation to assure good hygiene, but a rite of passage in which the young boy begins to learn the values of his people. The rite is not complicated—that is, it is not one of the most elaborate Gbaya rituals—but neither are its actions and objects in any way arbitrarily conceived. The importance, for example, of *soré* and the observance of the food taboos fit neatly into the symbolic reality of the Gbaya world.

GBAYA DANCES RELATED TO THE RITES OF PASSAGE

Dance, too, belongs to these early initiation rites, or rites of passage. Not all dances are fun and games, however, nor are they performed as an unmitigated pleasure. The freedom manifested in dance is not an effortless freedom, but a hard-won and costly freedom gained only through self-discipline. Gbaya initiation rites involve the protection of life and society, but Gbaya oral tradition, like all narrative, depends on the coincidence of opposing characteristics: the happy-go-lucky Wanto, for example, and his careful, responsible wife. It is this "holding together" that is celebrated in the dance.

A. The Dances of Diang and To

Diang is the first dance of Gbaya children, says Yadji André. A boy who *gbea diang*, successfully endures the initiation process of *diang*, shows that he is able to separate himself from his mother; he is, we would say, "no longer tied to his mother's apron strings." *Diang* teaches a boy courage, and in *diang* he also learns rules about abstinence and fasting.

When the time for *diang* has come, which, according to Yadji, is always during the dry season, the village elders (one of whom is leader of the rites) assemble all the boys who are between the ages of six and eight years old and are beginning to understand about life. They lead the boys to a nearby stream, where they wash themselves, after which they climb out of the water and kneel down by the bank of the stream. The elders explain to the boys that they must now receive *diang* medicine, and the leader says, "You must not scratch yourselves when I put this medicine on your bodies!" This medicine is *nguru*, the fruit of the *mbiro* vine; it is covered with hairy bristles that cause a violent itching sensation.

The medicine is rubbed on the boys' bare bottoms and may be supplemented by similar medicines from the *yoyongo* and *mbambale* vines. If one of the boys succumbs to the itch and starts to scratch his bottom, the leader swats him, saying, "You have no courage! You're breaking one of the rules of *diang*!" The boys remain kneeling until the medicine has dried and the itching has subsided, and then they are brought to their feet for the return to the village. They make their way home singing:

Yaa! Bamboo-sprout meat!
Gezengere, don't come up empty,
We do ours in the Mbal!
Diang-e, bamboo-sprout meat!
Gezengere, don't come up empty,
We do ours in the Mbal!

When they arrive back in the village, the elder tells the boys, "You're going to spend the rest of the day in the cold house!" Yadji explains that a *gee-tua* is a cool or peaceful place, an empty, abandoned house in which there is no fire and no food. It is a "fasting" place, says Yadji, like the one used by hunters who have killed a leopard; other villagers do not gather there.

When the boys are in the cold house, the elders tell them, "Today you must not go into your mothers' kitchens where there is *gui!*" *Gui* is a basket or pot of food suspended over their mothers' fires. This is the first rule given to the boys, explains Yadji. Then they learn a few phrases of the "*diang* language." Noss's informants told him there was no "*diang* language," but Yadji recalls a few phrases that appear to represent a kind of rehearsal for the far more serious task of learning the *labi* language during the boys' adolescent years. The boys are taught, for example, *Diang me na bubu, diang me na tuutuu!* These words mean "*Diang* wants *kam, diang* wants meat!" When the boys are hungry, they can go to their mothers for food, but only if they use these phrases to ask for it.

In the evening, the elders lead the boys out of the cold house and their parents assemble to watch them dance. First the boys are invited to share in a meal of manioc and bamboo sprouts with the elders. Then the *diang* dances are "consecrated," or set apart for this festival occasion. The boys sing as they dance:

Oh honeycomb, *diang kpol-e*
Kpol! Kpol!
Look at what the children do with themselves,
Kpol! Kpol!

As the boys dance and sing several numbers in the *diang* repertoire, the audience distinguishes between those who dance the right way and those who are slow to learn. According to Yadji, the important thing about *diang* is that it leads boys from irresponsible to responsible behavior, and the boys also get something "to swear by," just as they will later swear an oath by their *labi* incision. Gbaya initiation rites, beginning with *diang*, are, like the blacksmith's tools, "powerful" and "truthful"—thus something "to swear by."

According to Noss, "There was no unity among young and old, no interdependence between generations, no society until the elders called the children together to share a meal of cassava and bamboo sprouts. After eating this meal, they taught the children songs and urged them to dance, and this was the origin of the festival of *diang*—a celebration of the creation of Gbaya community and society."[6]

The *diang* "dance" is not unambiguously the celebration of life. As ritual performance it is also an expression of concern about the constant threat of death. In this way, *diang* appears to be linked to *labi* as the *baminga* dance is related to washing *simbo*: *diang* is a rehearsal or foreshadowing of more serious things to come.

Another male initiation rite among the Gbaya is the rite called *to*, last practiced about two generations ago by boys between the ages of eight and ten. *To* begins by a ritual death of the boys under water, followed by their resurrection and the cutting of an incision on the stomach of each initiate. An initiation camp is established near the village; there the boys learn the *to* language, a repertoire of dances and lore focused especially on hunting skills.

Death and resurrection, separation from the normal flow of society for the intense learning of Gbaya skills and Gbaya wisdom, including communication in a new language, and reintegration into society marked by a festive dance—these are the elements of the *to* dance and *labi*.

B. Dances for Girls and Young Women

Gbaya tradition encompasses several initiation rites for girls and young women. *Naa-yeng*, a female equivalent of *diang*, at least among Yaayuwee-speaking Gbaya clans, is a dance for girls between the ages of eight and ten. It is directed by adult women at the center of the village, lasts only one day, and focuses on the learning of songs and dances. Some of the songs allude to women's tasks and burdens in life; one invokes and praises the "spirit of *naa-yeng*," imploring it to have mercy on the initiates. The *labi* initiation also includes a "spirit," *so-labi*, although I have found no reference to any sacrifices or offerings presented explicitly to this spirit.

Oumarou Joseph explains the *bé-bokoo*, another initiation rite for girls that was practiced especially among Dooka-speaking Gbaya clans. It is probably not a *gasa yoya*, or a "great important dance," but several of its elements are nevertheless worth noting. Girls between the ages of ten and twelve are led to a stream and washed by a village elder, whose ritual title is *singmo*. After the washing, the girls wrap a *yoyongo* vine around their waists and return to the village. According to Oumarou, when these vines dry out, they are gathered and placed in the roof over the threshold of the house in which the *singmo*'s father lives. His father in turn takes the dry vines to the foot of a *soré* tree to cool the *simbo* of this dance.

The leaders of *bé-bokoo* then gather *giti* vines. They strip off the dirty outer layer of the vine to reveal a white bark from which fibrous strings are taken and fashioned into skirts for the initiates. The white skirts, says

Oumarou, show that the girls have left their old place for a new place, their new "dance house." He notes that this corresponds to a move of *labi* initiates from their first camp to a more permanent camp.

Oumarou distinguishes between *gbea-yoya*, "enduring or suffering" the dance, symbolized by the girls' going under the water to be washed by *Singmo*, and *zuia-yoya*, washing the dance. The girls wait in their mothers' houses before being led to the stream for a second washing. This one Oumarou calls a *kpasa zuiaa*, a "real" washing. A dam was built for the first washing because it was for *simbo*, says Oumarou; but at the second washing no dam is needed because this time they wash simply for their good health. Thus his reference to this as a "real" washing becomes clear; the first (*simbo*) washing was symbolic; the second washing is really to wash their bodies clean, since, as betwixt-and-between persons, they did not bathe. The girls then return to the village where they are presented to their families and begin the dance festivals.

Oumarou's recollections are the only data I have on the *bé-bokoo*, and they appear to be only a fragment of that ritual process. The question that it prompts concerns the reference to *simbo*: What offense occasioned the taking of these young girls? The food taboos of the ritual are clues to the probable answer. As the prohibition of red-colored antelopes and a red-colored mushroom suggest blood, it is reasonable to assume that the girls' *simbo*-thing is menstrual blood. If we relate this assumption to the slippery foods prohibited to *wi-simbo* during the time of purification, then the relationship is clear between those food taboos and sexual intercourse. The frequent appearance of *yoo*, the (slippery) catfish, as a food taboo for liminal persons becomes linked to the simultaneous prohibition of sexual intercourse for such persons.

ZAABOLO

Azimi Pauline, now a Gbaya Christian about forty-five years old, was initiated in the *zaabolo* rite as "Zek," the leader of her peer group. She subsequently helped direct several other *zaabolo* dances. The following description is her own narrative of this rite.

When the village fathers want their daughters to be initiated into *zaa*, they build a grass hut near the village. Then one afternoon at the beginning of the rainy season they lead the girls (as many as thirty or forty at a time) down to the stream for *gbea ne zaa*, initiating *zaa*. The leader of *zaa* is a man called *Waa-yi-zaa*. On the way to the stream he gathers scrapings from many trees and vines. He does not, however, circle the trees. When the girls arrive at the stream with their mothers and all the village women previously initiated into *zaa*, the leaders make a small shelter over the water called a house-for-initiating-*zaa*.

While they make a little dam under the shelter to create a pool, the girls wait on the bank.

When the shelter is ready the older women remove the girls' clothing and give each one a *yoyongo* vine to tie around her waist; each girl also ties on leaves as a skirt. Some men have brought a drum to the stream, and now the girls dance to its beat—indeed the men come only because women do not know how to beat a drum. A young man is chosen to be initiated along with the girls, and he is called *Lingi*.

Before the girls go down into the water, they dance and sing this song: "*Dikiḍi-kpee, gé noi gé ndé? | Noi'i baa ne zaa. | Me wo!*" *Dikiḍi* is the Gbaya name of the orange-cheeked waxbill, a tiny sociable bird who feeds on grains, and *kpee* is an ideophone designating an attitude of silence. Thus the song is "*Dikiḍi kpee,* what bird is that? The right one for initiates. Welcome!"

Each of the older women (former initiates themselves) chooses a girl who is known for her careful and responsible behavior to take as her own initiate, thus becoming the girl's "godmother" or "sponsor." When the song has ended, all the girls raise their arms over their heads, looking toward the east, their fists first closed and then opened toward the east. Then they are led silently into the water and under the shelter. Everyone is silent. The first girl taken into the shelter is called "Zek" and she is a leader among all the girls. The godmothers accompany their charges into the shelter, where they sit on the little sticks that form the dam. *Waa-yi-zaa* burns most of his medicinal scrapings and puts the ashes in the horns of a red duiker. He adds the leftover scrapings to a calabash of water.

When a girl enters the shelter and sits down, *Waa-yi-zaa* cuts two incisions in the small of her back, one on each side, and rubs medicine from the horns into these incisions. Then he dips water four times from the pool, washing each girl and saying, "I hereby initiate you into the *zaa* dance! May you be well and strong as you dance! May nothing make you sick! May nothing harm you!"

As each girl climbs out of the water, she is followed by another until all have been washed. The Gbaya never wash two at a time in the shelter, only one by one. The reason they make these incisions is to give the girls good health during the dance; it is to make their bodies soft and flexible for dancing.

The older initiates who are not godmothers wait on the bank of the stream; when the girls emerge from the water they kneel before these women to be whipped. The godmothers intervene, however, saying, "Don't beat my child! Beat me instead!" In this way the godmothers bear the suffering of their children. The girls' own mothers keep a distance, watching everything but not coming near. When all the girls have been washed and whipped (though it is the godmothers who endure the whipping), the shelter and dam are broken down, and the girls are led back to the village.

They go single file, each girl wrapping her arms tightly around the girl who precedes her, with the godmothers at their side to protect them from the old initiates' whips. The drummers bring up the rear of this procession, singing and beating their drums all the way to a new grass hut that has been built near the village. On the way, they sing, "The *zaa* maidens of *Waa-yi*, he! Good morning, greetings, to you, *Waa-yi*!" The girls will sleep together in this hut during the three or four months of *zaabolo*, and they are not allowed to enter their mothers' kitchens. Their food taboos during this time include red duiker, bushbuck and oribi—all the red-colored antelopes—and reddish-colored mushrooms.

The girls enter their hut and wait until evening, when their mothers bring them food. After they have eaten, the old initiates reappear, each with a calabash of cold water. They extinguish the fire in the girls' hut, then proceed to pour cold water all over the girls and all over the floor of the hut, singing all the while, "The *zaa* maidens of *Waa-yi*! Greetings to you, *Waa-yi*!" When the floor of the hut and everything and everyone in it are completely soaked, the girls are led outside, where they again form a single file, wrapping their arms around each other. The girls move from house to house in the village singing the same song and being doused with cold water by the old initiates all along the way.

When night falls, the girls are again led into the gallery forest, but this time they go to a different stream. No shelter is built over the running water as before, and they are simply told, "Go play in the water so that the cold water bothers you or causes you grief!" They remain there for some time, playing together in the cold, running water during the dark of night. The leaders of the rite and other old initiates cry out, "Give us some money and we'll let you get out of the water!" The girls' mothers, godmothers, and suitors give money to the old initiates, after which the girls finally emerge from the water and return to their hut.

According to Azimi, the girls remain in their *zaabolo* camp for several months. During this time, their mothers regularly prepare corn beer and generous portions of *kam* for the godmothers. Festive dancing marks these months, often lasting all night. Their mothers' kitchens are strictly off-limits for the girls, and they must also keep their distance from the little pools where freshly dug manioc tubers are being soaked. Every day during *zaabolo* the girls are assigned tasks to help their godmothers and other old initiates with domestic duties, but they never help their own mothers during this time.

The night before the girls return to their own families an especially vigorous dance is celebrated, during which "Zek," the girls' leader, must not fall asleep. If "Zek" falls asleep that night, the dance is ruined! "Zek" leads her peers through all the *zaabolo* dances learned during the initiation. This stage in the rite is an occasion for all the villagers to share in communal dancing, eating and drinking. In the morning, the girls are led first to the mother of "Zek," share a big meal with her and "after words" go home to their own mothers.

In the following days and weeks, the girls continue to practice their *zaabolo* dances with *Waa-yi-zaa* and to serve the domestic needs of their godmothers and other old initiates. When at last the time comes for the culmination of the dance a tall *kutu* tree is cut and planted as a pole in front of the chief's house. The *kutu* tree grows in the gallery forest and produces (oozes) a milky, sticky latex substance; initiates refer to it as the *lingi-zaa*.

According to Hamada Samuel, on the day of final celebrations, *Waa-yi-zaa* leads the girls down to the water and washes them; after which the girls return to the village, hidden under new mats. When they arrive at the foot of the *lingi-zaa*, the girls emerge and burst into dance, led by *Waa-yi-zaa*, who climbs the pole. High on the pole, he performs acrobatics and dance movements, holding onto the pole with his legs and feet. He descends slowly to the rhythm of the dance until he finally releases his hold and drops into the outstretched arms of the *zaa* maidens. His performance inspires the girls, who demonstrate the dances they have learned during the *zaabolo* ritual process until they are exhausted; then they kneel by their mats to receive gifts and congratulations from the villagers. Those who not only danced well but also worked obediently for the old initiates receive the best rewards.

Azimi concludes her description of the *zaabolo* with an account of the washings and anointings that take place as each girl is "graduated" from *zaabolo*. Alternately, the entire group of girls may undergo these rites as a grand finale. According to Azimi's own experience, on the day of final celebration, *Waa-yi-zaa* cuts a *soré* branch and throws it on the threshold of each girl's house. Each godmother leads her girl into the bush, holding *soré* between them. Circling trees and a fresh termitary, they process to the stream and are washed four times by *Waa-yi-zaa*. Their ritual gestures are very similar to washing *simbo*: they climb out of the water, pass through a *zee* plant, jump over a little fire on the path and, without looking back, strike out for the village.

Before entering the village each girl puts on a new skirt or fresh leaves and, when all arrive, *Waa-yi-zaa* anoints each girl with sesame or *zénga* oil between the toes, on the knees, in the palm of the hand, and on the breast. The oil is then wiped away with a *soré* leaf and all remnants of the anointing rite are thrown after a bird, "Hooooo!" Henceforth, the young girls are initiates.

Azimi explains that these final rites of *zaabolo* are the same rites performed for *labi* initiates at the very end of *labi*. She agrees with Hamada that dancing characterizes the culmination of *zaabolo*, but she insists its true denouement is the rite from the circling of trees and washing to the anointing. "The anointing rite must end it all." Azimi also offers the following reflections on *zaabolo*: "Today some of my friends swear by my name, 'My Zek-Azimi!' *Zaabolo* was a good thing, because none of us who were initiated together can ever forget each other! If you are not initiated, you remain in your old birth as you were born into this world, and you won't learn anything new. *Zaabolo* is like being born anew.

"The Gbaya used to laugh at girls who were not initiated. They said, 'Dekereke pours out "Zek's" mother's vegetable sauce!' The *bé-zaa*, initiates, must never quarrel with each other or they will get sick and skinny. When the leaders see that quarrels are causing poor health among the girls, they rub *soré* scrapings on the girls to cool them, saying, 'Since you've been quarreling during the rites, we cool you with *soré*! May your quarreling stop and may your health be restored!' "

A comparison of Azimi and Hamada's accounts with Mircea Eliade's discussion of girls' initiation rites confirms that Gbaya tradition is in line with other cultures and the wider arena of scholarship on initiatory practices. Eliade also refers, for example, to "the mystery of blood" and the "mystical interconnection between food, blood, and sexuality."[7]

The importance of *soré* in these rites recalls its appearance in purificatory rites and supports the interpretation of initiatory rites as "*simbo*-things." *Soré* appears to provide and to symbolize safe passage from one "state" to another: it also keeps the girls cool as they experience the danger of "hot blood" and "hot words." *Zaabolo* exhibits a striking preoccupation with the need for cold, running water to bother or to cause pain and grief to the young girls. And the girls' existence on the threshold, their time between the old and new life, is charged with *simbo*: they must not enter their mothers' kitchens or go near soaking manioc.

The *dikidi* bird as a symbol for *zaabolo* initiates successfully incorporates the elements of seriousness and play, endurance and "bursting" celebrative dance that characterize the ritual process. The *dikidi* is attractive and sociable, but not impudent; it works busily and silently building its individual nest, but its shrill twitterings keep the flock together. As *zaabolo* takes place at the beginning of the rainy season, so also the *dikidi*'s elaborate courtship behavior occurs chiefly during the rains.

Zaabolo is an expressive experience of Gbaya tradition and education. Its significance is symbolized by the girls before they go down into the water: they raise their arms together toward the east with their fists closed, then gesture toward the east with open hands, as though to anticipate the new day dawning in their young lives.

8

Going under the Water:
The Gbaya Dance of Laḅi

Laḅi, the Gbaya initiation rite for boys, has not been practiced in most Gbaya areas of Cameroon and the Central African Republic since the 1960s. It is well known, however, because many present-day leaders in Gbaya society (village chiefs, elders, and many Christians) are *kpang-laḅi*, old initiates. These men are our teachers as we seek to understand, describe, and interpret this rite and its prominence in the Gbaya tradition. It may be argued, especially from a Gbaya perspective, that Western-style schooling has not been able to take its place in the transformation of children into responsible adults.

Laḅi is the Gbaya way for providing a comprehensive education for adolescent boys. A boy who does not participate successfully in *laḅi* cannot become a genuine person. *Laḅi* is a school, but it is a school marked by deep Gbaya symbols. Haman Matthieu describes *laḅi* as *dina*, an Arabic term meaning "a religious practice." I use the term "spiritual" for *laḅi* to relate it to the development of a person's character and spirit, not to make any particular reference to worship. Worship and sacrifice were not part of the *laḅi* of my informants, but their training was not only physical and mental; it was also spiritual.

Laḅi teaches boys how to live and how to distinguish between right and wrong. Haman uses the term *dukaa*, rather than *dante*, to refer to *laḅi*'s influence on everyday life. He does not use *dante* in descriptions of *laḅi* because it has become so closely associated with Christian interpretations of eternal life. How does *laḅi* change the boys into intelligent men? Any *laḅi* initiate will explain that the change happens when the boy "goes under the water to die."

GOING AWAY TO DIE

The fathers of adolescent boys meet with the old initiates at the beginning of the hunting season (the dry season) in order to create a new initiation camp. The men may be from one or several villages; the minimum age of the boys is twelve, with most of them between the ages of twelve and fifteen. Some initiates may be as old as twenty, however, and even young married men can be included in the group.

The men inform *Narninga*, "the one who holds the spear," of their intentions. He is the man in charge; he represents the laws of *labi* and makes all the necessary preparations. Everything having to do with *labi* depends on him. He directs the former initiates to build a dam at a nearby stream in order to form a pond about 1.5 meters deep. They also clear the area around the dam of sharp rocks, tree stumps, and other obstacles that might interfere with the activities of *labi*.

Other initiates in the village prepare the boys for their departure, counseling them, "You are going away to die. You must take leave of your parents and be sure that all is well between you. You are going to learn how to live as a genuine person. Those who are not initiated into *labi* do not know anything about life; they are worthless!"

The novices enter initiation completely naked. Their heads are shaved and their clothing left behind. They are about to begin a new life and a separate existence; as everything will be completely different, they must not bring anything from the old life with them. Excitement mounts in the village as the old initiates begin to teach the novices a few elements of the *labi* dance, which will be the most demanding and exacting requirement of the entire initiation.

"The one who holds the spear" prepares his spear and other ceremonial accoutrements; he puts on an enormous straw hat and an assortment of ragged clothes to disguise and conceal his identity. Following the rites, these objects will be taboo—for having served as instruments of death. They will hang on a *soré* tree and no one will go near them. The spear especially will become a purely ritual object; it will never be used for hunting.

When the pond is ready and the boys have been shaved, the old initiates cover their heads with white ashes as a sign of death and begin to chant an invocation that signals their departure for the pond.

> Tomorrow these children will be changed;
> They will no longer be in the village.
> They will suffer,
> They will no longer do what they've been doing,
> They will be real *labi*!
> The leopard has already taken them;
> The lion has already taken them!

The old initiates lead the novices on a run to the pond, followed at a distance by the women and the uninitiated. The men sing, proud that their sons will become men; the women wail, fearing the death of their boys. The old initiates sing and dance to the accompaniment of drums, xylophones, and harps.

At the pond, they beat the water furiously with branches, and sing about the mortal wound that *Narninga*'s spear will inflict:

> *Narninga* stabs with a poisoned spear!
> Let *Narninga* come!
> Let us go into the water;
> *Narninga* is hiding among the trees,
> They set a trap under the water.
>
> *Refrain*
> Are the uninitiated coming?
> Is *Narninga* coming?
> Do you see *Narninga* coming?

The men continue to stir up the water of the pool, working their way toward the dam. Then they return to the far end of the pool. After the second complete round of this increasingly vigorous activity, the novices are carried into the water and submerged.

The boys are held by their "godfathers," their *daa-kasi-zu*, or "father-hold-heads," who keep each boy immersed, careful of course to see that his nose is above water, but pretending at the same time to drown him. The godfathers go up and down the pool twice, and as they approach the dam for the third time, "the one who holds the spear" arrives.

Narninga breaks out of hiding and jumps into the water from the dam, hotly pursued by the old initiates who circle the pond, going after him with branches and sticks. But *Narninga* is too quick for them, and he thrashes his way toward the boys. As he approaches the boys, who are lying on their backs in the water, the godfathers wash the boys' abdomens in preparation for the death that is to come. *Narninga* then thrusts his spear at the abdomen of each novice, and when he has thus "killed" all of them, he climbs up the dam and disappears into the bush.

During the entire drama, the uninitiated and the women must remain at some distance from the pool, the women wailing over the death of their sons. "The one who holds the spear" having left, the godfathers carry the boys out of the water and lay them face down on the ground, careful not to expose their "mortal wounds" to the uninitiated and the women. The initiates cover the bodies of the novices with straw as though to bury them. If a boy has the reputation of being a nuisance, stubborn, and disobedient in the village, he is severely bound up in the straw to make him believe that he will indeed be buried.

The old initiates then carry the novices to the "House of Blood," still accompanied by singing and wailing. Their chant expresses their grief over these deaths:

> The children's dance! The children's dance!
> The *labi* children are crying for food.
> The children's mothers! The children's mothers!
> The *labi* children want to dance!

The House of Blood, built in the shape of a horseshoe or a womb, is a simple construction of poles and leaves that faces away from the village. The novices, still dead, are laid out in front of the house. They may now be severely whipped and beaten by the old initiates, especially the boys who are known to have a rebellious character. Such boys may even undergo torture by fire. In terms of punishment, this is potentially the most dangerous moment during the entire period of initiation.

Lying face down in front of the House of Blood, the novices endure their suffering without murmur or complaint, for to complain would only intensify the beatings. Relief comes when the old initiates bring forward a small leaf rolled up to form a cone. This leaf contains medicine sent by "the one who holds the spear." The boys are on the threshold of a new existence, for *Narninga*'s medicine will raise them from the dead! The men pour this medicine into the nostrils of each boy, the immediate effect of which is a violent sneeze. All the old initiates shout, "To your health!" and "You are saved [resurrected]!"

The resurrection of the dead has been accomplished. But only the initiated are witnesses to it; the uninitiated and the women must believe that the boys are dead. In the eyes of the initiated, the life that follows this event is a new one—it is life after death! The novices sing:

> We died, we died, bring us food!
> Didn't we die?
> The *labi* children who died under water are saved;
> The *labi* children suffered under water;
> Stubborn children cannot become *labi* children!

The last line in this song says, literally, "The buffalo does not like *labi*"; my translation is according to Haman's interpretation.

THE NEWBORN CHILDREN

The novices enter the House of Blood one by one, and several old initiates leave for the village to find food for the risen boys. During the relatively brief time they will spend in the House of Blood, possibly several weeks but usually less, they will receive all their food from the village.

Next, *Gandimba* appears; he is "the one of blood," the director and chief teacher of initiation. He will instruct the "newborn children" during the next three or four years. The boys are smeared from head to foot with kaolin and become known for a time as "white *labi*." The color white indicates death and separation. The boys are no longer related to the rest of Gbaya society but belong, rather, to themselves. During this period they remain naked. White *labi* are not yet mature. "The one of blood" counsels the boys: "Beginning today, you are *labi*; you are no longer of the village, you know nothing about the village. You died and rose again. From now on you must not have any contact with women. They must not see you, they must never recognize you, especially pregnant women.

"If you touch a woman, you will die! You must not go to the places village people go. You must not lie or steal or quarrel with one another. You must obey and submit yourselves without question to the old initiates. You must not eat eggplant, because if you eat eggplant, you will no longer be able to speak the *labi* language.

"You must carry wood to women and other incapacitated people in the village. You must carry wood to *Narninga* and other old initiates. You must leave wood behind their houses and never be seen by anyone in the village.

"When you walk along the path, lower your head, and if someone speaks to you in Gbaya, you must never answer. If you speak Gbaya, you will be sent back to the village, and you will be full of shame all your life. Never explain a word about *labi* during your entire life, or you will die!"

DRINKING BLOOD, THE *LABI* COVENANT

When he has finished giving the exhortations above, *Gandimba* makes an incision four or five centimeters long on the abdomen of each boy. The place of the incision varies. Occasionally it is on the left side of the abdomen, but sometimes a mark is made on the novice's back to indicate that he has been run through by *Narninga*'s spear. In other words, *Gandimba* traces the mortal wound that "the one with the spear" inflicted on the boy in the pool. Then he dips a raw manioc tuber into the bloody incision and gives it to the boy to eat.

"This is your blood," he says. "Now that you eat this blood, if you ever reveal the secrets of *labi* to anyone who is not an initiate, may your own blood kill you! May you die by the knife! May the buffalo kill you with his horns! May the spear run you through! If you reveal the secrets of *labi*, may all that God has made kill you!"

This is the solemn and fearful covenant of *labi*, kept by the initiated during their entire lifetime. The boy eats the manioc that has been dipped in his blood. If he simply licks the blood, he does not make a covenant. Manioc and blood are genuine food; they must be consumed to seal a genuine covenant. The novice makes this covenant with *Narninga*, "the one who holds the spear"; one cannot seal a genuine covenant with oneself.

Following the covenant rite and while their incisions are healing, the white *labi* begin to learn the *labi* language. Vocabulary comparisons reveal numerous cognates between the *labi* language and the Laka languages spoken to the north. Indeed, the Gbaya maintain that the *labi* initiation came originally from the Laka peoples. During the two weeks they spend in the House of Blood, the boys must completely replace the Gbaya language with the *labi* language. They do not speak another word in Gbaya until the day they leave the initiation camp to return to the village.

THE TASKS OF *LABI*

During these weeks the boys also receive their titles, tasks and nicknames. The titles indicate a certain hierarchy among the boys: for example, *Mbélé* is the "president" of the novices, chosen for his superior leadership qualities. His name means "dance" in the *labi* language. *Ninga* or "spear," is the vice president; *Doko* is *Ninga*'s assistant, and *Ndanga* is a counselor who has the right to act as judge when there are problems among the boys. *Ndanga* can replace *Mbélé* and *Ninga* in their absence, and he has the right to beat his comrades if they fail to obey. *Bétaré* is also a counselor; his task is to exhort his comrades, and only "the one of blood" can counsel him. *Béloko* is the "sergeant-at-arms"; he keeps order among the boys.

Labi nicknames often highlight a boy's physical build or mannerisms. Thus, for example, "Boo-kom" is the boy with deep-set eyes; "Koya-siré" is an intelligent boy who acts well and adroitly; "Kpang-dom" has a large head; "Kpang-mbitaré's" ears are large and fanned out; and "Poro" loves to sit near the fire.

The novices begin a serious study and practice of *labi* dances during their stay in the House of Blood. The two most talented dancers are named *Ko-Mbélé* and *Yelem-Mbélé*, and it is their task to help the other boys learn the multitude of *labi* dance steps.

Among the elders who assist the teacher is one called *Séré-Ndimba*, the "man of blood." It is his task to terrify the boys at night. He is equipped with a "bull-roarer," which consists of two different-sized wooden plaques attached to a single cord. He swings the cord vigorously to simulate a lion's roar and shouts at the top of his lungs, "A lion is attacking us!" The boys run off in all directions; and later they are told that the lion swallowed one of their friends. The old initiates procure some well-peppered peanut butter from the boys' mothers to feed to the lion to induce it to vomit up its victim. The elder's name, "man of blood," indicates that he is preoccupied with drinking his victim's blood.

The study of the *labi* language is not carried out on the benches of a school classroom, but as the novices work together. The white *labi* engage in the construction of a more permanent camp, which will be their home for at least three years. When this permanent camp, or *gbang-lai*, is ready, they disassemble and abandon the House of Blood. This change of residence marks an important step in the initiation; it requires anointings and dances, and the elders summon the *okoo-pi-gangmo*, "the woman who throws peace," to invoke and establish peace among the novices.

CHANGING CAMPS, CHANGING STATUS

The boys form a circle. Their fathers and godfathers present them with simple clothing, and they are permitted to dress for the first time since the initiation began. They also receive some accoutrements for dance, for example, dried pods from the *mbuti* vine are attached to the boys' ankles. The old initiates again smear the boys with kaolin, but this time they are also anointed with *kui*, camwood. Camwood shavings are reduced to powder and mixed with oil to make a paste. Then the paste is rolled into a ball and used as a cosmetic to beautify the body.

The white anointing (kaolin) signifies that the *labi* are separated from the rest of Gbaya society; they must not come into contact with women, but remain pure and undefiled. The red anointing (camwood) indicates a change in status, an evolution; the boys are beginning to mature. The color red indicates that the boys have passed through a veil of blood; they have left their past lives behind to be reborn in freedom through their participation in the *labi* rites. Each of the three phases in the initiation rite — separation, liminality, and reintegration — is accompanied by appropriate ritual gestures, objects and colors. White, the sign of their separation, is still prominent in their move to the permanent camp, but the introduction of red signifies a progression in the novices' status.

As the boys dance to celebrate their new residence and status, the men offer them money. The first of these gifts is placed in the water pot of the woman peace-thrower to invoke peace, success, and well-being during the initiation. The pot will be carefully looked after in the Initiation House, especially by *Mbélé*, the president of the novices. Its water must never completely evaporate, as that would destroy the blessing. The woman sprinkles the novices, using water from her pot and a branch from the *soré* tree, the tree whose name and work she bears. This rite is her exclusive province.

The novices move to their new quarters. Like the House of Blood, the Initiation House is also horseshoe- or womb-shaped. It is protected by an enclosure and faces away from the village. The time consecrated to serious disciplinary beatings is past, and the boys apply themselves to the various lessons involved in the *labi* initiation. Not that discipline and punishment are abolished! The previous beatings have had their effect, however, and continuation of the initiation takes place in a more relaxed atmosphere. "The one of blood" was always with the boys during their weeks at the House of Blood, but he does not usually spend his nights at the Initiation House. He goes to the village in the evening and returns to the camp each morning.

The boys are equipped with spears, bow and arrows, knives, and poisons for hunting and fishing. They also have sticks with which they may defend themselves, for example, if an old initiate is drunk and unduly threatens them. If they do not receive enough food from their families, they are permitted to invade the village and make off with whatever food they can grab. For such raids, they disguise themselves and symbolize their distress and anger at having been neglected by rubbing their bodies with blackened tree bark.

The hungry boys hide behind a large black, white, and red shield and always carry a stick, which is referred to in the *labi* language as the "food stick." The shield is not a weapon, but simply a device to discourage recognition by the uninitiated and the women. The armed boys often go in search of food. They crouch back of the village and whistle, waiting behind their shields for their families to bring them *kam*, the life-sustaining food.

LEARNING TO DANCE

The boys receive training in a number of subjects during their time spent in the second camp. They continue to learn and perfect their knowledge and use of the *labi* language. But the *labi* dances and songs take precedent over all *labi* activities. The worth of each boy is measured first and foremost by his ability to execute the dance steps. He can be excused if he is not particularly agile in other matters, but not if he is unable to perform the dances as required by the teacher. If he fails to achieve competence in the dances, he fails the *labi* initiation altogether; and if beatings and harassment do not succeed in producing the desired results, he is sent back to his village in shame.

The essential thing in dance is a person's well-being in relation to his or her fellows. Dance as it should be is not just a matter of jumping and leaping around; it is *mboo-zu*, or obedience. A good dancer is of one heart and mind with his fellows, and no one can know how to dance unless he or she has worked hard to achieve competence in the intricate steps of each dance, that is, in life. Success in executing these steps brings great joy!

Labi dances reveal all the secrets of the bush. As each animal has its own way of walking and running and talking and singing, the *labi* dance steps reveal these in all their detail. The dance is both drama and pantomime. Genuine dancing is a "bursting forth" in dance. If there is no dancing in a Gbaya village, that village is simply not healthy. If there is no dancing, there is sickness and hunger in the village. Not even hunting is as significant as dancing because one cannot exhibit one's power as a hunter among people as effectively as one can show one's competence as a dancer.

HUNTING SKILLS

The time spent in the Initiation House is a great time if there is plenty to eat. The novices learn the art of making and setting a variety of animal traps, and also the art of making and setting fish nets and traps. They become expert in the art of avoiding danger. Evasive and cunning action is more highly valued in the hunt or in fighting than is the straightforward locking of horns. The boys must learn to be highly attentive and discreet. If a boy is excessively timid when he enters *labi*, he leaves it having acquired courage; if he enters with a rebellious and cantankerous character, he goes home having acquired humility and the ability to work with others.

The boys come to know and to understand the nature that surrounds them. In the *labi* language, they learn the names and characteristics of significant plants and trees, their usefulness and their danger. They learn the names of Gbaya clans, taboos, and omens and the names and character of other ethnic groups in the area. Although the night is especially for dancing, they also tell tales and learn the wisdom of their fathers.

The elders insist that the novices learn self-control. They must shed tears on command and stop the flow of tears as quickly as asked. If they do not succeed, they must eat charcoal with their manioc rather than meat sauce.

All oaths are forbidden, with the exception "God is witness!" Sorcery is strictly forbidden; if it appears, it is severely punished. The boy who utters a curse or uses the sorcerer's medicine is beaten and expelled immediately because the work and fruit of sorcery are death, and *labi* is for life. There are no secrets among the novices; they eat together and live together in harmony, with love and mutual respect. Sorcery shows hatred, and hatred has no place in the *labi* initiation.

PROVERBS FOR LIFE

After two months in the Initiation House, the novices arrive at another important step in their initiation, the rite called "cut the stick to call the name." All the old initiates assemble in the Initiation House, including "the one who holds the spear." His ritual and symbolic importance is greater than *Gandimba's*, "the one of blood," because death under the water is the real death. The incision made by "the one of blood" is only a sign of its accomplishment.

The presence of "the woman who clicks rocks" is also required at this rite. She is a young virgin who will live with the novices in the Initiation House, learn the *labi* language, and prepare their food. She is a "little mother" to the boys, and she has a solemn task to perform at the end of the initiation period.

The "cut the stick to call the name" rite is an examination, and the boys' godfathers are the principal witnesses. A single stick cut from the *soré* tree serves as the "blackboard" where the secrets of *labi* are recorded. Notches are cut in the stick, and each successive notch represents a secret lesson, which the boys must recite. The middle of the stick is "the way of *Narninga*," which leads to the Initiation House; the right side is "the way of *labi*"; the left is "the way of death." Although a single stick is sufficient for the rite, each novice carries his own notched stick into the bush. When he has chosen a certain path, he leaves the stick in the middle of it as a barrier to warn the uninitiated and women not to follow him. They must not "jump over *soré*."

"Cut the stick" begins when *Gandimba* says, "Today the novices will show us that they are mature. We will therefore give them their true *labi* names today." He places the notched stick on the ground before the first boy, and the recitation begins:

Gandimba: *Labi*, speak!
Novice: I'll tell all.
Gandimba: Speak!
Novice: Tell everything. Tell about *labi*. Look at the people. Look at the man with the spear. Look at *Narninga*, look only at *Narninga*.

As he speaks, *Gandimba* indicates successive notches on the stick. The novice then recites a series of insightful one-line proverbs or brief parables and puzzles based on the values embraced by *labi*. The following paragraphs are a rough translation and brief interpretation of each proverb.

1. "One cannot know *labi* from outside; one can only know *labi* under the water." Only the boy who dies under the water during the *labi* initiation really knows the secrets of *labi* and understands what it is all about. Herein lies the fundamental myth about *labi*.

2. "The insects join hands to cross the river together." The Gbaya must help one another overcome difficulties and obstacles. Once a boy knows the secrets of *labi*, he will not suffer as he did, because knowledge of the *labi* way changes everything. Mutual help rendered by initiated brothers forms a bridge that enables one to pass from death to life.

3. "Look at the color of the genet and the partridge, and these colors will show you about *labi*." *Labi* helps one to distinguish between right and wrong, between good and bad. The genet is a taboo animal, not because of *simbo*, but because of witchcraft; its white coloring is a sign of death. The partridge has good colorings, which indicate that steadiness and obedience will be rewarded. The genet's colors change, but the partridge's remain constant.

4. "One who drinks his brother's blood drinks bitterness." This proverb is directed against the witch, the most destructive element in Gbaya society. Witchcraft is anathema to *labi*.

5. "The virgin girl knows *labi*, but she will never breathe a word of it to anyone or she will die." The "little mother" of the novices knows the *labi* secrets, but she cannot reveal them to anyone. In a more general sense, this proverb is the law that forbids the revelation of a neighbor's secrets. Even if someone's secrets involve serious evils, the brother or sister who

knows this must forgive the evil and end the affair rather than reveal anything to other people.

6. "If someone tries to kill you, you must survive [escape]." Evasive action and avoidance of danger are highly valued in Gbaya society, since anyone who looks for trouble will surely find it. If a person has been wronged, he or she must avoid death rather than seek revenge.

7. "What happens when you show off your strength? You'll find a battle." This proverb in the form of a riddle counsels the novice against an imprudent and proud display of strength. The strongest person is the one who avoids death, not the one who shows off his muscles. Quarreling always leads to death.

8. "The one who begins his work knows how to finish it." This word is meant especially to praise "the one of blood." He has begun the *labi* initiation, and he knows how to bring it to a successful conclusion. It also suggests, however, that before anyone acts, he should think about the consequences of his deed. This interpretation yields the more familiar proverb, "You've made your own bed; now you can lie in it."

9. "What medicine do you take when you're cold? Fire." This proverb is another riddle; it suggests that doing good keeps a person from doing evil.

10. "The ax that cuts the wood will not remain next to the fire." No one who does evil can expect to achieve a good result. In this proverb the ax bears the curse of death because it is an instrument of death. If the *labi* initiate sows evil, he will reap evil.

11. "The knife that cuts the meat will never eat the meat." The hatred that causes a person to kill his or her brother must cease; it must not be allowed to continue until the hated one is eaten! This proverb is another allusion to witchcraft. The lips that pronounce evil words against a brother can never help anyone.

When these proverbs have been satisfactorily recited by the novice, the teacher responds, "Now this *labi* knows what is necessary." The novice receives his initiation name, and when all have passed the examination, their success is celebrated by dance and a festive meal.

CLIMBING *LINGI*

Another important event in the *labi* initiation is the rite called *danga-lingi*, which means "climbing *lingi*." The novices must be mature before this rite can take place; that is, it cannot precede the "cut the stick" examination. Climbing *lingi* is a ritual similar to the dance of the *lingi* pole in the girls' initiation rites.

The novices dig a hole in the middle of their initiation camp, then meet with the old initiates in the gallery forest. There they place the peace-thrower's water pot at the foot of a *kutu* tree, a tall straight tree, known in *labi* as the "dance tree." The boys fell the tree and remove its bark so that it becomes quite smooth; they do not, however, remove the leaves at the very tip of the tree. Instead, they tie a small packet of medicine to the tip of the tree, tying it to the leaves with a *yoyongo* vine.

Then they carry the tree to their camp, singing all the way. Even if there are fifty or a hundred boys, they carry the tree together, hoisting it to one shoulder. They replant the tree in the middle of their camp and again bury the water pot at its foot. When it stands tall and firm before them, they break forth in joyful singing and dancing.

One of the leaders among the boys, the counselor *Ndanga*, for example, is designated to climb the tree. *Ndanga* shinnies to the top of the tree and peeks inside the little packet of *labi* medicine. This packet, which looks like a little bird's nest, has nothing whatsoever to do with a sorcerer's medicine; it contains goat and chicken dung, fingernails, and clippings of hair. *Ndanga*'s courage to look into this package is extremely important; it gives strength and courage to his brother novices, whom he represents, so that he, in fact, seals a covenant on their behalf.

If quarreling and hatred had dominated among the novices, *Ndanga* could not have reached the top of the tree. His success is a sign that well-being and harmony reign in the initiation camp. It is also a sign of blessing on all the brothers and another occasion for them to manifest their joy in wild dancing at the foot of the tree. The old initiates embrace the boys and each other.

Ndanga must come down head first. When he is halfway down the tree, he stops in order to give a recitation, similar to the recitation of the "cut the stick to call the name" rite. He explains the songs of the robin chat, the bird of *labi*. No bird can compete with the robin chat's songs; he sings the secrets of *labi*, telling you the good things you should do and the bad things you should avoid doing. I was not familiar with this spectacular whistler until after I had collected my notes on *labi*; then, as I worked to interpret them, he made a point of singing every day in the garden outside my office window. To be fair, he should be listed first among my informants on *labi*.

All genuine *labi* initiates know how to interpret the robin chat's songs. He tells about the arrival of the moon and also the year; in other words, he is a kind of prophet, or seer, who helps one look into the future. The robin chat explains how one should "lie on his back at night with his eyes open," to reflect on what has happened today and to think about what will happen tomorrow. My students and Gbaya friends complain that this quality is no longer evident among Gbaya youth who "do everything today, with no consciousness of why they're doing it, or where it will lead."

Haman Matthieu supplied this version of *Ndanga*'s recitation:

I climbed up the tree in order to reach heaven, but I found death in the basket. I went up and found death, and now I am coming back to tell you. We must be careful lest we die from telling the secrets of *laḅi*, because what I found in that basket was death, and what I learned was this: death is a dangerous thing and heaven is far away.

Only through dying can a person go to heaven. As *laḅi* initiates, we must be obedient to what we have seen in the basket. I went and saw it on your behalf, because it was not possible for all of us to go, and now we must all be obedient. I did not go without a reason; I went because you sent me to look at it in your place. Now let us be careful because of death. Death is not something to play with, death is something dangerous.

Ndanga then completes his descent and is welcomed back to earth by his brothers. "The woman who throws peace" may be there to sprinkle the boys with benediction, and her water pot remains at the foot of the tree throughout the remainder of the initiation. When the time comes to disassemble the Initiation House, this important tree will also be pulled up.

The boys continue their education in hunting skills and the *laḅi* dances for a period of time that may be as long as three years. Examinations and dances around the *lingi* tree are interspersed with ordinary tasks and games. The old initiates delight in tricking and frightening the novices, as their trick with the lion proved. Another game they enjoy makes reference to the *laḅi* spirit. The old initiates use it to gain forced labor from the boys, but its obvious purpose is to teach the boys to do their share for the well-being of the community.

During the rainy season it becomes increasingly difficult to find good dry wood. The men warn the boys that the *laḅi* spirit is displeased with their laziness and will soon be upon them to punish them for not carrying the wood as they should. In the middle of the night, they encircle the boys' camp and raise a terrible noise. The boys, believing that the *laḅi* spirit has indeed come to carry them off, disperse in all directions and remain in the bush until encouraged by the old initiates to return. It is hoped that they will henceforth take more seriously their responsibility to provide wood.

WASHING AWAY *LAḄI*

Finally the day arrives when "the one of blood" and the old initiates decide that the boys are ready for graduation. They are told to disassemble the Initiation House and meet, very early in the morning, next to a stream with "the one who holds the spear" and "the one of blood." Leading them into the stream, *Gandimba* washes each boy, telling him in the Gbaya language, "We wash you to take away *laḅi*; you are a new person now." *Narninga* also washes each boy because, if they are not washed, they will be unable to relearn the Gbaya language. After this the boys also wash themselves before they return to the banks of the stream.

The old initiates prepare a grass fire, which the boys jump over one after the other, and which the last boy extinguishes with his bare feet, thereby putting an end to the trials and suffering of *labi*. Each boy also jumps over a branch of the *soré* tree to signify that now the boys are passing over the threshold from their ambiguous existence as *labi* persons into the normal flow of Gbaya society. The *soré* branch calms *simbo* so that the boys can reenter the village purified and cooled of *simbo-labi*.

In addition to the rites of washing and of jumping over the fire and the *soré* branch, the boys also stomp a goat to death. They jump on the victim one by one until it succumbs. Unlike the scapegoat of Hebrew tradition, however, the *labi* goat is eaten by the old initiates as a protection against witchcraft.

If the initiation does not last its full term—for example, if it lasts less than one year, as happened during the 1950s and 1960s (during which time the government put intense pressure on the Gbaya to abolish the *labi* rites entirely)—the foregoing rites precede the initiates' triumphal reentry into the village. But if the initiation goes its full several-year term, the following graduation rites are observed.

The "little mother" takes two white stones and dips them in oil, as the boys lie down in a row before her. *Narninga*, the "one who holds the spear," takes *Mbélé*'s right hand; *Gandimba*, the "one of blood," takes his left hand, and "little mother" says, "Here are the *labi* stones, which I touch over you." She touches the stones together, and their firm click is a sign that the boy has succeeded well during the initiation. The oil from the stones runs down the neck of the first candidate as a sign of blessing, and the "little mother" moves to the next boy in the line.

Now these boys are *labi* over whom the stones have been touched; they have received their diploma with honors. *Narninga* washes his hands in front of the old initiates and the boys' fathers, signifying again that the dangers of *labi*, its *simbo*, have been effectively washed away and the boys are free to reenter normal village life in Gbaya society. Before they are fully reintegrated into Gbaya society, however, they must undergo several more rites.

CLIMBING UP FROM *LABI*

The moment for the initiates to reenter the village arrives at last. Known as *danga-labi*, "climbing up from *labi*" or as *daka-labi*, "pulling *labi*," the boys' return is an event of general celebration and rejoicing for the initiates and the entire community. The old initiates, especially the godfathers and fathers, adorn the boys with all the accoutrements of dance and anoint them with camwood and oil.

Kaolin is not part of this anointing, since it is a sign of death. The returning boys are hidden, however, under newly woven grass mats as a symbol of their death and resurrection. The Gbaya wrap their dead in new mats and, thus "buried," the boys are not immediately identified by their families. The procession of the new graduates is accompanied by this song:

All you *labi*, hide under your mats, come quickly!
Oh, you mothers of *labi*,
Your children have come to dance!

When the boys are all assembled before the villagers, while they are still crouching under their mats, *Narninga* again appears in his ragged disguise and repeats the same performance that marked the death of the boys under the water. As his spear approaches the boys for the third time, they throw off their mats, resurrecting from the dead, and the dance breaks forth. The entire population is consumed by a frenzy of joy that indeed bears witness to the raising of the dead.

If the boys have not succeeded in learning their lessons, especially if they show no competence in dancing, their godfathers are quite unhappy and the boys themselves are mocked by everyone. On the other hand, success is generously rewarded by gifts of money and clothes.

The boys have emerged from their status as novices to become initiates. Their characters and behavior must henceforth witness to this fundamental change; from now on they must conduct themselves wisely and judiciously as sensible men who contribute to the well-being of Gbaya society. Those who have suffered the trials of *labi* together and who have honorably succeeded have a special fraternal relationship for the remainder of their days. They should respect and help one another and never deceive each other.

In order for a Gbaya boy to achieve genuine adulthood, he must follow the path indicated by *labi* and the old initiates. But what about someone who, for a valid reason, has never been able to participate in the *labi* initiation? Compassion is occasionally shown to such men as the initiates take them to the House of Blood and, without making the *labi* incision, reveal the secrets of *labi* to them. They have not actually been killed under water and cannot be considered genuine *labi* initiates, but the shame of total exclusion has nevertheless been removed.

On the day of climbing up from *labi*, when the boys have performed the *labi* dances and have been rewarded by the villagers, they are again taken to the chief's shelter or to a cold house, where they will spend three nights together as they did several years earlier at the beginning of *labi*. During this time they practice speaking the Gbaya language. The food taboos are lifted, and the old initiates bring the boys eggplant and catfish to eat. The raw eggplant enables them to speak Gbaya again.

After three nights in the cold house, *Narninga* takes them down to the stream to wash *simbo-labi*. They circle *simbo* trees, gather medicine, and speak to the trees as in the *zuia-simbo* rites. *Narninga* builds a little dam and washes each boy, after which they all climb out of the water and pass through a *zee* leaf. Then they jump over a small fire on the path and return to the village, picking *zobo* leaves and cutting *soré* sticks on the way to the *kpaiamo*, anointing rite. After everyone has been anointed, they eat *zobo* together and throw their ritual instruments and leftovers after a bird flying west, "Hooo!" At last they are free to return to their homes in the village, where they are anointed with red camwood. Now they can start looking around their own and surrounding villages for wives.

9

Reconciliation Rites:
The Place of Words

The Gbaya proverb, *Fara wén ne fara fio*, "The place of words is the place of death," indicates the importance of resolving and reconciling potential and actual words, or quarrels, among people, the ancestors (the living-dead), and territorial spirits. We have seen how this principle works in the ritual contexts of sacrifice, purification, and initiation. Our focus in this chapter will be on conflict and resolution in Gbaya society itself. The role of *soré* in mediating and transforming the chaos of everyday life is an important reminder to Westerners that *soré* is not confined only to esoteric and religious domains; it is also found where it is most needed—at the heart of human life.

Soré transforms intolerable human relationships into constructive, harmonious, life-oriented relationships. If the place of words is the place of death for the Gbaya, it is clear that *soré* also changes that place into a place of life. *Soré* generates harmony where there is dissonance among those who share the same living space. It mediates life by making everyday living secure from death.

Soré exorcises malignant, malevolent and ambivalent forces and influences in, with, and through common words, gestures and objects. It witnesses to the truth that there can be no peace in human relationships unless the specific factors creating dissonance are dealt with constructively by the community. As *soré* is the way to cool and cleanse the sins or curse of *simbo*, so it is also the way to exorcise the evils of *dua*, witchcraft, and *nyina*, harmful medicine. By exorcism, I mean that *soré* frees people from domination by witchcraft and harmful medicine, not in the sense of casting out evil beings, but in the sense of seeking an accommodation with powerful beings of an ambivalent nature.

Soré is the people's advocate as it works through ritual processes to achieve harmony and peace. The symbolic structure of *soré* is a structure that works against dissonance and disease for harmony and the generation of new life. Thus, *soré* points to such Gbaya values as openness, vulnerability, wholesomeness, truthfulness, and trustworthiness. These life- and community-oriented values stand in the sharpest contrast to the sinister values in witchcraft and harmful medicine.

The examples in this chapter illustrate, above all, that *soré* is not esoteric. Its physical and symbolic presence is eminently common, accessible, and approachable, and it collaborates with the foundational stuff of human life: water, blood, oil, and "good trees." *Soré* not only cautions people against sin; it also bears people's sins. *Soré* calls people home again to words and deeds that will assure and save the ongoing life of the Gbaya community.

RECONCILIATION IN DAILY LIFE

When words involving accusations of wrongdoing break out between two men in a village and threaten to disrupt peace between the families, a village *wi-to-mboro*, a counselor, comes forward to mediate between the two men. The counselor is self-appointed, yet the villagers recognize his gifts for this task and respect him as a *soré* person in their midst.

The *wi-to-mboro* goes first to one person, then to the other, and when they have both calmed down, they greet each other in words like these: "Brother, the words that upset us are finished. I don't hold any words in my heart against you. What you said made me angry, and we quarreled, but now it's finished." Ideally, they will embrace, forget the matter and resume a normal relationship.

If a person with less tact than the counselor becomes involved in the affair, *soré* may be thrown to that person. Thus, for example, if the casual words of one Gbaya offend another, he or she may say to the offended one, "Look, your *soré* that I'm hereby throwing to you! I did not say those words about you! It's not your affair!"

One does not actually take a *soré* branch in hand; the words alone are sufficient. But if the offended person jumps over *soré* by ignoring these words, things will turn out badly for that one. The Gbaya do not say in so many words, "Forgive me," or "Pardon my sin against you," but when the quarreling parties can freely say, "I no longer hold those words in my heart," they are reconciled.

Again, if a person accidentally offends another, he or she may kneel or crouch respectfully before the offended person, saying, "Father, I beat hand to you! What happened was not my intention! I did not prepare this thing!" *Goma-er*, beating hand, is a Gbaya gesture of supplication and request for forgiveness. The supplicant softly touches his (or her) hands together in a noiseless "clapping" gesture while speaking. The offended person responds to the gesture, saying that he no longer holds this offense in his heart, and the two greet each other to signify that peace is restored between them. The one who "beats hand" to another usually does not have to face being brought before the village court.

Yet another means of reconciliation between individuals is for the offended person to send a counselor to the offender. Suppose Garba, for example, damages Adamou's garden. Adamou will send an elder to Garba "to cover those words" or "to repair the affair." In turn, Garba will kneel before the elder and "beat hand" to him, asking him to go back to Adamou and beg for mercy on his behalf. Garba speaks no harsh words and does not deny his fault because such acts would encourage Adamou to bring him before the village court. Finally, if Adamou accepts the request for mercy transmitted by the elder, Garba must appear in person to thank Adamou for his compassion.

GBAYA JUSTICE AND PEACE

The Gbaya who has been summoned to appear before a judge or a village chief may first pick a fresh, new *soré* leaf and place it under his tongue. When the accused arrives before the judge and explains the case, say the Gbaya, the case will be dropped. But if the accused is guilty and holds that guilt in his heart, *soré* will not absolve it. *Soré* sees the intentions of the heart and never condones an evil way of life; it is a person's best advocate.

Soré is for calming murder. If a person has killed someone from another family in the village, a *soré* branch (a real one this time) may be thrown between the two families or between members of the same family to restore peace in their midst and to prevent revenge. *Soré* may also temporarily protect the murderer. For example, a man who has just killed someone will probably leave the village by the nearest path. If he throws a *soré* branch behind him on the path, those wishing to follow him confront the *soré* as a barrier before them; they must give up the chase and return to their village.

Soré's cooling property imposes peace regardless of one's guilt or innocence, but it is not unconcerned about justice and fairness. The peace achieved through the barrier of *soré* protects the other villagers as well as the murderer, lest further innocent blood be shed. *Soré* cools "hotheads," allowing for more effective measures to bring the criminal to justice. In any case, the murderer will pay the consequences of his act, since *simbo* is bound to "take" him for it.

Soré also warns, alerts, cautions, and advises people in other ways. A branch of *soré* leaves placed openly in someone's manioc field warns against thievery. When a woman puts her manioc to soak in a little pool, she throws *soré* leaves on the water over the manioc; then, if a man steals this manioc, explain the Gbaya, his wife will die. If *soré* leaves have been placed over the threshold of a person's house, no one goes near that house until inquiries have been made; the *soré* may indicate that a purification rite is taking place there. If a young woman dies, her husband takes a new mat, puts *soré* leaves on it, and sends it to his father-in-law to announce the death of his child. Likewise, if one sees a fellow madly pedaling a bicycle with *soré* leaves tied to the handlebars, one can be sure that he is on his way to announce a death.

If strangers choose to pass through a village in which many have died or in which there is a generally unhealthy air, they will be given a *soré* branch to avert afflictions. As they are not implicated in the village's affairs, they should not be subjected to its problems. If, for example, a harmful medicine is planted over someone's grave to avenge a murder, strangers are given *soré* branches for protection.

Soré is also for entering a village, especially a large village, where one has never before set foot. A woman, for example, may tie a *soré* leaf to her wrist, discreetly concealed under her clothing. She does this in order to eat freely in this village, without fear of being poisoned. After she has spent some time in the village, she can discard the *soré* and nothing bad will happen to her. The Gbaya use *soré* to lead people to new places and through experiences that are potentially dangerous; no one should enter such places without taking precautions.

CONFLICTS IN VILLAGE LIFE

Earlier I described the *zanga-nu* rite, a rite of purification that washes away hard words and curses. Because this rite is so important for the resolution of interpersonal conflicts in village life, I present another example of it here. Haman Matthieu supplied this description and verified my understanding of *zanga-nu* as a Gbaya way to confess sins.

Haman's narrative describes an incident that occurred in his home village, Bindiba, when the chief became angry with everyone and cursed them, saying, "If I really am chief here, may you no longer succeed in anything you do! If I am not in fact your chief, then may you succeed. But since I am in truth your chief here, may all your success come to me!"

The chief taps the top of his head, naming all the bad things the village has done to him: "I told you to work in my fields, but you refused! I told you to repair the walls of my concession, but you didn't want to help! The authorities came to visit, but you did none of the work to receive them! You killed animals on the hunt and ate all the meat in the bush, not giving me my part! I curse the lot of you! May my curse take you!"

In the days that followed, no one in the village succeeded at anything. People died from much sickness, and many quarrels broke out. The manioc fields failed to produce, the corn crop was not enough even for the children. Over and over again bad words among the people destroyed relationships in the village. Even when the people found something to eat, they were still hungry; they became thin. There was no happiness.

But finally the chief's anger calmed down because the old men and women of the village told him, "Chief, if you stick to those hard words, everyone here will be destroyed! You'll find no more strong men in the village. Wash your heart so peace can be restored!"

Then the chief called everyone together early one morning, including all the old men. He took a new calabash and filled it with water. He also put manioc flour (*zeze*) into the water to make it white. All the elders gathered together and held the chief's calabash with their right hands while he spoke:

"I'm doing *zanga-nu*, the real thing, with all my people here today! I was angry with you because you did no work for me, so I cursed you, and you have all been afflicted. But today I'm happy to call you back to me. If it was not really my own father who gave me this village, as I told you before, then my words would have had no effect, because the arms are not stronger than the thigh [the chief is a thigh; the young men of the village, arms]. So I'm gathering you here today in order to put an end to our fighting and quarreling. I tell you, I'm not lying, the bad words I spoke before, I herewith throw them out *top*!

"My heart is at peace now, and I spit (*touffee*) into this water! I hereby wash my mouth and head, since I told you that all your wealth and animals should come to me! Now may you all succeed again! Kill many animals! Get rich!"

Then he carefully poured the water on the ground and anointed all the young men with fresh mud. He anointed their foreheads and hands, their chests and their feet. Then the village was at peace again.

As *soré* reconciles individuals within a single village, it also effects reconciliation between entire villages. For example, if Garoua Boulai and Bindiba are beginning a dangerous quarrel, the old people in one or both villages throw *soré* branches in the path between the villages, saying, "Do not jump over this!" Then unless the fight is immediately abandoned, death will occur, because jumping over *soré* is a *simbo*-thing.

Soré is also for breaking the strength of a dangerous person who threatens the community. When such a person menaces the village, villagers of lesser physical strength may swat the fellow with *soré* leaves and *tiya* branches. When the strong man's body turns soft from this action, his strength is broken; the villagers take him as easily as one takes a child and tie him up! *Tiya* is a thick, tough grass that resembles a small plant or tree. It works together with *soré* to protect the weak.

IN CASE OF ILLNESS

Soré is for well-being in a village and for *gaia-genga*, for quieting down or scaring away sickness. According to Abbo, *gai* means "to scare away" or "to surprise" someone—like jumping out at a person from behind a door. The *gaia-genga* is presided over by a priest of *so-kao* (the territorial spirits) or another village elder; it is "prescribed" for a village that has suffered from an epidemic of ill health, arguments, or other problems over a period of time.

The priest prepares a special ritual pot with the medicine of several trees and plants, some small red and white rocks and *zenga* oil. When all is ready, he rises very early one morning and walks through the village shouting, "Quiet down this epidemic, this sickness!" People wake throughout the village and shout in response and agreement, "Hooo!"

The priest calls on his departed father and grandfather, speaking their names with supplication, "Take away these problems from our village, hooo!" Everyone in the village follows the priest to the chief's house and they wash their faces with water from the chief's ritual pot. The priest dips water from that pot into his own, then kindles a fire under it. He uses a *soré* branch to stir the medicine in his pot; then he anoints and blesses the chief: "May you have good health! May this epidemic pass away!"

He anoints and blesses the village elders and all the villagers who have gathered. Then he extinguishes the fire and waits for a bird to fly overhead, going west. He throws the ritual objects after this bird, and all the people shout, "May this epidemic leave our village, hooo!" The priest may also blow his whistle, the horn of a small antelope, to "scare off" the sickness and problems. The exorcism restores well-being to the village.

If a great illness falls on a village, the old people rise very early and proclaim loudly to one or more residential quarters in the village, "Look at this *soré* we're throwing to you! You are not responsible for the cause of this sickness! Do not jump over *soré!*" Their action exhorts the innocent not to throw accusations around. In this rite a *soré* branch is not actually thrown to the people, but *soré* resides in the old people's spoken words, which both clarify and judge the situation. Those to whom *soré* is thrown are set free of illness; they have cool and peaceful hearts.

Soré itself is a helpful medicine; one who has a bad headache can cut strips from a *soré* branch and tie them over the forehead to cool the pain. One can also put *soré* leaves in water and use this mixture to wash an aching head. Strips of *soré* bark tied around a person's neck heal a sore throat, and *soré* roots are used medicinally for diarrhea and elephantiasis. The Gbaya drink water "flavored" with *soré* bark to kill stomach worms.

In the dry season, when the winds begin to blow dust over the savanna, Gbaya mothers collect a variety of leaves, including *soré*, and use them to wash their children whenever they have a fever. It is the cooling and slippery qualities of *soré* that the Gbaya trust to heal their bodies; *soré* cools fever; *soré* cleanses.

Soré also takes the *simbo* of a leper whose wounds have healed. The person who cared for the leper takes his clothes, mat, and eating utensils to the foot of a *soré* tree. The leper is then washed, clothed, and returned to normal life with other members of the community. Leprosy is a *simbo*-thing among the Gbaya, and lepers are avoided as *simbo*-persons; ordinary contacts and relationships are forbidden to them for as long as the disease is active.

MAKING PROMISES OR VOWS

Ndofé Nathaniel explains how *soré* is for *haa-nu*, for making promises or vows. He says that *soré* may witness a person's desire to acquire certain things. One can "swear" by *soré* for money, for good luck on the hunt, or for the resolution of family problems such as the release of someone in jail. *Soré* can also be used to desire the successful birth of a child, especially when this desire is expressed during a difficult pregnancy or delivery. The man who makes these vows to a *soré* tree risks death if he neglects to untie the vow after *soré* has fulfilled his desire.

Bura-haa-nu, untying the vow, is a very delicate matter. Suppose, for example, that a man's wife is in a long and difficult labor. If he stands before a *soré* tree or holds a *soré* branch in his hand and vows that after a successful birth, he will return to the *soré* and untie his vow the right way, then his wife will give birth without further problems, says Ndofé, because *soré* will not let such a promise pass unheeded.

On learning that the infant and mother are well, the father does not go first to see his child; he goes immediately to the *soré* tree with some animal bones, a fish, and a chicken. First, he kindles a fire and boils the bones in water; then he pours them on the ground before the *soré* to untie his vow. Next he boils the fish, after first removing its liver, and kills the chicken, as he had vowed. Then leaving the fish and chicken there, he returns to his village, where he cooks a second chicken and shares it with his family. Once he has kept his promise to *soré*, he is free to visit his wife and child.

THE WOMAN OF PEACE

The *okoo-pi-gangmo*, woman peace-thrower, is an important custodian of *soré*. She is at her ritual tasks constantly so that peace may reign in the village. A man who is quarreling with someone may go to the peace-thrower at night. She takes her calabash of water, *soré*, and other leaves and washes the face of her visitor, saying, "Let there be peace in our village," or "May our village grow and be strong!"

When a fight is so fierce that no one can stop it, the peace-thrower appears. She thrusts a *soré* branch into the water in her calabash and sprinkles all the fighters, cooling their anger. The fighting stops and everyone quiets down. She takes water in her mouth from the calabash and sprays it all over the ground where the villagers were fighting, saying, "May all this fighting stop right now!"

The *soré* of the woman peace-thrower also cools people who have been in war or prison. When such people return to the village, the peace-thrower meets them on the path outside the village. In her hand she carries a *soré* branch, which she uses to rub *soré* on them, saying, "May you be cool!" After this anointing, the branch is discarded and they are once again welcome in the village.

The help of the peace-thrower may also be sought in the event that a family member has been gone so long that no one knows where he now lives. She takes her calabash and accompanies the person seeking her help. They leave the village together on the path originally taken by the missing person. The *okoo-pi-gangmo* says, "Be still! I'm going to call him and listen for his voice!" She calls the missing person's name in a loud voice until an answer is heard: "Yeeeeee!" She asks, "Did you hear that! He's not dead!" Then she "changes that person's heart" that he will return to his own people.

RECONCILIATION AND EXORCISM IN THE QUEST FOR FOOD

Rituals involving *soré* often relate especially to hunting and fishing. They focus on the quest for food and the conditions necessary for its success, and they emphasize again the Gbaya notion that the place of words is the place of death. If two hunters quarrel in the bush, their words must be "fixed" before they return to the village. It would be shameful for such words to reach women's ears, and hard words and deceit can result in death.

Soré stands between an animal and its hunters. Hunters must stop tracking an animal that breaks off a *soré* branch in its flight, because if they jump over that *soré*, they may be killed. But *soré* is also for a wound inflicted by a buffalo; when the wound has healed, the hunter's body is cooled with *soré* leaves to prevent the same thing from happening again. Ideally, it is a priest who rubs this *soré* on the wounded hunter.

If a buffalo has killed a person in a territory that had been burned for the hunt, when the time comes to hunt in that territory again, an elder from the dead man's family assembles the village in order to invoke a blessing on the ground and on all who walk there, man and beast. The elder explains how the blood of his relative was shed on this land. He explains that now all will be well here as the dead man's blood has paid for this place, and he and his family have invoked a blessing on the land. This blessing, in consonance with the blood, is a sacrifice offered to the local spirits.

The same procedure is observed when a man has drowned. All subsequent fishing in that part of the river is suspended until a blessing is invoked by the family of the deceased. Families not related to the deceased must ask special permission to hunt or fish in areas that have been purchased by blood. The purchase becomes a blessing on the land when it is joined to the good intentions of the family whose ritual gesture transforms the death into a sacrifice. The hunter's blood itself becomes a *soré* thing.

Soré is also for cooling weapons. If a gun has killed a person, that gun is not used for hunting until it has been cooled by *soré*. The same applies to spears, knives, and machetes; no animal killed by these weapons is eaten unless the weapons were cooled by *soré* prior to the hunt. Such weapons must be taken to the foot of a *soré* tree in the evening, at sunset. Early the next morning a *simbo* priest goes to the *soré* and strips off pieces of its bark, saying, as he strokes the weapons with the bark, "Because you killed people I am cooling you! May there never be such a terrible thing like that killing again! May everything in our village be calm!"

Soré may be used for small hunts "back of the house." That is, if several men have been hunting cane rats near the village and have had no luck at all, before trying in another place their friends will anoint them with *soré* leaves for good luck, saying, "I'm rubbing away all your bad hunting! I'm rubbing away the darkness that covered your eyes!" The hunters' friends anoint them, their dogs, and their weapons, then discard the *soré* leaves. The hunters cry out, "May bad hunting remain behind us, hooo!"

Seeds from *soré* fruits are used as bait to catch cane rats, but *soré* leaves must never be put in a quiver of arrows, because *soré* will cool the poison on the arrow tips. Thus a certain ambiguity appears in *soré*'s involvement in the Gbaya hunt: the life of animals (or enemies in war) may be taken, "thanks" to *soré*'s protection. Here *soré* incorporates a touch or twist of irony; it is used to take life, yet it also remains a symbol for the protection of life in ordinary Gbaya society.

STRENGTH IN NEW PLACES

Soré is for leading people to see the body of a dead elephant. Someone who has never seen a dead elephant must find an elder who has to lead him to it. The elder takes a *soré* branch and both men hold it on their way. When they arrive, the elder says, "Since you have never before seen a dead elephant, I have led you here today! May you have good health! I rub this *soré* on you for your health, to cool you!" Then he throws the branch on the dead elephant, and the hunters proceed to butcher it. The Gbaya appear to have nurtured an awe for large, imposing objects and places (animals, hills, rocks, trees, rivers) in their ritual practice. They also reserve special consideration for unknown or new places and experiences, where the possibility of encountering danger, especially *simbo*-things, runs high. In all such circumstances, *soré* is a necessary companion.

Soré breaks the strength of unruly domestic animals. Garba André explains: "I worked with cattle for seven years. When a dangerous bull threatens to kill people, that bull must be thrown to the ground; someone must pull mightily on the rope attached to its neck and legs and throw it violently to the ground. The bull's legs are bound; then strips of *soré* bark from a young *soré* tree are tied to its tail, and the worker says to the bull, 'The strength that is in your body is coming to an end! May your strength be finished!' Then we swat the bull with *soré* leaves, and let it go. His dangerous strength is over and done! He will now be obedient!"

To cure a dog of biting people, the Gbaya dig up the roots of a *soré* tree and put them in the dog's food. *Soré* calms the dog's aggressive behavior but, since its strength is broken, it is no longer able to hunt either! *Soré* can also be used to prevent dogs from stealing food and from overeating. Several strips of *soré* bark are placed on top of each other on a pathway. When these strips dry, they curl into circles, like little crowns. When the strips are dried, they are burned, and the ashes are put in the dog's food. A dog who eats *soré* ashes will never steal again or prowl the village looking for food as it did before, because *soré* killed the strength of its liver; that is, it conquered the dog's unworthy desires. His appetite has dried and curled up like the *soré*.

Soré breaks the strength of a new canoe. When a new canoe is put into the water without having been cooled by *soré*, it will overturn, spilling people in the water and killing everyone. The boatmen must use *soré*, right from the beginning. An elder puts a ritual pot at the foot of the tree from which the canoe will be carved. *Soré* is in the ritual pot, and a *soré* branch is used to cool the men as they work. When the canoe is ready, the elder speaks to it and sprinkles it with water from the pot: "Canoe, I hereby cool you with *soré*! Be cool and calm like *soré*! Do not overturn and kill people in the water! May all the dangerous things you would have done be cooled!"

Soré is for breaking the strength of dangerous fish. *Mgbim*, a fish in the Kadei River, grows as big as a person's thigh and gives off an electric charge. My informants explain that if you are fishing with traps and a *mgbim* enters your trap, it will flop around so violently when it is pulled from the water that the fisherman is thrown to the ground. To avoid harm, he must strip the bark from a *soré* tree or take *soré* leaves in his hand and rub them over the fish trap, saying, "May the strength of this *mgbim* be broken right now!" Then the *mgbim*'s strength is broken and the fisherman can pull up the trap without any problem.

The examples above clearly reveal that *soré* protects the life and well-being of the Gbaya community. *Soré* restores the calm necessary for constructive activity; it breaks disruptive forces and threatening behavior. *Soré* exorcises, banishes, rubs out the harmful and dangerous evils of disease, misfortune, and dissension among people. Like a wise companion who knows from experience what lies ahead, *soré* leads people on the way through new places, circumstances, and experiences; it is simultaneously a boundary and a threshold: it achieves peace by separation or by inviting one toward new horizons.

RECONCILIATION AND EXORCISM RELATED TO *DUA* AND *NYINA*

Dua is a complex Gbaya term for experiences that Westerners typically associate with malevolent magic, witchcraft, and sorcery. For the Gbaya, however, *dua* designates any extraordinary power and behavior that is often but not always harmful, while *nyina* is a general term for medicines, whether they are helpful or harmful ones. I shall now attempt to describe the phenomena associated with these terms and their relationship to *soré*.

Bouba Enoch relates the following myth of origin to explain how *dua* started in the world. According to the Gbaya fathers, *dua* came from *dang-so*, an evil god or spirit, who used to live in the wilderness by himself. He had no family, no friends. One day he put a piece of meat in the *ngmana* tree, saying, "The person who comes along and eats this meat will become a member of my family." The meat stayed in the tree for a long time. At long last, two men came walking and saw the meat in the tree. The first man wanted to take the meat; the other man counseled against it. The first man refused to listen to his friend. He took the meat and ate it. That, says Bouba, is how *dua* got into his stomach, because he ate meat that had been put in the *ngmana* tree.

The man who refused to eat the meat had no *dua* in him; he was a *bubu-zang*, a man with a pure, unblemished stomach. But the one who ate the meat developed a craving to keep on eating; that is, he became increasingly covetous and jealous. Today, if words come between people, it is the *ngmana* tree that uncovers the *wi-dua*, the one who eats his brother. The *ngmana* distinguishes between the *wi-dua* and the *bubu-zang*.

Witchcraft, sorcery, and divination in African societies are notoriously complex phenomena. It is most convenient, therefore, to have discovered this etiological account, which appears to tell the whole story in a few words. The myth does not resolve every problem, however, though it does provide clues to current Gbaya thinking about *dua*.

On the one hand, Gbaya believe that *wi-dua* are extraordinary persons with unusual powers, for example, the power to transform themselves into animals or lightning. Such persons can be identified by opening their intestines, in which *dua* is said to reside as a little red hook, a headless black snake, or a black, furry, mole-like animal. The powers of *dua* can be used for good or evil. A *wi-dua* is someone who hurts people with deliberate and spiteful maliciousness, whereas those thought to possess and use the *dua* substance for good are *wan-gbana*: witchdoctors, seers, or diviners.

On the other hand, the *wi-dua* metaphor can be used with nasty intent or in fun. For example, a fortunate or well-accomplished person may be called a *wi-dua* in an innocuous sense. The fathers say, "Zeng ko tana aa ko zang tana," "The wiliness or cunning of the turtle is hidden in the turtle's stomach."

PROBLEMS ASSOCIATED WITH *DUA*

If *dua* kills a person, a surviving member of his or her family will throw a *soré* branch to villagers who are not involved in the death to prevent them from entering into the affair. If lightning kills a person, a member of the same family takes a *soré* branch in hand to show everyone that the cause of death was *dua*: a *dua*-person who had transformed him- or her-self into lightning. *Soré* here testifies that the death was not simply the result of an ordinary illness. It is a sign that dissonance has already occurred and a presence that effects a cooling of further violent acts. *Soré* cools the survivors, preventing at least their immediate plans for revenge.

Soré is for *fio-ngmana*, for cooling the death of a *dua*-person at a trial by ordeal. If a man accused of being a *wi-dua* dies as a result of drinking the bark of the *ngmana* tree, one of his friends holds a *soré* branch during the opening of the dead man's stomach. *Ngmana* reveals whether the man was a *wi-dua* or a *bubu-zang*. If *dua* is found in his stomach, it is clear the *ngmana* has accomplished its task; if no *dua* is found, the dead man's family requires recompense from his accusers. Compensation can be the gift of a young girl or boy to the dead man's family. *Soré* branches are laid on the child as he or she is led to the dead man's family, and that child is known as *soré-ga-mo*, *soré*-cool-thing.

In Gbaya tradition there may be many causes of death by *ngmana*: *dua*, theft, lying, adultery, murder not associated with *dua*, jealousy, refusing to confess the truth, hatred, covetousness, revenge, quarreling, hardheartedness. The accused person is required to drink *ngmana*, and is presumed innocent if he or she merely vomits. If death occurs, the person is guilty, and *soré* is used to cool the survivors. If a person does not die from *ngmana*, those who accused that person either throw a *soré* branch before the person or simply declare, "I throw *soré* to you!" That is, "Forgive me for accusing you! Do not jump over *soré* and seek to do me harm!" The chief may order the accusers to pay a large fine to the survivors.

Adzia Dénis explains that even if a man is a *wi-dua*, but not responsible for the death under investigation, *ngmana* will not kill the *wi-dua* who says, "If it was really me who killed that person, then may *ngmana* kill me!" Then he vomits and thereby proves his innocence, because *ngmana* does not kill anyone, even *wi-dua*, indiscriminately.

Or perhaps, says Adzia, you are a pure-stomach-person, but a *wi-dua* overhears you express the desire to kill someone. That *wi-dua* kills your enemy for you, but tells everyone that you killed him. You deny it but are required to drink *ngmana*, and you die. If, when your stomach is cut open, no *dua* is found, your family cuts off your lips and puts them at the foot of a *soré* tree. If the *soré* tree dries up and dies, then everyone knows that your lie has entered *soré*, and it must die just like you. But if *soré* lives, you did not lie. In that case, says Adzia, those who accused you caused your death and must pay a heavy fine, because sometimes *ngmana* lies, explains Adzia. *Soré* is the final justice.

If a *wan-gbana*, a diviner, is called into an affair to help determine the cause of death, he arrives with several assistants, a medicine bag, his dance rattle, a *soré* branch, and a *gbere* stem. His face is smeared white with kaolin, and often he will receive payment from the deceased's family before he asks the chief if he may begin his dance of divination. When the chief agrees, the villagers assemble and the diviner declares, "The person I indicate must drink *ngmana!*" Then he begins his dance.

During the dance he waves the *soré* branch and tears its leaves off one by one. These he places before representatives of the village residential groups to designate their innocence. At last he takes the *gbere* stem and throws it down before the man or woman who is guilty of murder. A verbal or physical battle may ensue between the accused family and the dead person's family, which can be cooled by throwing *soré* in their midst. But the accused must drink *ngmana*.

Doko Illa, the Muslim blacksmith and chief of Illa, near Garoua Boulai, relates another example. He explains that whenever lightning (that is, a *dua*-person) has killed someone, a week or two after the burial the deceased's family must be washed, because they had all been in contact with the victim: *simbo* has taken them. Doko himself has washed many people, because the "priest" for these rites is usually a blacksmith. He leads the victim's family to a stream, circling good trees in the savanna and certain grasses in the gallery forest.

Before going down to the stream, the priest cuts three *gbere* stems, indicating that the victim was a man, and when he arrives at the stream he plants these stems upright in the running water. One by one, members of the family come to the water and squat over the *gbere* stems. The priest washes them, saying, "I hereby wash away your lightning sickness. May you be well and strong!" When everyone has been washed, he uproots the stems, and the water carries them downstream, as the priest says, "May water carry all this dirt away, far out of sight!"

On the way home, he cuts three young *soré* stems and plants them in the village to prepare for the anointing rite. A fire is kindled underneath these *soré* stems, and a potsherd of oil is heated. The priest adds pieces of amaryllis to the oil and stirs it with a *soré* stick. Then he dips *soré* into the oil and anoints every member of the dead person's family, after which the fire is extinguished and the anointing paraphernalia is cast after a bird. If a pregnant woman is in the group, says Doko, the priest prepares a ritual pot for her, filling it with water and the leftover scrapings. This pot must be kept under the woman's bed until her child is born. She washes herself from the pot every day, and when her child is born it is also washed from this pot—for three days if a boy, four if a girl.

FALSE ACCUSATIONS

If a man has been falsely accused of being a *wi-dua* and successfully passed through the trial by ordeal, though he still lives, his entire family will be angry with the accuser. One day the accuser may inadvertently share a meal with someone from the same matriline (lineage transmitted through the mother) as the accused, without being aware of this relationship. He falls sick (perhaps from harmful medicine) and consults a diviner to determine the cause of his illness.

On the way he breaks a dry stick, about ten centimeters long, and takes it to the diviner, to rub on two white stones. The bottom stone is about fifty centimeters wide; the top one is quite small. A magnetic force or power in these stones makes them stick to each other. The diviner rubs the sick man with the stick, then shows the stick to his stones, saying, "This man came to 'see.' Speak to him!" The sick man speaks to the stones as the diviner rubs them together: "Should I drink medicine of the *dumgba* tree to get well?" or "Was it Garba who made me sick when I ate with him?" and "Is Garba of the same matriline as Dangye [the man he originally accused of being a *wi-dua*]?" If the question contains the wrong answer, the stones do not stick together and the diviner keeps on rubbing. But if the question is on target, the stones stick together so powerfully that no one can pull them apart. The sick man inquires further about the solution to this problem and learns that he should participate in the *zuia-zang* rite with the man who used harmful medicine to make him sick.

Then a *wi-zui-zang*, a person who washes stomachs, leads the sick man and the fellow who gave him harmful medicine into the bush where they circle several trees. They do not, however, go down to the stream, but return to the village where the priest digs a shallow grave. He pours ashes all around this grave to indicate that the sick person's accusations started the entire affair; such accusations invite death, because the accused die from *ngmana*.

As the false accusation requires washing, so does vengeance of the man who resorted to harmful medicine. In order to "untie" the affair, both must be washed next to the symbolic grave, lest a death really occur. The priest prepares a calabash and fills it with water and *soré*. He puts this calabash on an old mat next to the hole, saying, "I wash away your false accusation, by which you accused this man's family of *dua*. May revenge for that act also pass away. May no one seek to kill any more. May you eat together again, and may both of you remain in good health."

In his calabash are medicines from the trees they circled, *soré* leaves, and an ax-head. The hole itself is empty, and the priest kneels between the two men. He dips water from the calabash and washes the men once, then tells each of them to wash with the same water. The sick man who started the affair washes first, saying, "The *dua* that I said was in your stomach, I hereby wash those words into the ground right here! May I eat with you again! May I be healed. May I be saved." The other man washes himself, saying, "The anger that took hold of me when you said there was *dua* in my stomach, I was so angry that I did medicine against you, and I wash that anger away right here!" Then the priest pours the water and everything from the calabash into the grave. Next he puts a bit of dry manioc to their mouths, saying, "This food that I'm testing in your mouths, may you eat together again! May you be healed! May you be strong and well! Jump over the snake! Stamp the poisonous centipede under your feet! Jump over all obstacles in your path! Jump right over deep holes! Jump over big rocks!

Crush them underfoot! May no vines ensnare your feet!"

Then the two men eat *kam géḍa*, a "meal to cool things," to show that they have confessed their sins to each other. Their stomachs have been washed and their families are reconciled.

WITCHES AND SECRET WORK

Some persons are witches rather than mere sorcerers. That is, they may work with bad medicine as well as good, as Hamada Samuel explains. If a *wi-dua* is jealous of someone, he may secretly take corn or manioc from that person's garden or meat from an animal he has killed or a scrap of material from his clothes and combine it with sticks about the size of matches. According to Hamada, the *wi-dua* then does *husa-tom*, or secret work, with these objects.

When the harmful medicine is ready (the Gbaya and several other ethnic groups call it *mgbati*), he plants it in the floor of the "offender's" house, or next to the house or in the garden. The effects of *mgbati* are swift. Successful work now brings failure, and everyone in the family becomes sick and listless. A *wan-gbana* informs them that *mgbati* is behind these problems. He offers to remove the *mgbati* for a price and comes at night to perform his divining dance.

The *wi-dua* may be protecting that medicine, says Hamada; he may have changed himself into a snake and be hiding it under the ground or moving it from place to place when the *wan-gbana* is not looking. The *wan-gbana*, however, will succeed; the snake will slither away from the medicine unharmed because a *wan-gbana* will never kill his own brother or directly harm another person who also possesses *dua*.

When the *mgbati* is located, it is shown to everyone and thrown into a fire. The *wan-gbana*'s work is over, but the family must be anointed in order to restore its health and success. According to Hamada, the person who does this anointing is not the *wan-gbana*, because he is not a priest but a master of medicine and a seer. Although Hamada claims that *soré* is not necessarily used for this anointing, Haman Matthieu insists that *soré* is always used. After the anointing, the men hold their hands over the fire; the priest pours water over their hands, and the resulting smoke envelops them all. Objects used in the anointing are then cast after a bird.

Dua and harmful *nyina* are both distinguished by their fundamentally secretive, occult, and therefore untrustworthy character. *Soré* does not destroy them, but renders them ineffective by virtue of its openness, strength, and character. *Soré* is eminently trustworthy, and in its strength there is nothing to hide. *Soré* is the way to life for the Gbaya, whereas *dua* and harmful *nyina* are ways to death.

RECONCILIATION AND EXORCISM AFTER A DEATH

Ritual precautions must be taken during various burial circumstances, especially if the person died a *fio-simbo*, or *simbo* death. The Gbaya use *soré* to solve a great variety of problems, but as these rites indicate, death itself is their most persistent problem.

If, for example, a man, woman, or child has killed a person or a *simbo* animal and never been washed, his death is a *simbo* death. His grave is dug with a wooden instrument called a *gba-gozo*; metal tools are not used to dig this grave because these are the same tools used in the fields, and food touched by the gravediggers' metal makes people sick.

Only a *simbo* priest can preside at this burial, and he advises the dead man's family not to serve food to the mourners. The priest himself washes the body and sees that the man's clothes are buried with him, lest someone touch them and become ill. *Soré* leaves are thrown into the grave, and the body rests on them, covered by the same mat that the person had used during his illness. In ordinary circumstances, the mat would have been new, and the body would have been on the mat. The grave is filled with dirt, and the gravediggers' wooden tools are left on top as *simbo* things that must not be touched.

The priest then leads the deceased man's family to a stream to be washed. The man's possessions must also be cooled by *soré;* food from his fields, domestic animals, money, clothes, tools, and weapons are put on the ground to be cooled by *soré*.

BURYING *FIO-DONO*

When a man dies after swearing falsely on *dono*, a blacksmith presides at the burial. He digs the grave with metal tools and covers it with *soré* leaves. The body, wrapped in the same mat on which the man had died, is placed on *soré*. When the grave is half filled with dirt, the metal tools used to dig the grave are also buried with the body so that no one will touch them and get sick.

After the burial, the blacksmith summons two people: (1) someone from the dead person's family, to represent the man who swore falsely by *dono* — for example, he swore that he was not a *wi-dua* though his subsequent death proved him to be a liar; and (2) his accuser. The priest washes these persons to reconcile their entire families. He "tests" a bit of manioc to their mouths, anoints them, and tells them to eat together again.

BURYING A *LAḄI* OR A GIRL INITIATE

When a *laḅi* initiate dies in the Initiation House, *Narninga*, the man of the spear, presides over the burial, and the dead boy's companions dig the grave. First, they put *soré* and dry roofing grass into the grave, then the body of their friend. After the burial, the surviving initiates are washed by a *simbo* priest: the entire *zuia-simbo* ritual is performed. The dead boy's father may be present at the burial, but his mother does not learn of his death until the boys return to the village. On that day, *Narninga* puts *soré* leaves over her threshold to inform her that the boy is dead.

The burial procedure for a girl is different from that of the *laƀi*. She is buried well, with no need for *soré*; her body is prepared as though she were to celebrate the final dance of her initiation. After the burial, however, the other *zaabolo* initiates must be washed because "one of their members has abandoned them." The girls are washed and cooled with *soré* to prevent other deaths in their midst. My informants explain that *soré* is used to cool the girls because their friend's death is like *simbo*, and *soré* helps them to forget this death; it restores their health and good spirits.

BURIAL OF A HUNTER KILLED IN THE BUSH

A *simbo* priest presides over the burial of a hunter. He does not wash the body or put *soré* in the grave, which is, however, dug with wooden instruments. The body is placed head down in the grave, in a kneeling position. No mat covers the body because this man did not die lying down; he died the death of a real man in the bush, a hard and difficult death. To deny this hardship by burying him in a mat would portend the same death to other members of his family; they would eventually die the same way, killed by an animal in the bush.

Burying a man in a new mat indicates an expensive burial, one that is carried out with great care and consideration. A new mat is like a casket, say my informants, because a proper mat is a *bu-dere*, a white, unblemished mat that is clean before all the spirits. A man buried in such a mat has already gone to the spirits, before whom one cannot appear dirty. A new mat signifies a clean death. The spirit of a hunter who is killed by an animal, however, cannot be buried in a clean, white mat, because he did not die a clean death. Nevertheless, though his companions must be led through *zuia-simbo*, the place where the hunter was killed belongs to his family because his blood purchased that place.

THE MAN WHO DRINKS *NGMANA*

The man who dies from drinking *ngmana* is presumably a *wi-dua*; the family are present at his burial, however, and they continue to insist on his—and their—innocence. This one is buried at the foot of a low mound or hillock behind the village rather than next to his own house because, as a *wi-dua*, this man was an outcast who worked against life, against the good of society. A hillock behind the village is a place of shame, say my informants.

His family washes his body. The gravediggers are *wi-kofe*, the men who begged wives from the man who died, who married his daughters. They wear *soré* tied to their wrists to protect themselves from the spirit of their dead father-in-law, but they do not admit that he was a *wi-dua*. The *soré* indicates that this death resulted from *dua*, but the men themselves support the innocence of their father-in-law. By virtue of marriage, they are involved in this affair, although in an ambivalent way. *Soré* reconciles their ambivalent relationship with the dead man.

They dig the grave with metal tools and bury the man well, because they are family. If no family were present, a person who had died from drinking *ngmana* would be thrown into a grave, covered with dirt, and forgotten. The family, however, when they are present, do everything possible to resist the charges of *dua* leveled against them by the community.

This death involved hatred because the man died from *ngmana*. As *simbo* is involved, all those who accused the dead man of *dua* must be led through the *zuia-simbo* rites after the burial. Washing *simbo* is the only way to calm things after such a death.

BURYING A WOMAN KILLED BY LIGHTNING

When women are killed by lightning, they are never buried in clean, new mats, even if their families are present to guard the procedures. *Soré* and other leaves are thrown into the victim's grave; a woman's body is placed on these leaves, and the grave is filled with dirt. The metal tools used to dig and fill the grave are cooled by *soré*, and a *simbo* priest cools the woman's possessions before they are claimed and distributed. Members of the victim's family are not led through the *zuia-simbo* rites, but they are anointed by a *simbo* priest. Lightning is like a spear; it has pierced this family, and their health must be restored.

The rituals described in this chapter contribute especially to our understanding of *soré* as a tree of life in the midst of the ordinary conflicts and the deep problems of Gbaya existence. *Soré* enables the resolution of chaotic relationships; it makes everyday life secure from death and exorcises malevolent and ambivalent forces in the society. *Soré* is unambiguously for life; even in death, it is the way to order and freedom.

10

The Story of Karnu,
a Gbaya Prophet

Contemporary Gbaya Christians transform the *soré* metaphor in their interpretation of Karnu, the most famous person in their recent history. Karnu is well known not only in the Gbaya community but also among students of French colonial history; in the 1920s he was the leader of an unsuccessful revolt against the French administration and Fulbe power. Today he is revered in Cameroon and the Central African Republic as a prophet who announced a new religious orientation and the coming of a new social and economic order.

Gbaya Christians emphasize the fulfillment of Karnu's prophecies and the fundamentally peaceful, nonviolent intentions of his message and activities, which were largely misinterpreted by the French and ignored by his Gbaya followers. At the heart of his story lies a concern and advocacy for justice in colonial policies affecting the Gbaya people and a prophetic conviction that the shedding of blood in warfare is not the way to attain justice.

Karnu's story is an important part of Gbaya tradition, if only because it constitutes a model for the transformation of *soré* from its ritual contexts to its significance as a metaphor for revitalizing and interpreting recent Gbaya history. Karnu is referred to as *soré-ga-mo*, or *soré*-cool-thing, by those who lived with him and witnessed his teachings, but those who shed blood in Karnu's named jumped over *soré*, so that *simbo* took them and their entire resistance movement.

There are two versions of Karnu's history, one told by European (white) researchers, the other by native (Gbaya) researchers. The two versions diverge at crucial points in the narrative and arrive at different interpretations and conclusions. To describe the European perspective as objective and the Gbaya perspective as subjective is simplistic and exaggerated, if not false. Such distinctions do not help us to hear what the Gbaya are saying about Karnu. It is equally unfair to characterize the Gbaya account as the inside story, thereby suggesting that the European account is biased and unsympathetic. The truth is that both versions contribute to our knowledge of the Gbaya people, their culture, and their tradition.

THE EUROPEAN STORY OF KARNU

In 1928 a peasant revolt broke out against French colonial administration in the Oubangui-Shari (the Central African Republic) and continued for several years. The revolt centered among the Gbaya people, who had furnished a large number of laborers for the construction projects of their colonial masters, whose interests were primarily at stake. The administrators identified an individual named Karnu, who lived in the bush about fifty kilometers from Bouar, as instigator of the revolt. They described Karnu as a Gbaya chief and witchdoctor (diviner) who wished to rid the territory of all whites and Fulbe, an encroaching tribe. This man claimed that his mission had been revealed to him by a sign from heaven, a star, that had plunged into the Lobaye River.

Karnu refused to wear any clothes or use any objects imported and sold by whites. He announced that their departure was imminent, and that it could be hastened and encouraged by the application of a medicine he provided. The Gbaya would be freed from white domination, he said, if they bore the sign of the *kongo-wara*, the "handle of the hoe," on their bodies. This sign, a mixture of honey and ashes, was rubbed into an incision on the skin. The revolt became known as the *kongo-wara* among the Gbaya; to the French administration, it was the Gbaya War.

Karnu decreed a nonviolent resistance to the whites. He told the Gbaya not to pay taxes and not to perform any work in the white man's service or have any other dealings with them. Karnu himself, however, wanted to visit the Roman Catholic priests in Berberati, 200 kilometers south of his village. He said, "I'll pray; I'll discuss matters with the men of their God. Then they will go home and leave this land for the blacks. If they threaten me with their guns, I'll tell them to kill me, if they so wish. I will not defend myself. No blood must be shed."

In June 1928 violence erupted between Gbaya villagers and the Fulbe herders in the Bouar area. The Gbaya accused the French administrators of giving their land to the Fulbe, whose further immigration into Gbaya territory had been discouraged after a similar conflict in 1896. Village after village joined in the fight, which soon became a major insurrection. Some reports claim that Karnu intended to drive out the French and the Fulbe in order to divide the region among several Gbaya chiefs.

Whatever Karnu's intentions had been, they were frustrated by the

French decision to send more troops from Bangui. The administration's forces in the Bouar area were increased in October 1928. On December 11 Karnu himself was discovered. Reports from colonial archives indicate that he offered no resistance to the soldiers, who killed him as he had predicted they would. His death, however, only inspired the Gbaya to more active rebellion against French authority, and this rebellion continued for several years. The French pursued and arrested the disciples of Karnu for some years.

On the basis of its antiwhite character, some European interpreters have described the entire Karnu phenomenon as a nativistic or messianic movement. Others, however, pointing to Karnu's various successes as witchdoctor and miracle-worker, explain his authority among the Gbaya from a traditional and magical perspective. Philip Burnham, for example, emphasizes especially the political character of these events, but also notes the "mystical aspect" of Karnu's leadership and his charismatic ability to exercise leadership beyond clan ties.[1]

European social scientists have sought accurately to record the history of Karnu and faithfully to uncover what actually happened. But their version is considerably different from the story now being told in the Gbaya community. The Gbaya version of Karnu's story is a small part of their contemporary oral tradition.

The tradition that follows was researched and narrated by Yongoro Etienne, whom I interviewed in Baboua in July 1976. At that time, he was a student at the Lutheran seminary in Baboua. He comes from the same town in which these events took place, and he worked with several eyewitnesses, including Saaré Joseph and Naahii Abraham. As I continue to research the Karnu story among many Gbaya, I am increasingly aware that Yongoro's account is an exemplary model of their understanding of this event.

YONGORO'S STORY OF KARNU

The story of Karnu and his last year begins with his wife Naayargunu, who was Chief Naahii's daughter. When she dreamed that she heard the voice of God, she was struck with fear, as women are not expected to understand such things. She said to God, "Show these things to my husband. He'll know what to do about it, won't he?"

Thereafter, Karnu himself began hearing God's voice in his dreams. Karnu's name at that time was Barka, which indicates that the bearer will someday receive a great honor; he will be a prince among men. These events began as Barka worked in his gardens in his wife's village. There he was troubled by a huge *ndende* tree, a tree so large that it was impossible for a man to think of cutting it down. Barka began pleading in these words: "Who will cut down this tree for me? What will I do? This tree is too much for my field. Who will cut it down for me?"

The next morning when Barka went out to the field, the *ndende* tree had been pulled up by the roots and thrown out of the field, roots and all, into the grass. Barka thanked the one who had done this and knew that it was God. When he returned to the village, he told everyone what God had done. He said, "It was God who did this; God worked for me in my garden."

After Barka had cleared and hoed the field, it was time to plant the manioc. He took manioc sticks from his old field and brought them to the new field for planting. Then he said, "Who will plant this manioc for me?" The next morning when Barka went out to the field, all the manioc was planted. He was very grateful and thanked God before returning to the village with news of this event.

At this time no one outside the immediate Bodoe area knew what was happening. Barka continued to work in his gardens and to fish. God spoke to him while he went about his work, and Barka never failed to share these revelations with everyone in the village.

One day Barka went down to the river to check his traps. One trap was very heavy, and Barka had to struggle with it. He pulled on it with all his strength and finally managed to get it out of the water. And there in that trap was a spectacular fish—a catfish—that had no head and no tail! It had feet like a human being, and in fact, it was wearing shoes. There were three things in Barka's trap: one fish and two white stones.

The fish spoke to Barka, saying, "You shall no longer be called Barka. From now on your name is Karnu [*kar*, roll up; *nu*, earth]. One day you will roll up this earth like a sleeping mat and take it away to heaven. Take these two stones home and put them in your box. They will show you everything; they will tell you what is going to happen." Karnu happily agreed to do as he was told.

Karnu took the stones to the village and put them in his box; then things began to happen. The stones spoke to Karnu when no one else was present, and he began to share his visions with other people. He showed people many things that were going to happen, miraculous dreamlike things. It was at this time that word about Karnu began to spread.

As these revelations took place in his own house, Karnu asked the villagers to help him build a new one. With their help, he made a very large house, ten meters square, though Gbaya houses are traditionally round. Karnu's square construction was an architectural innovation—a sign, the Gbaya said, of things to come. Many people from the Bodoe area brought him grass for the roof.

By the time the house was completed, word about Karnu had spread as far as Bouar, Carnot, Gbayanga-Didi, Baboua and Berberati, and the white administrators began to circulate in the area to find out what Karnu was doing. He warned everyone, "When you see war coming, do not go to battle with those who bring it. My only weapon is this *tikin*, my bamboo stirring stick. My soldiers are the bees of the forest. When my bees chase away those who bring war, you may whip those men; but you must not cut them with sword or knife. You must not shed blood. Do not refuse to work for them. Work for them happily, because you will get many things when you work for them."

Karnu baptized four people: Dedeng and his wife, his own wife, and himself. It happened this way. Early one morning Karnu, Dedeng, and their wives went out to the bush and found the hole of a giant rat. They sat down and sang this song to call the giant rat out of its hole:

> Giant Rat, Giant Rat, come quickly,
> O Giant Rat, O Giant Rat, come with your child.
> O Giant Rat, Giant Rat, come quickly,
> O Giant Rat, O Giant Rat, come with your child.

When they had captured the giant rat, Karnu cut open its stomach with his knife. He took out its liver and squeezed it in water, changing the water into blood. Then he dipped a manioc root in the blood and gave it to his three companions to eat. Karnu told them, "Do not worship false gods any longer. There is but one God in heaven. Get rid of all those things next to your house that you keep for the ancestors." After their baptism, they told everyone, "There is but one God in heaven."

Karnu abandoned his gardens and fish traps. He spent all his time telling people about the one God in heaven and performing many miracles that people had never seen before. Sometimes he called all the people together and taught them, sitting on top of a mortar that was normally used for pounding manioc. He drove that mortar around as though it were a truck! Sometimes he sat on top of a large rock, and he also drove that rock all over town. This was a great miracle that no one has seen before or since.

At that time cattle had not yet been brought into the area, nor had the locust appeared. When Karnu entered the bush in back of his house and came out again, he was covered with cow manure up to his knees. He showed everyone and said, "Look at this. An animal will come among us that we'll be able to eat. You won't have to look all over for meat; there will be enough for everyone." He went back into the grass and emerged again with hands full of locust wings. He said, "Let me tell you, you will receive many, many good things. Just remember to live in harmony with one another."

These are the things that Karnu used in his work. The large rock and the mortar were his trucks. The *tikin* was his weapon. The two white rocks were his telephones. The bees were his soldiers. He baptized three people and himself. He blessed many people and gave them each a *kongi*, a simple hooked stick. Everyone who received a stick from Karnu's hand also received Karnu's blessing and power and protection for the coming battles. Karnu also gave people small manioc and *soré* sticks in addition to the *kongi*.

Many people from the entire region came to see Karnu and to witness his miracles. They always brought him gifts, especially goats and chickens.

They also brought him young girls as wives, but Karnu refused to marry these girls, though he kept them as servants.

Karnu often spoke to the people, saying, "Never shed the blood of the white men and their soldiers with your spears and knives. Just let the bees chase them away." But they did not listen to him. They said, "We have his power, so now we'll show those whites a thing or two. Let's not be afraid; Karnu is behind us." Karnu spoke to them in vain about not going to war.

When the administrators sent their soldiers, Karnu held out his *tikin* to them, and they fell to the ground, their bullets turned to water. The soldiers' guns were powerless against Karnu. Then Karnu's friends started beating the soldiers. They killed some soldiers, and the bees chased away the rest, so far that they could not think of returning. This encouraged the Gbaya to pursue the battle, and they increasingly looked to Karnu as their chief.

Karnu continued to work miracles among the Bodoe people. But when they heard that the soldiers were coming back, they hid in the bush, waiting to ambush them. Karnu insisted that no blood be shed, because his *tikin* was stronger than the soldiers' guns. When the soldiers attacked the third time, things went badly for the Gbaya because Karnu refused to help them. He wanted no killing. Karnu told all those who looked to him for strength, "Do not stay with me any longer. Take your wives and children and escape into the bush, because there is no longer hope for us to win this battle.

"My power over the soldiers is finished, because blood has been shed. The one God will no longer bless me, so don't put your trust in me any longer. As for me, if they kill me, even if they burn me with fire and drown my ashes under water, I shall go home to heaven. But you will suffer for a long time. Everyone now living will die; then I shall return to roll up this land like a sleeping mat and take it away with me, and in that day your children will receive good things. But I shall not die; I shall go home to heaven. On the day of my return, these things will take place."

On his last day, Karnu saw the soldiers coming and said, "The time has come! Flee!" Karnu gathered up his goatskin and entered his house.

A white Catholic priest who had accompanied the soldiers entered the house after Karnu. Before any shots were fired, the house caught fire. Only when it had burned to the ground, did they start shooting. Karnu's brother was killed. When the soldiers entered the house, they did not find Karnu's body, nor the priest's body. They found Karnu's son Yolai still alive and took him away with the body of Karnu's brother.

When the people heard that Karnu had been killed by the soldiers, they all fled into the bush. In those days there were no roads, just bush. The fighting continued. Wherever the administrators and their soldiers went, they found people ready to do battle with them. The Gbaya filled the bush for war, "the war of Karnu."

AFTER THE WAR

In the abandoned village where Karnu used to live, strange things still happen, continues Yongoro, and all that Karnu foretold happened, just as he said it would. Karnu talked about "Naazi-Krist," for example, and it was only a short time later that "Naazi-Krist's" people arrived among us. Eyewitnesses report that Karnu used this term to designate Jesus Christ, and they insist that Karnu had no access to anyone who could have told him about Christ. They say that God revealed this name to him.

Karnu also talked about baptism and even baptized some people; today aren't we all baptized? Karnu preached against "choosing wormy nuts," a Gbaya expression that reminds one to distinguish between right and wrong, and don't we all follow his advice today? It is not yet a hundred years since he was here, and look how all these things have taken place. After all, Karnu did not lie; he spoke the truth!

Karnu did not want war with the whites. But his words and his power attracted Gbaya from all directions; they wanted to use his power against the French. When Karnu blessed people in the hook-splitting rite, that was no *wan-gbana*'s medicine he used, absolutely not! *Dua* had nothing to do with Karnu's power. He simply wanted to bless people and protect them from danger.

Karnu himself was just a little runt, a fisherman, who had no pretensions about leading the Gbaya. His strength came from God, who chose Karnu to help the Gbaya distinguish right from wrong. Maybe the French called Karnu a "sorcerer," but that is not what the Gbaya say.

Barthelemy Boganda, the father of the Central African Republic and a charismatic leader until his tragic death in 1959, visited Bingue-Bodoe in 1950 or 1951. According to Yongoro, the Gbaya point to Boganda's coming as proof of Karnu's word about his own return. "He said he would return and wasn't that Boganda? And doesn't Karnu continue to send the whites out to see where he lived and worked? If it's not Karnu, then why do the whites still come from Bangui and France to see his house? Didn't they carry that log out of here with them?" (The Gbaya who live near Naahii report that whites and government people visited the site of Karnu's house in 1975 and carried off a large beam from the remnants of its foundation.)

Remember what happened in the 1950s, Yongoro continues. "The French soldiers in Bouar looked through their binoculars at Karnu's old village and saw a huge city with tall buildings. For two weeks those Frenchmen tore around here in their trucks looking for that city. For two weeks they kept flying over this area in their planes. And they didn't find a single thing. Just the old house where Karnu had lived. Well, we know the miracles that our people are still seeing right there by Karnu's house. It is really something to think about!"

COMPARING THE TWO ACCOUNTS

Western observers and social scientists describe and evaluate the Karnu event as an important historical phenomenon, which, they say, is significant for an understanding of the French colonial presence in West Africa and for understanding African attitudes toward the whites. Their account gives us the Karnu of history through the medium of written documents.

The Gbaya, on the other hand, relate the Karnu event through their traditional oral medium; they tell each other about Karnu, and in the process of telling and retelling the Karnu story, some extraordinary assertions about him are made in a language that incorporates their mythic and ritual symbols.

The Gbaya version is not simply a history of Karnu, at least not as Europeans understand history, and yet it is faithful to what actually happened. The Gbaya version narrates the true and essential story of the Karnu event, but from their perspective as Gbaya Christians. Since their version is no less plausible to them than the historical account is to Europeans, it demands to be taken just as seriously as the European version.

The accounts diverge at two crucial points. The European version describes Karnu as an antiwhite, anti-Fulbe sorcerer; the Gbaya version describes him as a prophet who encourages the Gbaya to accept both the whites and the Fulbe. The European version notes that Karnu encouraged the Gbaya to reject whatever goods the whites imported, whereas the Gbaya version encourages the acceptance of all these new things.

Both versions agree that Karnu preached nonviolence and that Karnu's disciples failed to live up to this principle. Based on this notion, the Gbaya insist that Karnu was not antiwhite, but they are divided on whether or not he actually preached cooperation with them. Some say he did; others, that more recent Gbaya experience, especially since independence, requires this interpretation. As white and Fulbe presence shifted from threat to useful benefit, so the description of Karnu also shifted from aloofness to cooperation. (The white presence was neutralized by the coming of independence in 1960, and the Fulani presence became economically important. Today the two ethnic groups coexist in a relationship that is ambivalent, but mutually beneficial.)

Although the Gbaya account is pro-white, there is a profound ambivalence among the Gbaya for things, values, and people that are not their own, and the Gbaya version of Karnu's story is an example of how this ambivalence finds contemporary expression. Their ambivalence expresses itself at three levels: at the cognitive level, in their ideas of the ultimate; at the evaluative level, for it touches on morality; and at the aesthetic or expressive level of existence, for it is taught and transmitted in story form. Often Karnu himself assumes heroic proportions comparable to Wanto, the hero of Gbaya tales.

The other major difference between the two accounts is the Gbaya refusal to accept the European assertion that Karnu was a *wan-gbana*. Gbaya Christians state flatly that Karnu's power and message came from God and could not be associated with one who had *dua*. Gbaya Christians identify *dua* as witchcraft, as an evil power associated with evil purposes. Karnu, they say, could not have been a *wi-dua*, because his work and message were dedicated to helping the Gbaya community. Nor was he a *wan-gbana*, because such a person will do nothing useful or good unless he or she is well paid. Karnu solicited no payment; he did nothing for personal gain or enrichment.

Thus the Gbaya find it more appropriate to speak of Karnu as a genuine prophet—as one who had a message from God. They say he prepared the Gbaya community for the reception of the Christian message. For some interpreters Karnu is either a Gbaya John the Baptist or a political figure like Boganda, or both. They note that Boganda himself had studied for the priesthood before entering politics and remained close to the Roman Catholic Church throughout his career. But, if Boganda was a political and a religious figure, then so was Karnu. His significance as a political hero cannot be separated from his role as a religious leader. The Gbaya do not identify Karnu and Boganda as the same person, but their stories indicate that they have at least thought about the possibility.

THE KARNU NARRATIVE AND GBAYA RITUAL SYMBOLISM

Can the Gbaya account of Karnu be included in the large body of Gbaya narratives called *to*? The Gbaya themselves say No, because eyewitnesses saw all that Karnu did and said. In other words, the Karnu narrative has a firm historical core, whereas the tales of Wanto have no historical basis. Wanto narratives come from the dark; that is, from a past that no one really knows.

The Gbaya account of Karnu is not an ancient tale. It is mythologized or theologized history in the sense that the Gbaya have drawn on their own symbolic vocabulary to express the history of Karnu. That is, as a contemporary embodiment of symbols whose many meanings relate to both ultimate and existential issues of Gbaya life, the Karnu narrative is history and myth: its power stems from its ability to make sense of life from colonial domination to the present. Karnu's symbolic words and deeds would not be meaningful to the Gbaya if they did not fit a familiar universe of symbolic meaning. The ambiguity of the symbols is, however, both inherent and received, and the Gbaya do not necessarily interpret and heed Karnu's message exactly as it was received in his lifetime.

Eyewitnesses have stressed the elements of novelty and innovation in Karnu's words and deeds. The legitimacy of this claim should not be minimized, but neither can we ignore a certain regional variation in Gbaya beliefs or the inherent complexity in all symbols. Tellers of the Karnu narrative also manifest a modern tendency to recast Karnu's message to fit the present—thus the strong Christian gloss provided by my informants, all of whom are Christians.

The narrative gives little information about the origins or early career of Karnu, but it is generally agreed that he was not a native of Naahii. He came there from his home village a short distance away to take a wife, and remained in Naahii rather than follow the patrilocal norm of Gbaya habitation. As Karnu's influence grew, he established an independent hamlet near Naahii, but he was always considered to be a *wi-kofe*, suitor, in Naahii. A *wi-kofe* is a *soré* person in his wife's family, although he may also have an ambiguous status, especially if he chooses to rise among his in-laws. One of my eyewitnesses, Gbalaa Sorobana Rebecca, suggests that as Karnu's influence expanded and his wealth increased, Naahii people became jealous because he, though a stranger, had become like a chief in their midst.

My sources maintain resolutely that Karnu had no contact with Christian missionaries. They attribute not only his innovative square house but also his baptism and monotheism to a unique revelatory source. The narrative identifies his wife, Naayargunu, as the initial recipient of the messages that subsequently came to Karnu. This reference invites comparison with the woman peace-thrower, especially as it suggests the importance of woman's role in giving birth to a new reality.

The revelatory dreams and oracular media in the Karnu narrative have strong soteriological overtones, and the woman's role at the very beginning of the narrative does not appear to be merely incidental. Instead, it should be seen within the wider context of symbols related to birth and salvation: as the woman peace-thrower washes her vagina over her ritual pot, for example, its *soré* waters bless and protect her community, and hunters and warriors pass between her legs, going forward to new encounters without looking back. In the same way, the peace-thrower's participation in *labi* underscores the presence of women and the significance of their role in new beginnings undertaken by the Gbaya.

Gbaya oral tradition depicts Wanto's wife, Laaiso, as a counselor whose advice Wanto ignores at his own peril; and Zoyang Jean told me a story about his father, in which the woman's role and a fish trap are present as revelatory media. Zoyang's father was Beka Dumyi; he was called *dum-yi*, or "jump under water," says Zoyang, because he had the extraordinary power of being able to stay submerged under water for hours at a time.

Dumyi was a fisherman along the Kadei River near Batouri, Cameroon, in 1941. One day he pulled up his fish trap and found a heavy load of white stones, which he threw back into the water. He put the trap under water and returned three days later; this time it was full of rotten leaves. Again he put the trap under water and three days later, when he pulled it up, it was full of dried fish, the kind that have been dried over a fire. He got rid of all these things and put his trap back into the water.

At last he decided to tell his wife about these strange events, and she told him to give up fishing. Dumyi refused to listen to his wife, however, and kept on fishing. The next time he went to check his fish trap, he became sick and soon died. He died, says Zoyang, because he refused to listen to his wife. Zoyang's mother explained Dumyi's death to her son this way: "He found God under the water. That's why he died. He found all sorts of things under the water that he should not have found; they were not meant for him!" Zoyang says that Karnu's story is quite different from Dumyi's because Karnu received those things from God, "who gave him those things for his work."

Karnu listened to his wife. He did not jump over *soré* as Dumyi did, but received his wife's word and learned from the things he found in his fish trap: the catfish and the two white stones. As we have already encountered the slippery catfish as a food taboo in several purification and initiation rites, we know that its slipperiness is related to sexual intercourse and fertility. The Karnu story extends the metaphor of the catfish into the domain of new birth and fresh beginnings. There is, however, an ironic twist to Karnu's fish. It had neither head nor tail—no beginning and no end.

The two white stones, on the other hand, have the character of oracular authority. Contemporary Gbaya call these stones Karnu's telephones to emphasize his link with God. Their color, *zeze*, is ritually important: pure, unblemished water, pure, clean mats and pure, unblemished stomachs—all are also white. Although white may be a symbol of death in these instances, it also indicates a spiritual condition: no words, no arguments separate these things (or their bearers) from the presence of all the spirits.

Tani, a Gbaya rite of divination, also uses two white stones, which "see things" by sticking to each other at appropriate times. Though none of my informants believes that Karnu was either a *wi-dua* or a *gbana*-person, many will consent, albeit with little enthusiasm, that he may have been a *wi-zok-mo*, a person-seeing-thing, or seer. Although a seer may be a diviner, and therefore possess *dua*, the term itself does not imply the power and possession of *dua*.

The nuances of Karnu's use of the stones, compared with the deceit and venality of contemporary Gbaya seers, suggests that Karnu is less a seer than a *wi-to-wén oi-nu-So*, that is, a prophet or a "person speaking for God." This term meets with ready approval. Both familiar and innovative symbolic elements are manifested here: common Gbaya symbols are invested with new meanings by virtue of Karnu's way of receiving and using these symbols.

Gbalaa Sorobana Rebecca, one of Karnu's wives although she describes her role as a servant (she was a "gift" to him), is especially adamant in disclaiming any association of *dua* with Karnu, and she is also the principal informant who refers to Karnu as *soré*-cool-thing. She says that Karnu always recognized a *wi-dua*, even as he or she approached his village, and sent an army of bees to chase that person away. Karnu appears to have been a formidable exorcist.

THE *TIKIN*

Eyewitnesses to the events in Naahii, including Europeans, affirm that the most important object used by Karnu was his *tikin*, a simple bamboo stick about four feet long. Karnu held the stick in his hand day and night, and his powers were centered in this stick. When he waved the *tikin* in the direction of his aggressors, they were thrown to the ground as though caught in a whirlwind; their guns failed to function, and they were rendered powerless. The *tikin* did not kill anyone, however. Its purpose was to break the aggressors' power and cool their aggression.

Karnu's *tikin* is the key to his peaceful and nonviolent intentions, yet it also suggests that his purpose was to seek well-being and justice for the Gbaya people. To him well-being began with adequate health and food for all people, but it also included the freedom to procure that food without words with the French or Fulbe invaders. The *tikin* was an ideal symbol for such well-being, since its first and highest purpose is to stir manioc and meat sauce; it is the Gbaya woman's principal tool, the queen of her kitchen utensils.

I have described the use of the *tikin* in the important *zanga-nu* rite of reconciliation, in which it is dipped in *soré* mud and used for anointing. *Tikin* works with *zeze*, pure water, and with leaves of healing; it is a ritual sister to the woman peace-thrower's clay pot. The *tikin* has power over lightning, that is, over the *dua* person who changes him- or her-self into lightning; and it is related symbolically to *dono*, the blacksmith's tools and products, which also exist to procure food and well-being.

When lightning threatens, a Gbaya woman throws her *tikin* on the ground in its direction, then throws cool water on the *tikin* with an accompanying invocation to calm the lightning. A blacksmith may wave his hammer or ax toward lightning to break its aggression. During a lightning storm, a Gbaya may sink his ax or hoe in the ground next to *deng-koro*, the amaryllis that protects against lightning. Then he may place a *tikin* next to the ax or hoe and speak an invocation over these three objects to calm the lightning.

Gbaya oral tradition complements these rites: it tells how the original blacksmith, Tortoise, in a fight with Lightning over Dove's beautiful daughter, waved his hammer at Lightning and thereby subdued him. Many Gbaya still keep tortoise shells over the threshold of their houses; when lightning threatens, they burn the shells, and the resulting smoke protects them from the lightning's aggression.

Informed Gbaya note that both *tikin* and *dono* possess electricity, but with a significant distinction: whereas *dono* may kill an aggressor, *tikin* cools and disables the aggressor. The fundamental purpose of the tools is to procure (*dono*) or prepare (*tikin*) food. When the integrity of this purpose is violated, *simbo* takes the violator. Neither is basically a tool of violence; although *dono* on the hunt takes life, *simbo* always keeps it within the perspective of a respect for life, justice, and judgment. If an oath is uttered with *tikin* or *dono* in hand, that oath is particularly weighty and the guilty party is sure to suffer hard consequences if truth and integrity are violated.

Tikin's symbolic link with *dono* is not without a certain ambiguity whereas its link with *soré* is free of that ambiguity. It must also be noted, however, that neither *tikin* nor *soré* is merely a passive symbol; both are liminal, antistructural, and transformative symbols that also include elements of irony and ambiguity. Neither simply absorbs violence. *Tikin* and *soré* are alert, enterprising, and vigilant symbols that actively work to cool off words, deeds, and situations. They are full of intentionality and straightforward purpose when put to use in ritual acts. Karnu did not wave his *tikin* ceremonially; he waved it ritually in order to achieve his goal of peace with justice or harmonious relationships. Karnu's use of the *tikin* represents the surprising power of softness and coolness over hardness and heat. There was greater strength and wisdom in his *tikin* than in the violent bloodshed resorted to by French and Gbaya warriors.

THE *KONGI*

Many Gbaya went to see Karnu for the medicine that would help them prevail in their struggle for independence from the French and the Fulbe. The struggle itself took its name from this medicine. It was called "the War of the Hoe-handle" in reference to the hooked stick that Karnu gave to those who visited him in Naahii. The *kongi* is used to pick fruit or to pull something toward oneself, for example, when cutting tall grass with a machete, a preliminary task in the preparation of a new field. It has the same hooked form as a *ngomba*, a heavier stick used as a hoe-handle, and as a *kongo*, used as a hoe-handle or as a mallet for pounding the bark of *gba-do*, a tree from which poison is extracted for fishing. Splitting or ripping the hook apart at the joint is a symbol of reconciliation; it reestablishes peace among people because, when the hook is in two pieces, it can no longer be used to cut or to stir. The hook and handle may be interpreted as symbols of Karnu's pacifism, on the basis of the Gbaya rite *aka-ngomba-ari*, "ripping the handle of revenge," a rite that puts an end to warfare between Gbaya groups. Those who split the hook cut their forearms until they bleed, then dip pieces of manioc root in each other's blood and eat it as a covenant. This rite takes place in a stream where the flowing water can cool and carry away revenge. *Koya-saḍi* is another rite in which the *kongi* symbolism is present; it is performed after a kill to ensure success on future hunts. When the animal is dead or dying, the hunter takes the blade of his knife and touches it to the animal's throat, then to the joint of the *kongi*—three times for a male animal, four times for a female animal. He also touches the knife to the animal's breast and between its hind legs in the same way. Then he puts the *kongi* in his quiver with his arrows.

When the hunter is ready to set out on a new hunt, he stands in the path before leaving, puts the *kongi* to his forehead and splits it, speaking the invocation: "As my *koya-saḍi*, lucky animal, is in the *ḍere* [the name of the tree from which the *kongi* is fashioned], so I now split it on my forehead!" The hunter's performance of this rite "splits apart" the dangers and bad fortune that might otherwise befall him.

The *kongi* that Karnu gave to his visitors from other villages was not a genuine tool but only a small stick cut from virtually any available tree. Karnu kept dozens of *kongi* in his possession for those who came to see him. The widely attested miracles performed by Karnu suggest that the *kongi* participated in his power. It was interpreted as Karnu's medicine or source of power in the coming struggle against the white men and the Fulbe. Even the Gbaya who were not able to use the *kongi* as a power against the white men attest to the miracles that Karnu did with it.

But what exactly were Karnu's own intentions? Gbalaa Sorobana Rebecca and members of Karnu's family still residing in Naahii say that Karnu conceived of the *kongi* primarily as a symbol of the covenant between himself and those to whom he gave it, symbolizing that blood was not to be shed. Karnu gave the *kongi* to people as a symbol of pacifism or non-violent resistance. The Gbaya who shed blood in the rebellion broke this covenant, his family says, and therefore forfeited the protection of Karnu's God.

I have discovered no other examples in which the Gbaya use the *kongi* as a symbol or medicine. Many witnesses claim that Karnu used it in a unique and innovative way. Its power as a symbol was derived from the familiar *aka-ngomba-ari* rite, which focuses on peace. Karnu reinterpreted this symbol. He told all who took the *kongi* not to shed blood and, according to eyewitnesses, accompanied the gift of the *kongi* with other familiar objects: amaryllis, and manioc and *soré* sticks. Taken together, these objects point to Karnu's desire that the encounter with the white aggressors be nonviolent and the aggressors nonexploitive.

Doko Badan says that Karnu gave him amaryllis with the *kongi*. The complexities of amaryllis as a symbol and medicine cannot be treated here. It should be noted, however, that in giving it to his followers, Karnu was making use of a familiar African symbol. Amaryllis is used with the peace-thrower's ritual pot to restore good fortunes to a village; it is also used as a protection against snakes and many illnesses and to reestablish peace in a family.

Emissaries who went to see Karnu requested a chicken from their in-laws and took it to Karnu as a gift in return for the *kongi*. Karnu ate these chickens carefully; he never broke any of their bones lest his followers be harmed. Those who received the *kongi* then returned home and took a second chicken from their in-laws (with whom they lived in covenant relationship). They ate this chicken, then buried its bones and the amaryllis that Karnu had given them on the village path which led to the area of danger. Everyone who left the village to participate in enemy encounters stepped on this ground in which the bones were buried. The rest of Karnu's amaryllis was planted in the village, and still other amaryllis and chicken bones were placed in small baskets and hung over the threshold of villagers' homes.

The Gbaya use chickens in a wide variety of ritual contexts, for example, to ensure success in war or on the hunt or to ward off illness and misfortune.

A man preparing for war prepares a chicken and delivers its bones and feathers covertly to the war leader, who then calls a peace-thrower to prepare the way for battle. The peace-thrower invokes a blessing over the chicken bones and feathers and puts them in a small basket; then she takes water from her ritual pot and washes the man who sought her blessing. She washes him over the basket so that the water falls on the bones and the feathers.

The man then takes the basket back to his house, adds some amaryllis leaves provided by the peace-thrower, and hangs it above the threshold inside the door. He also plants amaryllis next to his house. When he is ready to leave for battle, the peace-thrower counsels his wife: "Woman, your husband is going to battle! Do not commit adultery! Do not speak to another man! We have prepared the way for this battle as it must be prepared!" Then she directs the man's wife to take her *tikin* and point it, first away from the door of the house, then back into the house, to indicate that her husband has gone to battle and will return safely.

Bernard Zama reports that his father and older brothers returned from Naahii with gifts of *kongi*, and manioc and *soré* sticks. The manioc sticks represent Gbaya food in general; their presence in the Karnu narrative suggests a link to the familiar Gbaya rite of washing away curses. Thus, if a woman discovers that her fields have been violated, she may seek revenge by cursing the thief after she has collected leaves of the *ndoya* tree and manioc sticks to represent that which was stolen. Her curse will result in the premature death of all the thief's children, unless he or she is appropriately washed and anointed.

The words spoken over the manioc when a person curses a thief indicate the person's intention to call down justice and judgment on the guilty party. Thus, if the manioc sticks that Karnu gave his visitors symbolized the food eaten by the *nasara*, the white men in Gbaya land, the "curse" they invoked on the white "thieves" was this: "If you, whites, have never eaten any of our food, then may you win over us! But if we Gbaya planted this manioc with our own hands and you came along to steal it, then the Gbaya will surely win over you!"

Manioc and *soré* worked symbolically together in an innovative, nonviolent way. Manioc, whether as sticks or as flour, is an ingredient in many medicines and signs of blessing. When a Gbaya has built a new house, for example, he takes ritual measures involving both manioc and *soré* before sleeping in that house. In the evening he makes *zeze*, pure water, and sprinkles a mixture of water and manioc flour on each side of the doorway. He then places a *soré* branch across the threshold. *Zeze* symbolizes the desire for health and sufficient food for this household; *soré* symbolizes peace and well-being for the family. The two together constitute a visible word—a prayer and an invocation of blessing for this family.

Karnu's use of *soré* may also be interpreted as a visible word and prayer for peace and harmonious relationships. Karnu and his followers were convinced that no one who violated or jumped over the manioc and *soré* sticks could expect to win in the end, because *simbo* would eventually take such violators. As for the manioc, it was as though Karnu posed the question to both the Fulbe and the white men: "Don't you eat manioc? Do we step on the food you eat?"

The Karnu narrative includes an event that the Gbaya in Naahii still refer to as a baptism, namely, the eating of the blood of a giant rat. Recalling previous examples of blood covenants—for example, in the *laḅi* rite— it is clear that Karnu's baptism has the character of a Gbaya covenant meal. The rat, however, is a puzzling element in the story. Rats are a prized delicacy for the Gbaya but potentially dangerous because they belong to the *wi-dua*, who especially savors the rat's liver as a source of power. If a *bubu-zang* (that is, an ordinary person) captures a rat, he or she should kill it in the bush and bring only its meat to the village, because if a *wi-dua* hears about it, he or she may seek revenge. If a man finds a dead rat in the bush his discovery is a *zap*, or evil omen; it indicates that a death will soon occur in his family unless protection is sought from an amaryllis.

Does Karnu's baptism in the rat's blood mark him as a *wi-dua*? All my witnesses vigorously deny such a possibility, and especially his servant Sorobana, who tells how incensed Karnu became whenever *dua* persons approached him. Contemporary Gbaya Christians interpret Karnu's use of the rat as a sign of his fundamental integrity and God-given powers, which immunized him from the dangers of *dua*. He handled the rat with impunity and even transformed its destructive power. Although Karnu may be referred to as a *wi-dua* in a metaphorical sense because of his extraordinary accomplishments, Gbaya Christians interpret him as a prophet. They say he is a Gbaya John the Baptist.

The association of Karnu with John the Baptist is a Gbaya Christian assessment rather than an element of my own interpretation. Sorobana says that although she has heard about Karnu's baptism in the rat's blood, she did not witness it. She claims, however, that a remarkable natural spring bubbled up immediately behind Karnu's house. Here Karnu washed her and his other wives and servants.

The spring water was exceptionally clean and formed a shallow pool with a sandy bottom. Karnu could summon forth sheep, chickens, goats, and ducks from the water, says Sorobana. When someone approached the water, it heard the person and became agitated. Karnu called this spring "the water of his God."

Abbo Samuel and Adzia Dénis contribute to the interpretation of Karnu as a John-the-Baptist figure when they say that "he was like a voice crying in the wilderness!" The Gbaya did not understand him any better than the white men who killed him, yet he spoke well, says Abbo, and much of what he said has come to pass. In the 1970s a large movie theater, one of the first of its kind in northern Cameroon, was built in Meiganga and named "Cinema Karnu." The Gbaya entrepreneur who built it says "Karnu was a genuine Gbaya!" Abbo and Adzia are certain that Karnu actually contributed to Gbaya independence; it is, they say, as though Karnu's blood had bought this land.

Certain apocalyptic elements in the Karnu narrative—for example, his ascension and promise to return and "roll up the earth like a mat"—may be seen as the natural development and response of the Gbaya community to the extreme circumstances of colonial domination. Yet we should not overlook the innovative elements in the Karnu story. Simply to label the Karnu rebellion as a traditional movement fails to address a number of crucial points. Although it employed traditional symbolic and political mechanisms, the movement took place in a social context that had fundamentally altered since the advent of the precolonial period, and Karnu's message was addressed directly to this transformed situation.

Karnu's message presupposed a significant transformation in the Gbaya worldview. His words were designed to confront the emerging colonial order; he seemed to know that the Gbaya had to assert their rights in the new order without relying on the traditional solution of warfare. Karnu was a liminal, antistructural person—but only for the sake of structure and for the life of Gbaya society: he was a soré-person. This is the assessment of those who knew and lived with him. He was an extraordinary voice for peace and harmonious relationships among the Gbaya people.

THE COMING OF A NEW ORDER

In Gbaya society Karnu is a link between the old and the new. In political terms, he represents the possibility of a voice for the Gbaya in the modern political arena. In cultural terms, he suggests a logical transformation of Gbaya cosmology to encompass the flow of recent history; and in religious terms, he represents a contemporary theologizing of Gbaya history, centered in their most significant ritual symbol, soré. In the person of Karnu, soré is taken from its original ritual contexts and becomes a metaphor that Gbaya Christians can use to interpret key events in their corporate and individual lives.

For Gbaya Christians, Karnu prefigures Jesus. Karnu generated new meanings of soré, especially as a voice for peace, not only among the Gbaya themselves, but also as regards Gbaya relationships with other peoples whom they contact on a regular basis. Soré emerges from the Karnu narrative as a dynamic symbol deeply intertwined with the Gbaya capacity for change and adaptation. Soré participates in their move to new horizons.

11

Soré: *A Gbaya Tree of Life*

I have intended throughout this work to trace the journey of a metaphor, that is, to determine how one of the most common, ordinary trees of central Africa could become a root metaphor for the Gbaya people. The thick description of *soré*, which we pursued through a multiplicity of ritual and daily contexts must have appeared endlessly circular at times, but it was well suited to our purpose; it has enabled us to recapitulate the Gbaya practice of naming things not only for what they are, but for how they are related to one another for health and well-being. Now it will enable us to understand the journey's culmination and new beginning in the naming of Jesus as our *soré*-cool-thing.

My interpretation of *soré* is grounded in contemporary Gbaya linguistic usage—not in etymologies but in semantic correspondences. The Gbaya symbolic vocabulary, which is central to Gbaya self-definition, cosmology, and religious orientations, is not merely a traditional and unchanging core of meaning in a behavioral framework of similarly unchanging family and ritual structure. Rather, the opposite is true: many symbols, *soré* in particular, owe their persistent relevance to their continuous and constantly changing appearance in countless aspects of daily life, not just in traditional ritual or religion, narrowly defined. *Tikin* (stirring stick), chicken, catfish, *kongi* (hooked stick), manioc flour, blood, oil, clay pot, water, leaves, ashes, charcoal, threshold, path, the fork in a path or stream, *dono* (blacksmith's tools), eggs, and white stones—all of these things belong to the ordinary living space of the Gbaya people.

To deny an evolution among their symbols, therefore, is also to deny the phenomena of change and development in their society. Indeed the Karnu story and its current interpretations teach us that although the frequency and the open practice of traditional rites have greatly changed and continue to change, the traditional Gbaya vocabulary is still highly relevant and actively employed to explain the meaning of contemporary experience in communal and private life.

Symbolic meaning is contextual; that is, it is constructed from a series of reflections, beginning in the physical properties of a thing. Thus meanings yielded by the natural, physical properties of the *soré* tree constitute a certain symbolic content that is peculiar to *soré*. But *soré* is also always part of a particular ritual context and situation. Thus, using Victor Turner's language,[1] we can distinguish its meaning from three perspectives. The original metaphor expands through exegetical, operational, and positional meanings to handle a variety of themes.

EXEGETICAL, OPERATIONAL, AND POSITIONAL MEANINGS

The first level of symbolic meaning is yielded by exegesis. Participants in symbolic speech and ritual give us the "sense of the matter," which, in some cases, is obvious and manifest, and in others, latent or hidden below conscious expression, or both. My students describe the manifest sense of *soré*: it is for making a new village, for cooling murder, or for reconciling two villages. But their further descriptions or exegetical reflections also provide its latent sense: *soré* hates *dua*; Adamou has a soft heart like *soré*; *soré* never lies; Karnu was a *soré* person. The exegesis of the symbol moves from the concrete to the more abstract levels as our understanding progresses.

Those who describe the role of *soré* in ritual contexts are usually fully conscious of the manifest sense of their words because this sense relates directly to the symbol's purpose and intention. In the beginning, however, they may be only vaguely conscious of the symbol's latent sense, which emerges more clearly only after further reflection. The hidden sense in the symbol, its relationship to fundamental human experiences, remains an unconscious, third sense, which is never articulated in the informants' exegesis.

Operational meanings derive from the way in which a symbol is used in a particular ritual context. For example, *soré* may be thrown between people, rubbed on people, held in one's hand, used to wrap fresh meat, cut and notched for initiates to read, or decorated with *simbo* things. Again, we note the movement from the concrete to the abstract in the way that *soré* performs as an instrument in a great variety of ritual and nonritual contexts.

Soré carries an invariable, acknowledged meaning into each context in which it appears, but each new use may also generate new meanings. *Soré* transforms people and situations; it is antistructural for the very sake of structure. Many of its ritual contexts manifest an interlocking configuration of symbolic objects, words, actions, and motifs; yet these never constitute a fixed or inflexible configuration. *Soré* is for life; it is used to serve and promote life, and it manifests the ever fresh creativity and freedom of life. It is a living instrument and a growing tree of life.

Positional meanings of *soré* refer it to the totality of cultural elements and institutions in Gbaya society and illustrate that its meanings may vary in different contexts. In fact, *soré*'s position in ritual process manifests both a dynamic interrelationship and a galvanic interdependence between it and other symbols. *Soré* is placed on or over a threshold; in water at the foot of the *labi* initiates' climbing pole; beside *kongi* next to the fishing dam. *Soré* is fixed in the slits of *bui-so* in the form of a cross, and it is thrown on the ground between two quarreling people. Positional meanings of *soré* are further enriched by reflection on its place in the episodic flow and process of certain Gbaya rites, especially in washing and initiation.

In each of these three ways of looking at *soré*, it is possible to detect a potential for semantic movement from the concrete to the abstract, a movement that yields clusters of meanings or themes. New meanings, prompted by these exegetical, operational, and positional perspectives, open before *soré* as it journeys from one ritual context to another. Yet, without some singular, meaningful connecting link, all these new meanings would dissipate into nonsense. The characterization of *soré* as a tree of life is the organizing image that keeps together the rich growth of life-oriented themes emerging from its many ritual appearances.

The ritual uses of *soré* are as numerous as the leaves of a mature *soré* tree, and the thematic meanings of *soré* in each use clusterlike branches of that tree. These themes are all meaningfully interconnected; they find their center and focus in the root metaphor, *soré*-cool-thing. I shall attempt now to recapitulate the journey of this metaphor, which begins with a discussion of the common understandings of the verb *ga*, "to calm" or "to cool," and the way this verb is used to name and describe Gbaya experience. When this word is related to *soré*'s physical characteristics, it facilitates a gradual expansion of the root metaphor, "*soré*-cool-thing," and leads to the identification of themes that are associated with and symbolized by *soré*. These themes do not define *soré*, as one part of a metaphor does not define the other part. But they may be understood as pointers; they direct us to an object that can be seen, though not possessed. It is a matter of perception, rather than possession, when we allow the "*soré*-cool-thing" itself to help us glimpse the end of our journey in a new beginning.

SORÉ-COOL-THING

When the Gbaya are asked to tell about the *soré* tree, their response is immediate and very consistent: *soré duk wén gaa mo* (*soré* is for calming [or cooling] things). The Gbaya expression is straightforward: *soré* is for something; its explicit purpose in the broad context of human life and relationships is to cool or to calm things.

The verb *ga* has two basic meanings. The first is to calm or to comfort, as in "The mother *gaa* [comforts] her child," and *"Mo gaa me ndé?"* or "Are things peaceful [calm] for you?" The latter of these expressions is Gbaya for "Good evening." The second basic meaning of *gaa* is to pacify or to cool, as in "The sickness is pacified," or "The food is cool or cold."

As an adjective, *gaa* means calm, peaceful, or cool, as in "the water is cool." The noun, *gaa-mo*, means "peace" or "evening," and *gaa-see* means "internal peace of heart or mind." The Gbaya say, *"Ene duk ne gaa-see!"* "Peace be with you!" A *gaa-wi* is a calm, reasonable, and humble person, a person who is never involved in quarrels. The root metaphor, *soré-ga-mo*, *soré*-cool-thing, plays on the relationship between comfort or peace and coolness, and always incorporates both meanings. In a specific ritual context, however, one of these two meanings will be manifest while the other is present only marginally.

Why is the *soré* tree associated with coolness and peace? The most consistent Gbaya reply to this question refers us to the physical properties of *soré*; the Gbaya relate coolness to softness and, by implication, hotness to hardness. *Soré* is a soft tree of the savanna grasslands. Its soft, moist wood makes it utterly unlike the imposing hardwood trees of the gallery forest. The Gbaya say that the *soré* tree *aa ne moka-sée*, has a soft heart; and a Gbaya proverb says, *koro ba soré na*, lightning does not take the *soré* tree. *Moka-sée* means humility, and *soré*, literally, is a soft, insignificant, common little tree; it does not attract lightning as the tall hardwoods do. Thus the Gbaya link the physical softness and humble character of the *soré* tree to its capacity to cool and to pacify things.

The Gbaya also say that the *soré* tree is a *gaa-wi*, a calm or reasonable person. It is common Gbaya idiom to personify trees or to name people by reference to a tree, and any calm, reasonable person who contributes to the peace and general well-being of a community can be called a *soré-ga-mo*. As regards the character of a *soré* tree, the adjective *moka* refers not only to softness, but also to reason and calm.

Another important physical characteristic of *soré*, often referred to in this study because it links *soré* with other symbols, is the mucilaginous substance between its thin bark and soft wood. If *soré* is for washing *simbo* (manifest meaning), it is because bad things slip right off *soré* (latent meaning). Sickness, too, slips off *soré*; its slipperiness calms and cools a feverish, inflamed body.

The bad things that slip off *soré* may be hot or dirty. *Soré* cleans as it cools; it clears, cleans, and opens the way to fresh experiences in human life. *Soré* cools new beginnings to bless the Gbaya for life and it frees them from death. From these reflections, *soré* emerges as a way of life, and this theme is enriched by *soré*'s relationship with several other slippery symbols: blood, oil, eggs, the *zee* leaf, mud, *labi*'s slippery pole, catfish, *zobo* leaves, *woo*, and the passage through the peace-thrower's legs. The way to life must be cool, clean, and clear.

Soré's strong, odorless leaves support still another cluster of its symbolic meanings. Mature *soré* leaves are large and strong, ideal for wrapping fresh meat; young *soré* leaves are clean and absorbent, useful for wiping dirt from people. The plant itself is resistant and resilient, capable of taking much physical abuse. It can be burned, broken, or cut apart, but it will grow right back again. Moreover, *soré* yields an edible fruit, a favorite of hungry Gbaya children.

These characteristics relate to *soré*'s strength; it is humble but not fragile, and the strength it exhibits is echoed in two of the notches on the *labi* initiation stick: "If someone tries to kill you, you must survive"; and "What happens when you show off your strength? You'll find a battle!" The strongest person is not the one who shows off his muscles, but the one who takes evasive action; such is the one who remains cool, reasonable, and peaceful—like the *soré* tree.

The root metaphor, *soré*-cool-thing, may be said to consist of a principal subject and a subsidiary subject. *Soré* is the principal subject and "cool thing" is the subsidiary subject. Neither subject is defined by the other, but each one points to the other. The most explicit meaning of *soré* as principal subject is its distinction from any other identifiable tree; its subsidiary subject, cool thing, exists through hints and guesses, through the expressive perception of Gbaya who see it as meaningful. *Soré* as principal subject controls or limits the way its subsidiary subject, cool thing, expresses itself in a variety of ritual contexts; explicit meanings associated with *soré* direct and guide the particular way the Gbaya interpret it in each ritual context.

INTERPRETING *SORÉ*

The answers to the question "What is *soré* for?" come, as far as possible, from participants in the ritual process, supplemented by the observer's effort to elicit meaning from the data they provide. Consequently, the rites cited below have already been described and interpreted in these pages. Now, however, we must go beyond that which we can observe and push more systematically below the manifest level to discover the latent and even hidden meanings of *soré* in order to identify its principal themes. The semantic movement of a root metaphor will inevitably transcend the intentions of those who experience it as a symbol in their lives.

In thick description, the focus of meaning is on exegesis. That is, we look first at what the Gbaya tell us about *soré* in the context of a particular rite and then at what they say after further reflection. Their descriptions provide the manifest and latent meanings of *soré*-cool-thing. A second level of meaning derives from their description of the way that *soré* is used in particular rites. This kind of meaning is operational or instrumental, and it requires a focus on what the Gbaya do with *soré* rather than on what they say about it. Again taking my cue from Turner's *The Forest of Symbols*, in which he relates operational or instrumental meaning especially to problems of social dynamics, I shall consider not only how *soré* itself is used (for example, whether it is rubbed on a person or thrown on the ground), but also by whom it is used, with a sensitivity for the emotional disposition of those who use it (for example, whether they are angry, fearful, or happy).

Positional or locative meanings (a third semantic level) are so closely related to the operational or instrumental meaning that they may be viewed together. It is important to note, however, that a symbol's positional meanings can shift from one ritual context to another, and every change in the space it occupies changes its relationship to other symbols and its significance for the people who use it.

SORÉ IS FOR MAKING A NEW VILLAGE

Soré is *wén ḍafa yé*, for making a new village. The meaning of the term *ḍafa* cannot be fixed independently of its contexts. It can, for example, refer to cleaning up around one's house; preparing food; making sacrifices to the ancestors or spirits; arranging or putting a table in order; fixing the fire; dressing one's hair; repairing the roof of one's house; arranging or putting the village's affairs in order; getting a tool ready to use.

Therefore, the dispersion of villagers in response to a sickness that they believe is caused by *dua* creates a particular context in which certain of *ḍafa*'s meanings are more appropriate than others. The Gbaya manifestly need a new village, new beginnings, and *soré* meets that need. *Soré* is for making a new village in the sense that it cleans up and fixes what has been damaged, thus putting things into livable order again.

An implicit or latent meaning of *soré* in this situation is that the villagers need unity and harmony in order to enjoy adequate food and health; another is that *soré* has a relationship to the malignant forces that must be expelled if people are to be well and free. A cleansing is called for to get rid of the disruptive influences in the village, and *soré* is for making the way clean.

A deeper, hidden meaning in this circumstance is the villagers' unspoken but hopeful recognition and daring faith that new beginnings, the restoration of good health, and escape from danger and imminent death are even possible. These meanings, though unexpressed, provide the villagers' motivation for doing with *soré* what needs to be done, or rather, for letting *soré* do what it can do for them.

What the Gbaya do with *soré* for the making of a new village is inseparably linked to *soré*'s location in the rite. It is not brought to the site of a new village; rather, the new village is constituted at the site of a *soré* tree, conceived as "the center" for new beginnings. *Soré* is here an *axis mundi*, a center of unity, which people symbolize by tying a knot in a *soré* leaf.

The knotting or tying of the leaf not only draws people together; it also symbolizes a binding of those malignant forces that had disrupted the old village. Untying the leaf signifies that people have been reunited around a fresh center and are now free to live harmoniously in covenant around it.

Not just anyone may preside at the binding together of a new village; a *bé-noko*, a son or a daughter of the chief's sister, performs this task. As the *bé-noko* is related matrilineally to the chief, the new village itself may be said to issue from a woman (the *bé-noko*'s mother). The *bé-noko* can also be seen as a *soré* person, who is called to bind his or her mother's people together in peace and who represents the village's peaceful relationships with neighboring villages.

A mixture of solemnity and hopefulness marks the occasion, as the villagers expect this new beginning to restore their good fortune, adequate food, and health. *Soré* is located at the center of these expectations as the hub of a newly created arena of human life; it grows and works as a tree of life.

SORÉ IS FOR COOLING A FIGHT

Soré is for cooling, pacifying, or ending (*ga*) an argument between two men before they go for their machetes. In this context *soré*'s manifest meaning is to end the physical violence, but its latent meaning is its power to calm the fighters' hearts, to cool their anger, improve their basic dispositions, and thus to establish internal peace. In a hidden sense, *soré* understands that hatred and jealousy lie behind physical violence and lead ultimately to death. *Soré* is not only for throwing cold water on a hot fight; it is also for changing people's hearts in a fundamental way. *Soré* is for peace.

When *soré* is thrown on the ground between two fighters, it achieves peace first by separating them; that is, it constitutes a boundary or barrier between quarreling people. The actual separation is a penultimate measure on the way to ultimate peace and reconciliation. Just as the separation of two sources of heat is required to prevent an explosion, so *soré*-cool-thing is aggressively thrown into the midst of a hot situation, like cold water on a raging fire.

It is neither carefully placed nor planted, but vigorously thrown—again, not just by anyone, but by a cool person. That person may be the woman peace-thrower or any other man or woman of reasonable, humble, and prudent character. If a fighter jumps over *soré* with harmful intent, he will die, but his death will be suicide; it is not *soré*'s work. *Soré* is a barrier, but it is also a doorway, a threshold on which the fighters stand, compelled to assess their behavior.

If they jump over that barrier to fight, they die; if they walk through that doorway in peace, they live. *Soré* makes peace by deflecting the danger and heat at its source. The use of *soré* in this rite is ambiguous—it is both a barrier and a doorway—but the intentions behind its use and position are ultimately unambiguous. As doors are used, in any case, with double meaning, so *soré* is used: to keep out danger and to welcome new relationships.

SORÉ IS FOR *AMA-MO*, FOR RECONCILIATION BETWEEN VILLAGES

The verb *am* means "to suck" (as a nursing child sucks) or "to breathe"; it can also refer to the separation of two people or groups of people who are in conflict. *Ama-mo* involves the intervention of a third party in order to stop a conflict. Thus, for example, *soré* is manifestly for separating two groups of villagers whose fighting has reached a dangerous level. It is also, in a latent sense, for bringing villagers back together on reasonable terms; it encourages the establishment of a covenant to avoid future battles.

The Gbaya often describe *soré* in terms of another metaphor. They call it *wi-am-mo*, a person-reconciling-thing, because it is a mediator. *Soré* symbolizes the Gbaya preference of cooperation over competition. As the Gbaya fathers say, "The right hand washes the left hand as the left hand washes the right hand." *Soré*'s hidden meaning points to the common human experience of conflict, the inherent tendency of human beings to oppose each other, and the domination of self-interest in all areas of human life. Consciously or not, *soré* appears on the scene to mediate wholeness amid the mystery of human contentiousness.

We have seen how *soré* can be thrown as a barrier between two fighters. It can also be thrown on the ground between two villages, but in addition, it can be used with water by women peace-throwers. Old women from both villages will sprinkle their young warriors with wet *soré* branches to cool the fight. *Soré* appears initially as a closed door between people, but *soré* persons can open the door to renewed relationships.

Those who instigated the quarrel between the two villages must be cooled and cleansed of the heat and dirt of self-interest. Against the domination of self-interest, *soré* and *soré* water mediate wholeness and transform these two conflicting halves into one whole. Wholeness is achieved as the pursuit of self-interest is defeated, cooled, cleansed. *Soré* is in the middle where it can most effectively deflect bad things from both directions, impartial yet not passively neutral, because *soré* is for the life of both sides. There are two sides but only one *soré*, where the sides meet to be one.

SORÉ IS FOR WASHING *SIMBO*

Washing in *soré* water manifestly cleanses and purifies one from the dirt acquired in particular *simbo* violations; for example, when a hunter kills a leopard, he must be washed in *soré* water to become clean again and avoid death. There are certain taboos in Gbaya life that one simply cannot violate without suffering death; washing in *soré* water (*zuia-simbo*) is the only way to be saved from death, to keep on living.

Zuia-simbo generates many latent exegetical meanings of *soré*, but it is perhaps most significant that washing *simbo* in *soré* water involves obedience. It is a matter of doing things the right way so that a person's way through life may be clear and clean. The Gbaya explain this obedience in terms of intention; the constant desire of one's heart must be never to jump over *soré*. Otherwise, the washing is of no use, and *simbo* remains.

Soré knows the intentions of a person's heart; it is the way to life; it saves a person from death. For example, when a leopard has been killed, the hunter goes in search of help, carrying a *soré* branch in his hand. He carries *soré* to warn people that he has contacted contagious dirt; the sight of *soré* induces the appropriate response. In this way, *soré* deflects danger from the innocent community. The contagious person carries the *soré* to avoid endangering other people; his gesture is an expression of concern for the health of his family and friends. It may also be a confession of sin; it is an open, visible acknowledgment that he has violated sacred principles.

Before the hunter and his friends enter the village with the animal, a *simbo* priest meets them on the path and washes their shins with *soré* water. This washing is preventive medicine for the hunters who must handle the leopard. It deflects whatever danger they may encounter as they leave society and enter the betwixt-and-between liminal period in which the intentions of their hearts must be joined to the right ritual procedures, lest the washing be in vain.

Only the *simbo* priest can apply this medicine to *simbo* persons, because he has already been there. That is, he has previously trod this path, first as a *simbo* person, and now as a *soré* person, who alone can mediate between the hunter and the life that was violated.

Prior to the actual washings in running water, the hunter and his companions wait in a cold house, the threshold of which is covered by *soré* branches. This *soré* is a barrier, a warning, to those outside, but it also represents their options: one who jumps over *soré* knows what to expect as a consequence. *Soré* cools the danger within the cold house; it prevents the danger from spreading and cools those who are already afflicted, lest they die before they can be washed.

When the time has come for washing, the *soré* branches on the threshold represent the boundary that must be crossed in order to reach the most crucial phase of the washing process: *soré* marks the time and the space where washing as a transformative, regenerative rite takes place. *Soré* leads and guides the hunters on this passage to running water; they grasp a *soré* branch held out to them by the *simbo* priest and proceed together toward the stream, gathering *soré* and other medicine on the way.

In the stream, the priest makes a pool, a watery grave, for the hunters but, transformed by *soré* medicine, this pool becomes a womb in which they are reborn. They are not washed with mere water but with *soré* water, for it is *soré* that enables the water to give life even as it removes dirt. When the *simbo* dirt has been carried away by the stream, the hunters leave the womb and pass through a slippery *zee* leaf. Their return to the village is the beginning of their reintegration into the community. *Soré*'s use and presence in such liminal places carries important meanings for healing, cleansing, and regenerating life.

For a final rite of reintegration, a fireplace of three *soré* sticks is made to support a shard containing oil and *soré* medicine. This mixture is heated and stirred from time to time with a fourth *soré* stick, which is then used to anoint the hunters. The passage from death to new life culminates in this place, resting on *soré* as it began and progressed with *soré*.

The old piece of broken pottery (the shard) is yet capable of being a humble vessel for life-giving ingredients, especially *soré* medicine, and this medicine mixed in sesame oil cools the generative, resourceful parts of the hunter's person (forehead, breast, hands, and feet), blessing that person for whatever new encounters lie ahead. *Soré* washes away his *simbo* dirt; it transforms him from a *simbo* person into a *soré* person and clothes him with *soré* oil. That is, the hunter is not only cleansed of his *simbo* affliction, he is also equipped with the natural properties of *soré* itself so that bad things may henceforth slip right off him.

SORÉ IS FOR *GBEE YOYA*, UNDERGOING AN INITATION

The Gbaya are well aware that *labi* is for making a new and genuine person, but *soré* is also present in the midst of suffering and death for the sake of ongoing life. A hidden meaning of *soré* within the *labi* context may be related to questions about *soré*'s role in the birth and new birth of human beings.

Labi is not only a matter of new beginnings, but far more radically, of new birth, a process in which *soré*'s participation is indispensable. *Labi* has to do with the formation of genuinely new persons, and *soré*'s key role in that formation suggests that the values symbolized by the *soré* tree (for example, humility, the ability to repel lightning [*dua*], strength, softness, and flexibility) are the same values most revered in Gbaya society and life.

Soré is used in several crucial ways during *labi* initiation rites, some of which correspond to its use in *zuia-simbo* rites (for example, threshold and washing uses), and others that disclose new dimensions of *soré*'s meaning. Whereas the vast majority of operational and positional meanings of *soré* can be cross-referenced in various ritual contexts, the initiates' notched *soré* stick is a notable exception. Initiates "read" *soré* from the notches on their stick, as though the essence of *soré*'s symbolic content or semantic load could actually be revealed by *soré* itself.

This particular use of *soré* as well as its key position within the liminal phase of *labi* suggests that *soré* is a source and a way of wisdom. It is a practical, daily, life-oriented way, as the various proverbs recited by the initiates would indicate. The proverbs express values compatible with the uses of *soré* in ritual contexts. For example, mutual help is a bridge enabling passage from death to life; *dua* is the most destructive element in society and must be firmly resisted; forgiveness of someone's sins must replace gossip about those sins; quarreling leads to death; one reaps what one sows.

The way of *soré* is at once soft and strong, and it is revealed in a person's life, not merely in words. A fearful covenant invokes the injunction forbidding *labi* initiates to reveal the *soré* way to uninitiated people on pain of death. It is as if to say, "This way is too worthwhile to treat cheaply! Don't just talk about it, commit your life to it, let *soré* be your way of life, be a *soré* person!"

The *soré* way is a Gbaya treasure in an earthen vessel (much like the shard that contains *soré* medicine and sesame oil). It is not an esoteric knowledge—not a forbidden fruit on a forbidden tree (though we can compare the tree of knowledge in Paradise with Bouba Enoch's story about the origin of *dua*). Rather, *soré* is the way shown by a tree of life, and the fruit of the tree of life is not forbidden.

The notched stick appears on a path frequented by *labi* initiates; it warns the uninitiated against taking this path, and recommends the way of *labi*, the *soré* way, as the genuine path for the initiates. Again, the paradox or edifying puzzlement of *soré* appears in this rite: it is at once a barrier and an open door. And it appears as a threshold (in the threshold or liminal phase of *labi*) to symbolize the potential for human transformation. As a symbol, *soré* helps to constitute that toward which it points, and it can mean either judgment or salvation or both for the person relating to it, depending on whether one jumps over it or reads it into daily life.

The *soré* way leads to the Initiation House, a womb and a house of wisdom, at the center of which, a (slippery) pole is planted. The mystery of good and evil is hidden in the basket at the top of the pole, and the bottom of the pole is at the foot of a *soré* tree, which is hidden in the water of the peace-thrower's clay pot. The boys die under that water, and under the water *soré* leaves bring them back to life. They emerge from death under the water into a *soré* way of life.

Narninga has hung his hat and his ragged clothes and his spear in the *soré* tree: the tree is decorated with signs and instruments of death. But the *soré* way is a difficult, slippery way, strewn with signs of hardship; it leads inevitably through suffering and death to new life. The traveler on that way must be soft and flexible, equipped with resilient, determined strength. *Narninga*, who has himself gone that way before his initiates, is a resolute and purposeful teacher whose ultimate aim is to join in celebration with all the initiates at the end of their journey.

SORÉ IS FOR BLESSING THE HUNT

When the woman peace-thrower Helen Laka washed hunters and their weapons, "I blessed them," she says. "Go in peace! May no harm come to you! Kill many animals and bring them back to me! May your spears see clearly, may they hit the mark!" The explicit, manifest purpose of the peace-thrower's use of *soré* is for blessing: *soré* water blesses.

In the peace-thrower's blessing, some meanings that remain latent for the hunters themselves are manifest in the spoken word. Her words specify what blessing on the hunt really means, and indicate thereby what *soré* water is for. *Soré* is for peace (manifest): these men must not quarrel with each other as they hunt. In fact, *soré* is for establishing a covenant of peace among these hunters (latent): "May no harm come to you," she says. To say that *soré* protects them from danger and death on the hunt (manifest) is to say that *soré* cools the heat of danger. In addition, *soré* deflects danger because bad things slip right off *soré* (latent).

The peace-thrower tells the hunters, "Kill many animals and bring them back to me!" The blessing of *soré* water is for success on the hunt, that is, for bringing home food without being wounded or killed in the process (manifest). Since success is linked to the spears' "seeing clearly" and thus "hitting the mark," washing the spears in *soré* water enables them to accomplish the purpose for which they were made: *soré* "sees clearly"; *soré* "hits the mark" (latent).

Questions about how one takes life on the quest for food without thereby violating life reside at a hidden level. *Soré* protects from the inherent dangers of violating life (in an ultimate sense), and it provides for continuing life (in a penultimate sense). *Soré* is a way through the mysterious necessities involved with having to take life in order to live. Success on the hunt is thought to be achieved, first of all, when unharmed hunters return with food; success at a deeper level means going and returning in the peace or strength of *soré*.

"Everything we did with *kpana-zora*," says Helen Laka, "we did for peace and joy!" *Soré* always reaches into deeper, more intense levels of human understanding and interpretation to cool life and to help the Gbaya to glimpse a new thing at those depths. *Soré* can also be a reminder that peace does not just happen, for there is a way for peace to be established which involves human responsibility. Peace is not a passive state; it is created by people who walk the way of *soré*, and it is always linked to a Gbaya sensitivity for justice. That justice is *soré*-oriented justice, and therefore not without forgiveness. For example, a wronged hunter washes in *soré* water the one who stole from him, lest that thief die. A murderer may throw *soré* in his path to make his pursuers give up the chase.

Soré blesses the hunt as the principal ingredient in the peace-thrower's water pot. Here the most visible *soré* person in the Gbaya community washes village hunters with water from her ritual pot; she also takes a *soré* branch and dips it into the *soré* water, then sprinkles water on the hunters. Water and washing mean cleansing; they wipe out all the transgressions and words (quarrels) that would otherwise muddle and infect the daily flow of their lives.

Quarrels, after all, make people inept in the quest for food. Therefore, *soré* cleanses and cools the hunters; it even clothes the hunters with *soré* oil, not only to deflect danger, but also to wrap them in the integrity for which *soré* stands. The hunt must proceed in a just and fair way, and the hunters' concern for their mutual welfare must predominate over self-interest. (Other leaves in the peace-thrower's pot evidently symbolize related themes and call for closer investigation. For example, *danu* is related to curses and insults; working with *soré* in a ritual pot, it cools and softens such hard words.)

Certainly a latent intentionality is involved in the use of *soré*, because, from the Gbaya perspective, any rite is useless if the actions and use of symbolic objects are not joined to that deeper, life-oriented intentionality, which distinguishes rites and symbols from purely magical and strictly utilitarian performances that have no integrity. Helen Laka says she blessed the hunters with *soré* water for peace and joy; the operational and positional meanings of *soré* in her ritual performance must be interpreted in the light of her expressed intentions.

SORÉ IS FOR COOLING *DUA*, WITCHCRAFT

The death of a person who is struck by lightning triggers a string of accusations in the community. It may lead to *fio-ngmana*, death by ordeal (drinking poison made from the *ngmana* tree), then to an autopsy, and perhaps to cutting the lips from the corpse. *Soré* is for cooling or pacifying a death by lightning as well as in these concomitant circumstances, for such a death grows into a composite of sinister events revolving around *dua*.

The manifest aims of *soré* throughout these events, its explicit meaning within the entire scenario, is to bring calm into chaos. Whereas *dua* brings only hatred, jealousy, bitterness, revenge, and disorder into the community, *soré* restores the equilibrium between opposing forces lest they bring death and the disintegration of society. These latter meanings are for the most part latent, yet readily expressed by the Gbaya participants in the complex events that typically surround death by *dua*.

Other latent meanings of *soré* in this context may be associated with the speaking of truth in a situation heavily laden with false, vengeful accusations. Hidden behind the more obvious meanings of *soré* in the context of events inspired by *dua* is *soré*'s presence as an agent of truth and life. *Soré* stands unequivocally opposed to *dua* in all its evil manifestations; in particular, it witnesses to the truth that there can be no peace in human relationships without justice and truth among human beings. It exorcises lies and vengeance to free people from dueling for power and domination. Because *soré* is for openness and light in human society, it resists the secretive ways of *dua*, which leads to darkness.

Soré's use in the context of *dua* bears the message and meaning of innocence. A diviner throws *soré* at a person during a *dua* trial to proclaim that person's innocence. Individuals who hold *soré* branches during the autopsy of someone who died after drinking *ngmana* are also maintaining their innocence and lack of involvement in the *dua*-related events.

At the same time, *soré* is used to deflect the anger and vengeance of the victim's family and to cool their anger lest further violence occur. Placing the lips of a poisoning suspect at the foot of the *soré* tree means that *soré* is the final court of justice, not *ngmana*. If the tree shrivels and dies, the victim was indeed guilty of the other person's death. The *soré* tree laments and bears those deaths and gives its own life as a witness that death begets death. Indeed, as anything placed at the foot of the *soré* tree marks *soré* as the center, this gesture at the end of many rites suggests the finality and ultimacy of *soré*.

Another important meaning of *soré* is derived from the action taken by a family that has wrongly accused someone in another family of *dua*, thereby causing that person's death. For example, the accused may have plunged his knife into his stomach and pulled out his entrails to prove his innocence, to show that *dua* was not in his stomach. The accusers may then choose a young girl from their family, dress her in *soré* leaves and lead her to the grieving, angry family to be a *soré*-cool-thing in their midst. Such a young girl is ransom and compensation (payment) for the wrongful death of the accused.

The *soré* girl ransoms the family; she redeems the false witnesses from the threat of vengeance and opens their way to more constructive relationships with others. She personifies, constitutes, and symbolizes a new covenant between the two families that both must respect and never jump over.

SORÉ IS FOR BREAKING THE STRENGTH OF A DANGEROUS PERSON

Soré is for cooling the verbal and physical abuse of a bully or a tyrant. It disables but does not destroy abusive, hurtful people. *Soré* may take away the strength of people who misuse their strength; and it may subdue and tame those who violate the gift of life; but it is never *soré*'s intention to kill the violator. It may be that the violator will indeed die if he jumps over *soré*, but whoever jumps over *soré* actually takes his own life. *Soré* seeks, rather, to channel one's strength for service to the community.

Soré is tied to an unruly cow's tail, or rubbed on a bully to break his strength. Tying *soré* to the cow binds and subdues the malignant forces that animate the cow, the ultimate purpose of which is to transform harmful strength into useful strength. Such actions indicate that *soré* changes situations and persons by transmitting and communicating its own natural qualities to that which needs change. The action of binding or rubbing symbolically and actually transfers *soré*'s qualities into another physical object.

SORÉ IS FOR PROTECTING FOOD

When a woman who is putting her manioc out to dry is threatened by approaching rain, she may go to a small, nearby *soré* tree, split it down to the ground, and say, "May the rain go away and leave my manioc alone!" She expresses in her invocation what *soré* is for, its manifest meaning in this circumstance. But *soré* will also bear the rain and violence that would otherwise have taken her manioc. That is, in a latent sense, *soré* protects the woman's labors. In an extended, metaphorical sense, rain means lightning, which in turn means *dua*. Thus *soré* is for bearing, and putting an end to, the evil forces that threaten to take life and destroy society.

Soré bears violence in the stead of others. As regards a possible positional meaning suggested by this circumstance, the utter availability of *soré* in the living space of the Gbaya people must be considered. *Soré* grows where the Gbaya live. It is not just a tree of life in some abstract sense; it is a tree *for* their lives, always available in their midst to serve their everyday needs.

SORÉ IS FOR *MBANGA-TE-WI*, ANNOUNCING A DEATH

Soré is for cooling the anger and grief caused by death. *Soré* symbolizes an explicit cooling or pacifying of death. It offers comfort and consolation, not merely by cooling the potentially violent emotions involved, but by its sensitivity for the poignancy, the pathos, of death. *Soré* is for comforting emotionally afflicted people in an active, expectant way. Hidden meanings of *soré* in the circumstance of death suggest that *soré* is indeed a tree of life, a symbol for the human need to continue the ongoing struggle for life precisely in the face of death.

When a young woman dies, her husband places a *soré* branch on a new mat, curls it, and sends it to his in-laws; and *Narninga* places *soré* leaves over the threshold of a mother whose son died during *labi* initiation rites. The contexts are different, as are aspects of *soré*'s operation and position in them, but in each case, the *soré*-cool-thing manifests a single, fundamental meaning: it expresses the hope that human life may not be overcome by the death that surrounds it.

Soré is placed on the new mat, which is the Gbaya symbol of death. The rolled-up mat contains and surrounds *soré*, and *soré* fills up the gap in the middle. The death of the young woman leaves a gap in her husband's and her parents' lives. *Soré* means to fill up that gap, to bring them peace.

In the same way, when *Narninga* places *soré* leaves over the threshold of a mother whose son died during *labi*, he is placing *soré* in a gap that needs to be filled. The threshold itself is a betwixt-and-between place of enormous symbolic importance. It is a hopeful place and a temporary place; it precedes and promises fulfillment, but it is not free of danger and even death. Nevertheless, every threshold is a place in which, even in the midst of ambiguity, people still cling to signs of hope and salvation.

Soré is a tree of life in such a place. *Soré* placed over a threshold reminds people to look back, but with an eye to acting peacefully, constructively, and hopefully in the present, for a liberated future. The *soré* threshold is therefore a paradigmatic place of the ritual transformation of human lives.

The threshold meaning of *soré* is also linked to its meaning as a mediator. Thus *soré* is planted in the right hand of a dead chief. When the chief's grave is covered over, *soré* extends above the ground, and it soon takes root and grows there. It fills the gap between the living and the living-dead, and it mediates between them. *Soré* provides a means of communication between these two realms that affect the village.

SORÉ IS FOR *HAA-NU* (MAKING) PROMISES

Soré is for saving people in life-threatening circumstances, and it is also for keeping a person honest; it insists upon truthfulness. For example, if a man's wife has a difficult labor, he may stand before a *soré* tree and vow to return to it when his wife and child are out of danger. If the child is born well, he must return and untie his promise to *soré*. If he jumps over *soré* and neglects to return, he will suffer grave consequences.

Salvation and truthfulness are manifest meanings of *soré* in this case. Latent meanings relate to the kind of salvation being offered; it is conditional rather than unconditional or automatic salvation. *Soré* will not grant life when its own principle of truthfulness joined to the right intentions is violated. The hidden meanings of *soré* focus on the matter of human integrity; *soré* is for keeping words and deeds together as one.

Soré is used in the spoken word, and this word must not be spoken in vain. A promise spoken before a *soré* tree must be kept, lest the principles of life and truth for which *soré* stands be violated. *Soré* may also be "thrown" in the spoken word. When a person says to someone who has intervened in a matter that does not concern him, "I throw *soré* to you!" his words are as effective as the deed itself. *Soré* lives in the spoken word.

It should be noted that in many of the rites described in this study, a spoken word accompanies each ritual action or object to give each full meaning and power. Gestures and objects may be visible words, or they may be replaced or superseded by the spoken word. *Soré* works as a symbolic object, a gesture, or a word to bring integrity to Gbaya life at its most critical points.

SORÉ IS FOR CONDUCTING ONE TO A DEAD ELEPHANT

A person who has never before seen a dead elephant must be taken through this experience by *soré* and a *soré* person. The neophyte and his or her conductor hold a *soré* branch between them as they approach and circle the elephant. While a blessing for good health is spoken, *soré* leaves are rubbed on the initiate, then thrown on the body of the elephant.

Soré is thus for accompanying people into new, heretofore unexperienced circumstances (manifest meaning), especially into situations of an extraordinary character (latent meaning). That is, *soré* opens us to new and unprecedented possibilities for human existence, possibilities that we do not imagine apart from *soré* (hidden meaning).

Interstitial, mediating, and liminal meanings are all evoked by this passage-oriented use of *soré*. At least four interconnected aspects of its use may be noted in this context: (1) the newness of the circumstance itself is linked to the fact of *soré*; (2) the *soré* is grasped between the unexperienced and the experienced person; (3) the person of experience leads, conducts, or guides the neophyte; (4) *soré* protects them as they enter a new place. Taking all these aspects together, *soré* may be said to provide the kind of support human beings depend on whenever they embark on a new experience in life.

Soré is a kind of pioneer. It holds the new experience together as a piece within a larger whole, marks it off as somehow special, and integrates it within the whole of human experience. *Soré* is the known factor, the friend who helps us make sense of all the unknown, strange, new encounters and experiences. It is the object that people grasp and hold onto as they venture into mysterious new realms of physical, mental, and spiritual space.

Soré accompanies the Gbaya on their encounter with the mystery of a dead elephant, and it is there when they encounter the *labi* mystery of death under water. Indeed *soré* guides the Gbaya through all the mysteries of *simbo* washing, *dua*, hunting, fighting, making a new village. In each ritual in which *soré* appears, it is the way to newness and life. The Gbaya who are guided by it perceive it as a tree of life.

Soré mediates reconciliation and wholeness. It cleanses, saves, heals and frees people from *simbo* dirt, insisting upon obedience and the right intentions of one's heart. *Soré* does not resolve the ambiguities of life, but helps people to cope with ambiguity; it achieves by humility what cannot be achieved by violence: the renewal of human lives. *Soré* is for new birth.

In the course of daily life, *soré* establishes covenants of peace between people; it actively works at making, creating, and keeping peace. *Soré* is a way through the necessity of having to take life in order to live; *soré*-oriented justice incorporates the possibility of forgiveness and brings calm into the chaos created by *dua*. It speaks the truth openly in the light of day and resists all darkness.

Soré exorcises; that is, it takes away the strength of those who misuse their strength, but it disables rather than destroys. *Soré* bears abuse and violence in the stead of others; it renders destructive forces harmless in order to promote life and turns self-interest into community service. *Soré* comforts the grieving and gives hope in the face of death. *Soré* always intends life, yet it saves conditionally, insisting upon integrity. It leads people through new experiences and opens the way to new and unprecedented possibilities for human existence.

Operational and positional meanings of *soré* tend to be interdependent. For example, *soré* is a center to which people come, to which objects are brought. It is a center for new beginnings. *Soré* brings people together, binding and freeing them. *Soré* often achieves peace first by separation; but *soré* as a barrier to violence is a doorway to peace and reconciliation.

Soré makes itself visible, and the sight of *soré* induces an appropriate response. Its presence marks one's separation from the normal flow of life, but it also leads people through the gaps back into ordinary existence again. It is a medicine to protect people from danger, and a womb in which new life is generated; *soré* water not only cleanses a person, enabling new life to form, it also clothes or equips that person for living in a new way, as a new person.

Soré is a source and a way of wisdom. Its wisdom leads through hardship, suffering, and death to a new life rooted in integrity. *Soré* represents finality and ultimacy in the total human arena where truth and justice are at issue; yet it also pays for injustice and redeems unjust persons. *Soré*'s own qualities are symbolically and actually transmitted by physical contact in order to engender personal transformation.

Soré is utterly available as a tree of life; in the midst of everyday lives, it bears the people's burdens in their stead. *Soré* fills the gaps created by death; it is a sign of hope in betwixt-and-between places, and *soré* lives in the spoken word just as it lives in gestures and as an object to ensure Gbaya integrity and life. *Soré* holds new experiences of life together within the wider human experience; it is like a friend who makes sense out of all that is strange. *Soré* is the symbol that enlarges one's horizon and graces one's encounter with mystery. It lives for the Gbaya as a tree of life in their midst.

12

The Gbaya Naming of Jesus

"A new grass mat can [only] be woven over an old grass mat." The New Testament message of salvation and life through Jesus is a new thing among the Gbaya, but unless this new thing is perceived as fulfilling old needs, it is not likely to gain much recognition or serve the Gbaya effectively for life. Thus, when Gbaya Christians name Jesus their "*soré*-cool-thing," they are weaving a new grass mat over an old one. They are saying that Jesus fulfills needs previously met by *soré*.

The path we followed through Gbaya ritual practice has led us to the interior of Gbaya culture, which is one of many worlds in a vast universe of human cultures. In every culture, the deep things of life are mediated to us in symbols or, as I said earlier, life's energy and meaning come to us in word, water, meals, people, and trees that are the Spirit's mediators in every culture. The Gbaya words and trees that appear strange to us are not really strange—only simply and refreshingly new. Our own culture's words and trees make them less strange and help us to recognize them as meaningful and life-giving. Seen in the gospel's light, the *soré* tree draws us to attend with the Gbaya to God's deed for all people in and through the name of Jesus.

Gbaya Christianity is a constructive Christian theology in the making; that is, it is a local theology that seeks to articulate the absolute relatedness of all things to God. To name Jesus "our *soré*-cool-thing" is the act of one particular theology within the complex and pluralistic universe of faiths that Christian theology seeks to understand in relation to God.

Everywhere it occurs, Christians are compelled to investigate and evaluate the nature of salvation—whether or not the people who experience it ever name the name of Jesus. And if Gbaya rituals are indeed experiences of salvation, the question is urgent: In what sense is the Gbaya experience of salvation related to God and to God's salvation of the world in and through Jesus of Nazareth?

Important criteria for such a constructive theology can be discovered in the search for analogies between cultural and biblical materials. Investigation of the Gbaya tree metaphor reveals, for example, how similar it is to the Christian tree-of-life tradition, and, in turn, how close the correspondence is between Gbaya and Christian interpretations of salvation.

Symbols and events in Gbaya tradition provide us with new theological sources. Gbaya rituals are not merely interesting or captivating bits of folklore; they bear the message and the reality of salvation in Christ Jesus. Such symbols are evidence of revelation's presence in every culture and are channels for the special revelation of salvation contained in the New Testament; the revelation of God in Jesus always seeks and evokes new expressions in unheard-of places. The symbolic expressions of faith in cultures other than our own invite us with utmost seriousness to a fresh encounter with Jesus, the Lord of creation.

The Bible itself is a culturally conditioned document; its symbols and stories speak of God and God's saving act in Jesus of Nazareth. In the power of the Holy Spirit, it speaks of the transcendent one in the words and images of particular cultures. Not that we can simply and undialectically equate symbols with Jesus — two pieces of wood in the form of a cross are not less culturally specific than a living tree called *soré*. The tree and the cross are culturally conditioned symbols, and they are significant for all people and creation: both can be made to speak the name of Jesus, and both can convey his saving, hidden presence. Both are a new word of God for us.

Thus *soré* is not just a random metaphor for the Gbaya naming of Jesus. Rather, the tree symbol is a ritual element familiar to diverse cultures from earliest historic time to the present.[1] In Jewish and Christian tradition, the image is as old as the opening pages of the Hebrew Bible, and it continued to be developed in the New Testament and in the Christian theological literature of later centuries. Indeed, some of the imaginative and metaphorical theology of the early Christians, including this tradition, continues in the vital theology now being practiced in Gbaya and other African churches. Its resurgence can also bring new life to Western churches whose symbolic experience is sadly impoverished; too often we live in a world of canned words, on-the-run meals and plastic trees.

THE BIBLICAL TREE OF LIFE

The tree-of-life image makes its first biblical appearance in the midst of a garden watered by four rivers (Genesis 2:9–14) and reappears in both the prophetic literature and the Wisdom tradition. In Ezekiel 47:12 it is a tree growing in the midst of waters that flow from the temple, and in Proverbs

3:18: "[Wisdom] is a tree of life to those who lay hold of her; those who hold her fast are called happy."

In these passages the metaphor has at least two meanings; it represents messianic salvation and divine wisdom or righteousness: "The fruit of the righteous is a tree of life" (Proverbs 11:30a); "A desire fulfilled is a tree of life" (Proverbs 13:12b); "A gentle tongue is a tree of life (Proverbs 15:4a).

The tradition of comparing a person's strengths and weaknesses to the enduring or withering nature of trees is included in the biblical sources. Psalm 1:3 tells us that a righteous person is "like a tree planted by streams of water, that yields its fruit in its season"; and, in Ezekiel 31, Pharaoh is described as having attributes like a "cedar in Lebanon, with fair branches and forest shade, and of great height, its top among the clouds" (Ezekiel 31:3). Birds nest in its boughs, beasts bring forth their young in its shade, and its roots go down to abundant waters.

A similar personification occurs in Daniel 4:10–27, but this time the tree represents Nebuchadnezzar. These trees, like the men they represent, are proud and strong in the midst of the earth—and they are eventually cast out. They differ from the righteous ones, or the ultimate tree of life, which, though humble, endures forever. This aspect of the image was later appropriated by Christian authors to represent the eternal king, who was cut down but rose up again.

Isaiah's use of tree symbolism also conveys the theme of messianic salvation. Two references are especially significant: "There shall come forth a shoot from the stump of Jesse, and a branch shall grow out of his roots" (11:1); and, "the surviving remnant of the house of Judah shall again take root downward, and bear fruit upward" (37:31).

In New Testament passages, Peter writes that Christ "himself bore our sins in his body on the tree" (1 Peter 2:24); and Luke, that "they took him down from the tree" (Acts 13:29). These references indicate that even the earliest Christians interpreted the cross of Christ in relation to the tree of life. The full development of this theme, however, does not appear earlier than the book of Revelation, whose author used it to symbolize the fulfillment of redemption: "To him who conquers I will grant to eat of the tree of life, which is in the paradise of God" (2:7).

In Revelation 22:2 the prophet describes the tree of life that grows "with its twelve kinds of fruit" on either side of the river. It "yields its fruit each month; and the leaves of the tree were for the healing of the nations." The fruit and healing leaves are based on Ezekiel 47:12, but the twelve fruits are a new detail in Revelation, a symbol of the eschatological completeness of God's people, a metonymical expansion of the root metaphor, the tree of life.

Revelation 22:14 adds a crucial new element: "Blessed are those who wash their robes, that they may have the right to the tree of life." As numerous passages in Revelation make clear, the tree of life is closely related to water and blood. In the power of the Holy Spirit, it speaks of Jesus and of his cross as the new tree of life, which appears (proleptically) between the tree in Adam's Paradise and the tree in the New Jerusalem.

FROM IGNATIUS TO BONAVENTURE

Other early Christian writers continued to use this metaphor to illuminate central meanings of the cross of Christ. In the first century, for example, Ignatius of Antioch identified Christ with the tree of life and "the saved" with its fruits;[2] and, in the second century, Justin Martyr wrote in the *Dialogue* with Trypho, "There are various figures in the Old Testament of the wood of the cross by which Christ reigned," and "this Man . . . was symbolized . . . by the tree of life. . . ."[3]

Ambrose refers to Christ as a seed, who suddenly "unfolds as a tree," as "wisdom, in whose leafy branches" Christ's followers "now take their rest in safety." In the same sermon, Ambrose speaks of the "sap of the tree" from which Christ's apostles grew as branches.[4]

Gregory of Nyssa, also in the fourth century, interprets Proverbs 3:18 as a prophecy that "Paradise will be restored; that tree will be restored which is in truth the tree of life; there will be restored the grace and the dignity of rule. . . ."[5]

The most crucial resource for subsequent understanding and development of this metaphor during the Middle Ages is probably Augustine's allegorical interpretation of the Garden of Eden. Although Augustine himself took pains to affirm the historical truth of the Genesis narrative, he clearly saw it as a symbol for the life of the blessed and found the figure of the church in each of its parts: "Thus the Garden is the Church . . . the four rivers are the four Gospels; the fruit-bearing trees are the saints, as the fruits of their works; and the tree of life is, of course, the Saint of saints, Christ."[6]

The tree-of-life image reaches its zenith in the mid-thirteenth-century writings of Bonaventure, for whom the tree of life is especially Christ the divine king. Bonaventure's work includes a treatise, or sermon, called *The Tree of Life*,[7] in which he narrates the historical truths presented in the "four rivers," the Gospels, in a manner consistent with Augustine's views and sense of priorities concerning the interpretation of scripture.

In fact, Augustine and other patristic authors greatly influenced Bonaventure's thought. His hermeneutical principle and methods and the fundamental meanings that he assigned to the tree of life were clearly inherited from the early church, yet this inheritance supported his theological reflection in unprecedented ways.

For Bonaventure the tree of life not only speaks to the fundamental order in creation; it also points to new meanings of salvation in Christ. In some traditions the life and the death meanings of the tree symbol are presented as polarities; in Bonaventure, however, they are analogically unified in Christ, the tree of life who lends intelligibility to the entire universe and through whom all things are held together (Colossians 1:17).

In his sermon on the tree, Bonaventure inspires us to union with God by saying that Christ, as the tree of life, is the way to God. Such language suggests a ritual act, however, such as we find in the Johannine Gospel or the Letter to the Hebrews, both of which draw on the Hebrew Bible for their understanding of sacrifice. In turn, these scriptural meditations initiate us into the way that leads through purgation and illumination to union with God.

The traditional steps of mystical ascent correspond to a threefold ritual structure: separation, transition, reincorporation. The transitional, or liminal, stage is partly a stage of reflection. Bonaventure encourages such reflection as contemplation of Christ, the tree of life in whom are revealed all the archetypes of God's creation. Contemplation focuses on the cross, the tree of life, which is our salvation through Christ's exemplary act of love.

Bonaventure's thought reveals a central cluster of symbols: his tree of life is an archetype, a whole system of medieval Christian beliefs and values, a paradigm that reflects the ultimate measure of things. For Bonaventure, the tree-of-life metaphor is a symbolic template that, through metonymical expansion, communicates Christian wisdom, mystical and spiritual knowledge, and the values of faith, devotion, simplicity and love of the cross. It evokes the desire to cultivate the practice of those values, in contrast to the tree of knowledge, which evokes desire for reason, investigation, curiosity, and carnal feeling (or wisdom of the flesh).

Bonaventure's *Tree of Life* is in fact a striking example of the scriptural naming of Jesus in Christian tradition. The tree of life is a biblical symbol; it leads us into a deeper understanding of, and participation in, God's own life. The cross is at the center of this symbol, where images of a tree, water, and blood are merged and become living images of salvation. And the image continues — in scripture, in the classics of Christian literature, and in the developing theology of a young African church. Meanings familiar from traditional ritual reappear in contemporary Gbaya theology, often in spontaneous ways, always in dialectical continuity with the original gospel. The relationship between Jesus and *soré* is not fortuitous; it is metonymical.[8] The *soré* tree is a Gbaya Christian participation in a way of life that begins and ends at the foot of the tree that is the cross of Christ.

SORÉ IN A CHRISTIAN CONTEXT

Soré may be received within the Gbaya Christian community as a familiar, yet new, component of the community's symbolic vocabulary: a new mat is woven over an old mat. I shall attempt to extend reflection on *soré* to its potential role in a constructive theology, in which its task will be to engender fresh meanings and to enrich the universal church.

The metaphor "Jesus is our *soré*-cool-thing" may become meaningful, not only to Gbaya Christians but to all people who have or who may yet come to live in the eschatological time of God's kingdom. Christians live by faith always hoping and praying for God's own creative, redeeming, gracious, and transforming initiatives to reappear even in the midst of dissonance and sin.

In the very particularity of the metaphor "Jesus is our *soré*-cool-thing" lies the potential for its universal significance: the particular meanings associated with Jesus and *soré* are the promise of salvation and new life for all who struggle daily with life and the threat of death.

Jesus of Nazareth proclaimed an eschatological salvation for all human beings. God's kingdom is a kingdom of promise, to which we may belong by faith in the power of Jesus' name to make us worthy recipients of the reign that is yet to be fulfilled. In this betwixt-and-between time of eschatological tension, we are not only limited by the particular cultures in which we live; we are also liberated by the promise that salvation is a living reality in every culture.

To contextualize the promise of salvation in Jesus is to express it in the most meaningful terms available in a particular culture, and this process is always dynamic and open-ended. The Gbaya naming of Jesus contextualizes the promise of salvation in Jesus; it does not domesticate the name of the one who is above every name. As no single metaphor, nor all the metaphors in the world together, can express everything about God, a particular metaphor that draws our attention, even momentarily, to salvation in Jesus merits our attention and should have its moment in our midst. Christian theology must always be alive and attentive to such moments, which are moments "for life."

SORÉ AND JESUS: SOTERIOLOGY AS THE WAY TO CHRISTOLOGY

Theological issues involved in the Gbaya naming of Jesus involve a process of correlation, at the center of which stands the symbol of the cross as the ultimate Christian criterion for interpreting the meaning of God's relationship with us. The universality of the cross holds the semantic correspondences between *soré* and Jesus in dialectical tension. They do not exist in simple or unambiguous continuity, but in a dialectical connection that is potentially constructive and enlightening. So also, the character of our investigation, like the nature of the metaphor itself, must be inherently tentative, nondogmatic, and open-ended.

Because metaphors contrast two different categories of reality, they always shock our imagination and induce new possibilities of experience. Jesus himself used parables as metaphorical expressions; he overturned the expectations of his listeners, enabling them to hear and see something new in familiar and meaningful terms: the parables were his way of weaving a new mat over an old one. The Gbaya naming of Jesus entails a double newness: first, the newness of the metaphor itself, its linguistic components; and second, the way in which Jesus lives in the language to make *soré* a symbol of God's word addressed to human lives in a given situation.

The meaning that Jesus intends may vary from one life situation to another (for example, comfort, exhortation or judgment), but it is always new beyond our expectations: "Think not that I have come to abolish the law and the prophets; I have come not to abolish them but to fulfill them," Jesus said, after which he laid down a new law incomparably more exacting than the old one: "You, therefore, must be perfect, as your heavenly Father is perfect" (Matthew 5:17, 48). Something altogether different from what we normally understand by "fulfillment" is intended here, and so it is with the expectations expressed in *soré*, whose newness and fulfillment are accomplished in the cross; there our old expectations and symbols are broken and saved, judged and fulfilled in ways more wonderful than we can imagine or anticipate.

Gbaya meanings of *soré* draw us anew to Jesus, but these meanings, too, are always exceeded and transformed by the cross within the historical and transcendent dialectic of the kingdom that is already-but-not-yet-present. The Christ who lives in the language and meanings yielded by *soré* is the hidden Christ, who always slips away from the confines of language and meaning to affirm his own reality in the shock and scandal of the cross.

From the Gbaya perspective, *soré*'s use in ritual contexts is imbued with a salvific tenor and purpose. They enact rites of passage and purification, for example, for personal and communal survival. Having participated in such rites, a Gbaya describes his or her experience by saying, "Mi Kpasa!" "I'm saved!" A hunter who undergoes *zuia-simbo* says, "I was saved because of that washing!" And a *labi* initiate, "I was saved in the water!"

The verb *kpasi* and its cognates mean "to save," "to pull [someone] from a perilous situation," and "to heal." As a noun, *kpasi* means "life," for example, "he was between life and death." An important cognate is the adjective *kpasa*, which means "true, real or genuine, of good quality," "living," "awake." A *kpasa bii* is a truthful, loyal, and sincere person; *kpasa-wen* means "truth" or "true word."

The Gbaya experience of salvation is a holistic and truly life-giving experience. Ideas of truth and life are intertwined in the experience, and one's worth as a person is vindicated. And the "experience" is not one of "feeling" only, or even primarily; cognitive, evaluative, and expressive or aesthetic dimensions of personal existence are integral aspects of Gbaya salvation.

One principal message conveyed by the ensemble of Gbaya rites described in this study is that the only context, arena or universe of salvation that provides a life-giving experience of wholeness and integrity is relationship-in-community. This community includes the living, the living-dead, and territorial spirits. But it also includes animals, birds, fish, and insects as well as trees and plants, hills, rocks, and streams. It is in the midst of the natural created world of relationships that *soré* saves.

If the Gbaya naming of Jesus as our *soré*-cool-thing is expressed regularly in the preaching, teaching, and worship of the Gbaya Christian community, then their new experience of salvation in Jesus is analogous to their experience of salvation in *soré*. But this is not merely a linguistic analogy or only a name; rather, the metaphor *soré*-cool-thing posits a bond between itself and a dissimilar world: the reality of Jesus. Here *soré* means Jesus and brings these two worlds together, even if imperfectly. This can be accomplished initially only by an intuitive leap of the imagination as a hopeful act of faith. But when it is actually experienced within the Gbaya world of relationships, the metaphor itself may be expanded metonymically by Gbaya Christians as they reflect together on manifest, latent, and heretofore hidden meanings of *soré* and relate them to the biblical witness and description of Jesus. The resulting overlap or contiguity of the one world (*soré*) to the structures of the other (Jesus) extends the metaphor and so becomes a way of doing theology.

The Gbaya naming of Jesus constitutes a movement from the practical world of salvific relationships to the ever growing, expanding, and open-ended articulation of a Christology. That is, the structures of *soré* expand the world of Christological reflection. Always, the definitive measure we have for articulating a Christology is the biblical description of Jesus, whose life, death, and resurrection are symbolized in the cross. The cross as a tree of death extends over all creation and all relationships; it penetrates all human expectations and experiences of salvation. The cross as the tree of life, as Christ Jesus, grafts all things to Christ, who is the fullness of all things. "Grafting" is a New Testament image that suggests the transformation and enrichment of the life that receives it.

Israel did not historicize Canaanite myth; Israel theologized its own history by letting elements of Canaanite myth be the symbolic context for telling the story of God's acts in its own history as a particular people. This is an early example of contextualization; it involves a grafting of natural symbolic material to the historical core of lived experience. The new Israel, the church as the body of Christ, followed the same process: when the church is born in the lives of particular people, it acknowledges this people's mythic and ritual vocabulary as the context for telling the wholly new story of God in their midst.

The church is the sacrament of the world's salvation; its members live within particular human cultures, but their faith and hope in salvation is transcultural and transcendent. The metaphor "Jesus is our *soré*-cool-thing" reflects this understanding of the church in Gbaya culture. Gbaya Christians are members of the new Israel, of the body of Christ eschatologically present in their culture. They affirm this truth and interpret this reality each time they retell the story of their experience of salvation in Jesus in terms provided by their own symbolic and cultural vocabulary.

Some Gbaya Christians believe that it was the appearance of Karnu that gave general Gbaya history its transcendent and religious meaning. For these Christians, the Karnu story is introductory; it helps them to experience Jesus in whom historical and symbolic expressions are complementary.

Still, it is the natural, created properties of the *soré* tree that constitute the primary symbolic pattern for Gbaya imagination and reflection. By analogy, the soft and flexible character of *soré*, combined with the slippery substance found between its bark and core, yield meanings of humility and coolness. Because bad and dirty things slip right off *soré*, it is the way to make things clean and new again. *Soré* is humble, but not fragile; the plant itself is resistant and resilient.

The Gbaya condense these interrelated meanings of *soré* into the fundamental meaning of peace. There is only one *soré* whose ritual meanings, however diverse and contextual, are always related to its physical properties. And this connection, or link, between the root metaphor and new events brings peace to the Gbaya and saves them from death. Salvation is the one song and purpose that *soré*'s meanings yield.

"Jesus is our *soré*-cool-thing" names the one who brings peace for life and saves us from death. As St. Paul writes to the Ephesians: "But now in Christ Jesus you who once were far off have been brought near in the blood of Christ. For he is our peace, who made us both one ... by abolishing in his flesh the law of commandments and ordinances, ... for through him we both have access in one Spirit to the Father" (Ephesians 2:13–18).

Soré-cool-thing and all its expectations are broken on the cross of Jesus, but they live again in the new *soré*-cool-thing that is the word of God, Jesus, the one who comes to judge and to save: "For in him all the fullness of God was pleased to dwell, and through him to reconcile to himself all things, whether on earth or in heaven, making peace by the blood of his cross" (Colossians 1:19–20).

The peace of the *soré*-cool-thing, now interpreted as Jesus our *soré*-cool-thing, is the peace made by the blood of his cross. With this in mind, we must look again at each of the twelve ritual contexts described in the preceding chapter — as each one represents an episode in the drama of ordinary Gbaya life. *Soré*'s presence in many of these contexts corresponds in a striking way to the presence of Jesus in the New Testament. Yet there is a newness in Jesus that eludes any simple correspondence.

The ritual contexts remain as they were, but now the various meanings of *soré* apply to Jesus and his cross. In each context the subsidiary subject, *soré* of the metaphor "Jesus is our *soré*-cool-thing," is made to speak a new thing by the principal subject, Jesus. The original meanings are (1) retained, but (2) critiqued, (3) expanded metonymically or by analogy, and (4) transformed, in a process disclosing a genuine, yet dialectical, continuity between old and new meanings. The old meanings are given the jolt of a new center as Jesus becomes the content of *soré* for Gbaya Christians.

This is the grafting of *soré* branches to Christ, the tree of life; henceforth they will grow in the New Testament's expression of the gospel, enriching it as much as being transformed by it. The core of Christian faith is historical: that is, salvation in Jesus is an actual event within history, but it is also an event that happens throughout all subsequent history. The image of grafting is appropriate to a dynamic and pluralistic view of Christian history and particular cultures.

THE RITUALS OF JESUS OUR *SORÉ*-COOL-THING

In chapter 11 we discovered *soré*'s meaning in twelve ritual contexts; those same ritual contexts now yield the meaning of Jesus our *soré*-cool-thing.

As *soré* is for making a new village, Jesus our *soré*-cool-thing makes peace by the blood of his cross. His new village does not depend on the fragile ties of blood relation. Rather, he unites a people from hitherto scattered tribes and clans and calls them into a community of more enduring significance. The peace of Jesus our *soré*-cool-thing is a word that cuts across all human structures to open an unprecedented world of human relationships. It creates a village of far greater breadth and communion than we could ever imagine. Jesus, we remember, ate with the outcasts and those who were ritually impure.

At the center of all community and all relationships is Jesus our *soré*-cool-thing, in whom all things hold together. He comes from his father's village to judge and save his mother's, the whole inhabited earth. Jesus our *soré*-cool-thing grafts all peoples into one tree of life with many branches and countless leaves, to nourish and heal all people. Jesus as *soré*-cool-thing is the tree of life whose branches embrace the whole earth, in whose shade there is comfort and rest for all peoples and whose fruit gives life to the world.

As *soré* is for cooling a fight, so Jesus our *soré*-cool-thing pours forth his own blood to flow as a life-giving stream in the midst of all conflicts. He is present in those conflicts to receive the verbal and physical blows we rain on each other. Our sin does not, however, slip off Jesus but goes straight to his heart, and by his wounds we are healed, renewed, and transformed for life with each other in his new village. When we spurn our *soré*-cool-thing by jumping over the blood of his covenant and the spirit of grace, *simbo* takes us ("It is a fearful thing to fall into the hands of the living God" [Hebrews 10:31]). Jesus our *soré*-cool-thing is the mediator of a new covenant, and his blood purifies our conscience to serve the living God (Hebrews 9:14–15).

As *soré* is for reconciliation between two villages, so Jesus our *soré*-cool-thing looks out from his cross to all of us who put him there, saying, "Father, forgive them." He fills the gap between our villages in the east and our villages in the west, saying to us, "Woman, behold your son! Son, behold your mother!"

Jesus our *soré*-cool-thing lives on in the gaps between us to make intercession for us and to save those who can draw near to God only through him (Hebrews 7:25). He is in the middle, living and interceding for the life of both villages. There are two villages but only one *soré*-cool-thing, in whom our two villages meet as one. Fulfillment and life can be found, but only in the single village that Jesus called the kingdom of God.

As *soré* is for washing *simbo*, Jesus our *soré*-cool-thing is able to help us, his sisters and brothers, even when we kill one another with hard words and cruel deeds. Lest we fall into the hands of the living God, Jesus our *soré*-cool-thing invites us to enter life on his threshold. There, on his threshold, bodies are healed, minds restored, and human hearts can depend on the power of forgiveness. We are *simbo* persons called to repent; and Jesus is our high priest, the great *soré* person who leads us to his *soré* water. Confident in his promises, we are washed—drowned—in *soré* water, and our way home with him is clear and clean: "our hearts [are] sprinkled clean from an evil conscience and our bodies [are] washed with pure water" (Hebrews 10:22).

This threshold of Jesus our *soré*-cool-thing is a sacred place from which we remember and celebrate his salvation. It is a place of ritual, for the transformation of human lives, and a place for the sealing of covenant agreements; and from this threshold there flows a river of *soré* water deep enough to swim in.

As *soré* is for undergoing an initiation, Jesus our *soré*-cool-thing comes to be the way, the truth and the life for us here, yet ultimately to bring us into the kingdom of his Father. He makes our lives a passage, an initiation with him.

Jesus our *soré*-cool-thing is in the world but not of it, for he is the word who was in the beginning and with God before the world was created. He is the wisdom who reveals God's glory to us and lights our path. Jesus our *soré*-cool-thing teaches us the things that are above, instructing us in the truth and helping us to do what pleases God. He invites us to eat and drink of his life and wisdom in order that we may live as he lives eternally.

In his wisdom, Jesus our *soré*-cool-thing calls us together as brothers and sisters in discipleship. Together we learn the *soré* way and how to love one another. He purifies and sanctifies us in his word and truth, calling us friends. He issues constant warnings to those who would jump over him, lest they die. He did not come to condemn us but to save us, yet death is inevitable for those who reject his way and life.

The wisdom of Jesus our *soré*-cool-thing provokes division: some seek and find, others go their way to death. Jesus our *soré*-cool-thing reveals his strength in meekness; he is "peaceable, gentle, open to reason, full of mercy and good fruits, without uncertainty or insincerity" (James 3:17), and his wisdom is from above. He leads us through mystery and hardship and he will join in celebration with us, his friends, at the end of our passage. Jesus leads from death to new life. He takes us under the water to die, but his blood is in the water, and his life for us is in the blood. We shall rise with him.

As *soré* is for blessing the hunt, so Jesus our *soré*-cool-thing teaches us to pray for our daily bread, telling us that "the laborer deserves his food" (Matthew 10:10). But at the center of Jesus' life is the cross: "I give my life for my friends." One day his friends said to him, "Teacher, eat." But Jesus our *soré*-cool-thing answered, "I have food to eat of which you do not know; . . . [it is] to do the will of him who sent me, and to accomplish his work" (John 4:31–34). His food consists in feeding us, and he feeds us with food to share with others in our village.

When our *soré*-cool-thing blesses us and gives us what we need to eat, he also empowers us to share our food with people we never dreamed of joining at table. He blesses our quest for food and our giving of that food to others with unexpected joy: "It is more blessed to give than to receive" (Acts 20:35). Jesus our *soré*-cool-thing gives us his cross to be our joy—and so we pray, "Give us today our daily bread," seeking his strength to bear one another's burdens as he bears ours.

As *soré* is for cooling *dua*, witchcraft, Jesus our *soré*-cool-thing appeared among the mystifiers and the mystified in the region of Galilee and read God's word of life to them: "The Spirit of the Lord is upon me, because he has anointed me to preach good news to the poor. He has sent me to proclaim release to the captives and recovery of sight to the blind, to set at liberty those who are oppressed, to proclaim the acceptable year of the Lord" (Luke 4:18–19).

Every society is bedeviled by mystifications of one kind or another, not least the Gbaya by *dua*. Jesus our *soré*-cool-thing is himself the word of God, the word of perfect integrity, light, and life before whom "there is nothing hid, except to be made manifest; nor is anything secret, except to come to light" (Mark 4:22). He is good news for all who are oppressed, blinded, made prisoner by ideological or spiritual mystifications: he is our shalom, our peace, and our salvation.

Soré is for breaking the strength of a dangerous person. Our *soré*-cool-thing is a treasure hunter, and his treasure is people. By the power of his compassionate word, Jesus expelled demons from a man in the country of the Gerasenes, a man who had been under guard, naked, and bound with chains. When people came to see what had happened, they "found the man from whom the demons had gone, sitting at the feet of Jesus, clothed and in his right mind." This man begged Jesus "that he might be with him," but Jesus sent him on his way: "And he went away, proclaiming throughout the whole city how much Jesus had done for him" (Luke 8:35, 38–39). Our *soré*-cool-thing puts the treasure of his word into our hearts, a treasure too precious to hide, so that we may declare his wonderful deeds (1 Peter 2:9), secure in his peace that "passes all understanding" (Philippians 4:7).

Soré is for protecting food from rain, so Jesus our *soré*-cool-thing suffered for us, and "when he suffered, he did not threaten" but "himself bore our sins in his body on the tree" (1 Peter 2:23–24). Now we, like *soré*, must deflect the dangers that threaten our sisters and brothers: we "have been crucified with Christ; it is no longer [we] who live, but Christ who lives in [us]" (Galatians 2:20).

Soré is for announcing a death. Jesus our *soré*-cool-thing wept over the death of his friend Lazarus and for the violence that was to befall Jerusalem, saying, ". . . how often would I have gathered your children together as a hen gathers her brood under her wings, and you would not!" (Matthew 23:37). He calls down judgment on proud, unrepentant cities, but to his little ones, his disciples, he gives rest and ultimate consolation, saying, "Come to me, all who labor and are heavy laden, and I will give you rest. Take my yoke upon you, and learn from me; for I am gentle and lowly in heart, and you will find rest for your souls. For my yoke is easy and my burden is light" (Matthew 11:28–30).

Jesus our *soré*-cool-thing is himself this rest, and he is one with those whom he invites into the obedience of the kingdom. Receiving his yoke into our lives is receiving his cross, which bears our burdens, keeps us in grace, and yokes us to him until we rest on that great day.

Soré is for making promises. Jesus our *soré*-cool-thing is "the pioneer and perfecter of our faith, who for the joy that was set before him endured the cross, despising the shame, and is seated at the right hand of the throne of God" (Hebrews 12:2). To him, therefore, we may come with our deepest needs and supplications, for we share in Jesus our *soré*-cool-thing, "if only we hold our first confidence firm to the end" (Hebrews 3:14).

Jesus our *soré*-cool-thing "has obtained a ministry which is as much more excellent than the old as the covenant he mediates is better, since it is enacted on better promises. The better promise is the blood of Jesus, shed on the cross, by which we have been sanctified once for all" (Hebrews 10:8–10). We may, therefore, "hold fast the confession of our hope without wavering, for he who promised is faithful" (Hebrews 10:23).

Soré is for conducting someone to see a dead elephant. Jesus our *soré*-cool-thing opens before us the possibility of a gracious encounter with mystery; in the blood of his cross he leads us to salvation, by grace through faith. "For by a single offering he has perfected for all time those who are sanctified" (Hebrews 10:14), putting his laws on our hearts, writing them on our minds, and remembering our sins and misdeeds no more (Hebrews 10:16–17).

A GBAYA CHRISTIAN THEOLOGY

These reflections have only briefly illustrated the way that Christological thought can develop in tandem with the Gbaya experience of salvation. Such a development involves and presupposes a descriptive and critical reflection on Gbaya experience and deep reflection on the biblical and extrabiblical sources of Christian experience (in this case, the Gospel of John and the Letter to the Hebrews).

I stress again my belief that Gbaya Christians are the only Christians who can initiate this encounter, because they alone have the experience and sensitivity to know how the biblical word is heard in its connection to *soré*. When Gbaya Christians attend to and articulate the word in their midst, they help other Christians, in turn, to hear and to see new things. We may and we must share our deepest symbols if only to bring theological reflection to life in the global church.

Gbaya pastors, theological students, and lay leaders must be encouraged to work at grafting *soré* onto the historical core of the gospel. *Soré* is a branch, after all, of Christ, the tree of life; when its meanings are correlated with the gospel, they are transformed and the Gbaya hear new things in them. Gbaya Christians need only a free imagination to see how the ritual meanings of *soré* relate to the New Testament meanings of Jesus. Such imagining is a process of theological "play," in which the Gbaya discover their own meanings.

Their accomplishment is a "theology in a new key." Until now, "official" theological reflection has been nurtured almost exclusively by a single source: non-African Christian texts. The new Gbaya theology may have considerably more parable and metaphor than analysis; and it may be more doxological and homiletic than most Western theologies, if only because it must fit a society in which oral tradition is still very strong.

Gbaya Christians have the potential for retrieving material from their own cultural and religious sources and from traditional Christian sources in order to articulate their own kind of theology. The Gbaya naming of Jesus as *soré*-cool-thing can be a beginning; certainly it provides an appropriate symbolic vocabulary for the contextualization of Christological expression among the Gbaya.

13

Theology as the Way to Missiology

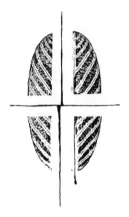

In chapter 12 I tried to follow a logical progression of thought, yet my argument continues to proceed on a circular path. Christian mission initially gave rise to Christian theology, and still does. But as Christian mission requires us to contextualize the good news of salvation in Jesus, it also gives rise to Christian theology by way of soteriology and Christology. The task of Christian theology is to deepen the communication of the gospel message in the most meaningful terms available to the local culture, and to let that communication expand both within and beyond the culture. Theology becomes missiology when it lives within the vision, faith, and dynamism of the kingdom, at the center of which stands the incarnate one whose kingdom it is.

The term "missiology" refers to a constructive, multidimensional theological discipline that serves to communicate the gospel of salvation to all human beings. Missiology is concerned with the meaning, interpretation, and practice of life as it appears in the kingdom of God and in the cross-cultural circumstances of the modern world; that is, it seeks to serve the kingdom by exploring and interpreting the appearance of God's reign in particular human contexts and histories. Missiology therefore requires the help of cultural, social and symbolic anthropology and the history of religions. I cite these disciplines as examples because they have played special roles in this book; they are ancillary disciplines uniquely suited for service in a cross-cultural concern. This book, too, is a missiological endeavor and a call to Christian mission. It is my reflection on the task and practice of such mission, and it embodies my conviction that Gbaya cultural and religious materials are a truly significant resource for Christian theology.

167

SORÉ AND THE IDENTITY OF JESUS

Gbaya Christians who say that Jesus is our *soré*-cool-thing are giving their own answer to the question, "Who is Jesus?" And their particular answer has universal implications. It represents for Europeans and Americans a kind of "mission in reverse," so that the word of God does not return to them empty.

The assertion that Gbaya symbolic materials serve as a source for Christian theology is associated with the overriding concern throughout this book for God's relation to all things in Jesus Christ. How, then, does God relate to us in and through the symbol of *soré*? We can, of course, ask the same question about such symbols as lamb, water, wine, bread, and the cross. In what sense do these symbols constitute the reality they symbolize?

In this study I have often referred to the way *soré* "draws our attention to Jesus." But we say more than that when we say, "This bread is the body of Christ" or "These words are the word of God." We comprehend how a symbol "constitutes" the reality it "means" by way of metaphor and analogy, but not by "definition," for the converse does not hold; we cannot say that "the body of Christ is this bread." Yet there is a univocal element, a logos that links together the two parts of the metaphor. Every metaphor, however, will eventually be broken, because we cannot ultimately understand the mystery of the logos that it bears. It is as though our analogies, symbols, and metaphors exist to be sacrificed in praise and doxology.[1]

Not even revelation can give us an immediate encounter with mystery, because all speech about God is indirect and necessarily mediated by symbol. Through God's revelation in Jesus Christ, however, we receive a new principle for analogy and doxology; in Christ we receive creation, not from the beginning but from the end—that is, the whole is already revealed in him. Thus our analogy is derived, not from the effects of God in creation in the sense understood by medieval theology, but from the parts of creation to the totality of all things proleptically fulfilled in Christ.[2] We do not know about the adequacy of our symbols, but we offer our speech, gestures, and ourselves doxologically, waiting for God.

In spite of the provisional and tentative character of the enterprise exemplified in the Gbaya naming of Jesus, we have a simple criterion for determining symbols and metaphors. The words we use must make us comfortable; they must be the familiar, "homey" words of our experience. When we hear them in a meaningful way, as in "Jesus is our *soré*-cool-thing," then we have some reasonable basis for speaking about God in a new language, in metaphors and symbols. And the symbols that we discover invite us to a new encounter and relationship with God in Jesus Christ.

Not all symbols are appropriate to name what God does for us in Jesus, and not all symbols help us to know who Jesus is. On the basis of thick description, however, it is clear that *soré* is appropriate for that naming and encounter. We can perceive, in faith, the connection between Jesus and *soré*; the ultimate tree of life (Jesus) stands in dialectical continuity and contiguity with its parts (of which *soré* is one). Jesus and *soré* in its ritual contexts stand to one another in a relationship of mutual participation. But *soré* by itself, whether as symbol or as tree, does not save us — nor does any symbol have such power. "Water," according to Martin Luther, "by itself is only water, but with the Word of God it is a life-giving water which by grace gives the new birth through the Holy Spirit."[3]

Jesus, revealed to us and for us as God's word, saves us. But when *soré* is grafted to that word and made by the Spirit to speak of Jesus, then this metaphor, this symbol, in its very particularity draws our attention to the truth and universality of Jesus as the Christ of God, in whom the fullness of God was pleased to dwell and in whom all things hold together. And what happens in *soré* is not an isolated circumstance in the history of religions. Other symbols, analogous to *soré*, also wait in other cultures to draw attention to salvation in Jesus. Thus *soré* becomes a paradigm for theological and missiological research in other cultures and for a new way to look at salvation in our own culture.

Theology as the way to missiology must trust the religious and traditional elements in local culture, as St. Paul trusted these elements in the Jewish and Hellenistic cultures in which he preached. Indeed, he counseled their continued use in Christian life: "Whatever is true, whatever is honorable, whatever is just, whatever is pure, whatever is lovely, whatever is gracious, if there is any excellence, if there is anything worthy of praise, think about these things" (Philippians 4:8). Such trusting and thinking does not mean that nature is simply completed by grace. A constructive theology is dialectical and critical; it is prepared to contract as well as to expand when it is enriched by newly discovered cultural sources.

African Christians encourage us to shift our theological paradigms from a cognitive, informational emphasis toward a more holistic one. Christian life is a totality. Gbaya ritual traditions renew our appreciation for life's integrity and humanize our existence by reminding us of the importance of interpersonal relationships and harmony in community life. When we participate in one another's lives through conversation and hospitality, we acknowledge that our common inheritance of all things overcomes our instincts for ownership and privacy.

Gbaya Christians know the difference between existence and presence; therefore, they also contribute to our understanding of personal, holistic development. Gbaya initiation rites, for example, center on the development of the whole person, not by emphasizing the acquisition of information or for the sake of making more money and possessing more things, but with a wider concern for practical wisdom and the "right way" to live in community. This dimension of African spirituality, with its concern for doing and saying things in the right way, the clear, clean way that leads to new birth and new life, has the potential for showing us the fullness and wholeness of a "simple" way of life. *Labi* images of the *soré* way help to deepen and broaden our longing for community, true names, and waters of blessing. These images help us to imagine the love that is beyond all imagination—the richness of God's love for us in the crucified Lord Jesus Christ.

Gbaya rituals are reverently utilitarian and communal because "to be" is to participate harmoniously in community. The behavior of a person who isolates himself or herself is not simply antisocial, but actually destroys community. The Africans' spirit of hospitality and the joy in sharing and celebrating life are significant among cultures that put such a high premium on individual privacy. So is their categorical refusal to separate experience into "sacred" and "profane" realms: these modes of existence cannot be dichotomized. For the Gbaya, reality is transparent, and "the universe is God's sanctuary."[4] Visible and invisible worlds coexist, and if God is understood as transcendent, God is also immanent.

At some levels of African experience, reality appears to have a monotheistic character; at other levels, it appears to be polytheistic. At every level, however, the African experience of God is intrinsically, intimately related to ordinary experience. Many Western theologians have noted the difficulty of presenting the concept of a "personal God" in a pluralistic and scientific age, but African Christian experience supports a commitment to the personal and gracious God who comes to us in Jesus. African concern for their ancestors has not been killed despite the missionaries' wars on "ancestor cults," and their idea of a continuity linking past, present, and future contributes to all peoples' livelier appreciation for the communion of saints. The Gbaya say that their interest in the ancestors is not to worship them but to communicate with the living-dead, the dead who are not dead. Belief in the living-dead is part of the Africans' worldview; it does not conflict with their belief in the resurrection of Jesus or negate their hope for their own bodily resurrection.

A crucial aspect of the Gbaya contribution to theology is the significance of symbolic discourse in their lives and religion. It is here especially that theology becomes the way to missiology. Symbols in Gbaya life are an invitation to participate in realities otherwise inaccessible to human beings. Not that such symbols are new sources of revelation. *Soré* and the gospel of Jesus Christ are from the one source of revelation, God, whose revelation always provokes new expressions in unheard-of places. Creation does not simply reveal God, but God is at work in the gospel and in creation and human culture, constantly giving birth to symbols like "Jesus our *soré*-cool-thing" that we may attend with utmost seriousness to the love and care for us that God works in our midst. In *soré* we find redemption moving dialectically, though not simply, within the orbit of creation to enlarge our Christian vocabulary and our commitment to the unity of all things in Christ. For this reason the theological proposal of this book goes far beyond being just another call for the translation of the Bible into culturally relevant terms. In Jesus our *soré*-cool-thing, God is at work, witnessing to the culmination of all our cultural symbols in the finality of God's self.

SORÉ AND THE WORD OF LIFE

The Gbaya naming of Jesus is a Gbaya Christian way of weaving a new mat over an old one: Jesus fulfills needs previously met by *soré*. Through the ministry of his body, the church, Jesus our *soré*-cool-thing is the eschatological word, water, and bread of life, in whom all things hold together, and the paradigmatic experiences of salvation among the Gbaya occur in the midst of married life, in times of mourning, and in the reconciliation that follows conflict.

The Gbaya plant this *soré* tree in the midst of their marriage relationships as an embodiment of everything that is truly valued. Formed in the *soré* way by the tales and dances of their youth and by their participation in initiation rites, they enter marriage knowing that society itself, which is centered in the institution of marriage, is a *simbo* thing. In fact, the dances and tales that narrate the story of Wanto are the very model of a Gbaya marriage.

At the heart of Wanto's struggle with death stands his wife, Laaiso. She purifies his errors and cools his *simbo*. Wanto is a *simbo* person, always violating the inviolable in spite of himself, but he is wedded to a *soré* person, so life goes on. On the other hand, the woman, Laaiso, is profoundly a *simbo* person; hot words stream from her mouth from time to time, and likewise from her comes a regular flow of blood — passion and violations of life — in spite of herself. At such times, her husband must be a *soré* person at her side, leading her through physical and spiritual danger.

In the tale, Wanto and Laaiso remind us of *soré*'s deep relationship with *simbo* and the sanctity of life. *Soré* gives human beings a way to cope with their limitations and fear of death, but though it serves *simbo* for life, it is also a Gbaya image for all that we strive for but cannot attain. The truth is that *soré* is not complete until it tells us both sides of the human condition and initiates us into a new way of life. Christ Jesus our *soré*-cool-thing comes to heal the brokenness of *soré* and to give us a new *soré* way.

As Jesus receives (because he has himself evoked) an old, yet new name among the Gbaya, he means a new thing for them and for all peoples. As a married person living in Christian faith, I may understand myself as a *soré* person wedded to a *simbo* person and, simultaneously, as a *simbo* person wedded to a *soré* person. My marriage embraces a deep ambiguity: the fear of death and the celebration of life. It is not an imaginary struggle with death; it is that struggle lived out with another person. Nor is my celebration of life in marriage imaginary either, for as I experience the threat of death, *simbo* person that I am, to me is given this *soré* person at my side, who accompanies me safely through all the dangers of my life.

When it is given to me to be with and for my spouse as God is with and for both of us in Christ Jesus our *soré*-cool-thing, it is by God's grace no longer we who live but Christ Jesus who lives in us. Because marriage brings to us the most intimate participation in the life of another person, its fullness is attained only insofar as we give ourselves to each other with the very love of Jesus our *soré*-cool-thing. And there is no genuine love of one's husband or wife without the cross of Christ, for the cross alone makes known the unsearchable depths of love; we live together at the foot of the cross.

The love of God in Christ Jesus, the word of life, has the amazing capacity to grow in the worst soils. The living Christ is incomparably resilient, though he receives the regular abuse of our bush fires; his new life springs up in us over and over again from charred stumps, like a holy seed. Jesus our *soré*-cool-thing heals our wounds and bears the brunt of our angry words in the midst of Christian marriage; he lives with us as husband for wife and wife for husband. At the deep level of sexual intimacy, we may, as *simbo* persons, violate one another, but we also have the power to transform dangerous, life-threatening encounters into life-giving, peaceable, and cooling moments of participation in each other's lives. Jesus our *soré*-cool-thing brings to marriage that which is meant for it, that which no amount of self-generated optimism from contemporary American consumer-oriented folk religion can provide: the gracious hope of living daily the fullness of human life in Jesus, the word of life.

Thus marriage is the paradigm of who Jesus is in the midst of any and all human relationships. In fact, the ensemble of Gbaya rites conveys the principal message: relationships in community are the truth of life, the context and universe of Gbaya salvation, and the source of their wholeness and integrity. Relationships in community may be marital, but office staffs, baseball teams, church councils, and other people or groups also forge deep ties for mutual help against dissonance and the threat of death. *Soré*, reinterpreted by Gbaya Christians and transformed by the Spirit into an image of Jesus, can make such relationships meaningful witnesses to the Lordship of Jesus Christ in this age.

SORÉ AND THE WATER OF LIFE

My second example of Gbaya Christian theology involves the ambiguity of *soré* in the context of death. The traditional purification rite called *zuia-gera*, the rite for washing mourning or grief, continues to exert a powerful influence on the Gbaya, regardless of their professed Christian or Muslim identity. Aware of its power, church leaders are seeking to weave a new mat over this old mat.

The continuing relevance of this rite raises the issue of parallel religious systems. When the gospel of Jesus Christ is perceived as unable to meet all the people's needs, the result is a resurgence of traditional Gbaya ritual. The continued practice of traditional rites by Gbaya Christians compromises the power of the gospel, but the rites will not disappear simply by forbidding Christians to believe in their efficacy and power. They will not be abandoned unless the Gbaya are offered Christian rites that truly meet their needs.

Traditional Gbaya mourning rites lead surviving spouses through the threat of death and back to life again. At heart, they are about washing *simbo*, making the way of life clear and clean. Gbaya Christians have struggled to make a clean break with such practices; they sense that these rites are no longer appropriate for them, but nothing else gives them as much comfort. They look for Christian ways to find peace and give God glory.

The liturgy of blessing and comfort that follows is for those who grieve and fear death. It attempts to lead people to a clear confession of faith in Jesus our *soré*-cool-thing. It is also a rite of baptismal renewal; it recalls the joy (in the midst of this new grief) and the finality (in the midst of this death) of our baptism in *soré* water, the cool water of abundant life.

A Rite for Those Who Mourn the Death of a Spouse

Several days after the death of Garba, mourners gather in front of his home to comfort his widow, Zoumai. After an appropriate hymn, the pastor addresses the mourners:

Brothers and sisters in Christ Jesus our *soré*-cool-thing: We know the ways our beloved ancestors taught us to mourn death. We know they were concerned about uncleanness and dirt, about the dangers associated with the spirit of the departed and about the causes of their death.

The people of Israel also had those concerns, and we still have them today. But God the heavenly father sent the gospel, the good new word, to the people of Israel, and now he has sent that same word of life to us. That word of life leads us to the water of life: "Let us draw near with a true heart in full assurance of faith, with our hearts sprinkled clean from an evil conscience and our bodies washed with pure water" [Hebrews 10:22].

A deaconess brings a pot of water and puts it on the ground in front of the widow. The leader continues:

Brothers and sisters, look at this water. Water is a great gift of God. We drink it, we wash with it. But when we drink it now, we are soon thirsty again. When we wash away today's dirt, tomorrow we shall have to wash again. When our fathers and mothers washed away *simbo* dirt one day, if *simbo* found them the next day, they had to wash again.

But when the goodness and loving kindness of God our *soré*-cool-thing appeared, he saved us, not because of deeds done by us in righteousness, but in virtue of his own mercy, by the washing of regeneration and renewal in the Holy Spirit, which he poured out upon us richly through Jesus Christ our *soré*-cool-thing, so that we might be justified by his grace and become heirs in hope of eternal life [cf. Titus 3:4–7].

Our sister, Zoumai, has been washed once for all in the waters of Christian baptism, which is the washing of regeneration and renewal in the Holy Spirit. She may take this water and wash her own body today, and every day, as we all wash the dirt from our bodies every day. But we cannot cleanse our own hearts. The gospel of Jesus our *soré*-cool-thing bids her today, as she grieves the loss of her partner, to draw near to Jesus with a true heart in full assurance of faith, with her heart sprinkled clean by the blood of Christ, and her body washed once for all with pure water in the name of Jesus our *soré*-cool-thing.

The pastor sprinkles the widow with water from the pot, after which he also sprinkles the other Christians who have assembled with her. He says:

Brothers and sisters, may this *soré* water remind us today of our baptism into the death and resurrection of our Lord Jesus Christ, so that as Christ was raised from the dead by the glory of the Father, we too might walk in newness of life. If we have died with Christ in baptism, we believe we shall also live with him!

Friends, we know how our ancestors imposed laws of abstinence on widows and widowers. But our Lord said, "There is nothing outside a person which by going into him can defile him; but the things which come out of a person are what defile him" [Mark 7:15]. This means for us today that the death of Garba does not defile Zoumai. She is simply exhorted by the word of God to live in newness of life, by God's grace and strength. She is free to abstain or not to abstain, but whatever she does in this regard, may it be out of love, not out of fear. For there is nothing in all creation that will be able to separate her from the love of God in Christ Jesus our Lord!

The pastor, deacons, deaconesses, and friends surround Zoumai, lay hands on her and pray for her, asking the Lord to give her comfort and strength. The pastor continues:

"None of us lives to himself, and none of us dies to himself. If we live, we live to the Lord, and if we die, we die to the Lord; so then, whether we live or whether we die, we are the Lord's. For to this end Christ died and lived again, that he might be Lord both of the dead and of the living!" [Romans 14:7ff.].

Receive the benediction: "Now may the God of peace who brought again from the dead our Lord Jesus, the great shepherd of the sheep, by the blood of the eternal covenant, equip you with everything good that you may do his will, working in you that which is pleasing in his sight, through Jesus Christ, to whom be glory forever and ever. Amen."

The pastor closes the ritual with exhortations to the community to surround Zoumai with words and acts of love.

SORÉ AND THE BREAD OF LIFE

In an earlier chapter, we met Yaya, a Lutheran catechist who is also the village blacksmith. Yaya preaches and teaches from the Bible, but he also washes the villagers when they ask him. He washes them in the traditional manner for *simbo-dono,* for the sickness caused by swearing falsely on a metal object. The catechist-blacksmith also presides at traditional Gbaya rites of purification.

A man may request Yaya's help after he has quarreled with a fellow villager—perhaps because he was accused of stealing a chicken. The accused man denies the charge by putting his hand on a piece of metal, either a tool or a weapon. Metal represents for him something "true"; it serves him for life in the field and on the hunt. With his hand on the metal, he swears he did not steal the chicken. But later, knowing that he is in trouble for his lie, he believes that he will die because he swore falsely on metal.

He therefore asks Yaya, the catechist-blacksmith, to wash him in a rite of purification. Yaya calls the two men together and digs two small holes in the ground into which he places some leaves, roots, and sticks from the *soré* tree. Then he washes the men's hands, which they have extended over these symbolic objects: he blesses them and washes away the threat of death that hangs over them in their quarrel and lies. Finally, he directs them to use their hands to feed one another as a symbol of their reconciliation.

Yaya says that he continues to wash his fellow villagers in this way, whatever their religious profession may be, because he does not want them to die. *Soré* is at the heart of this washing, and Yaya's way of telling us what this rite is "for" corresponds to its most central meaning, which is always "for life."

So long as Yaya continues to practice the rite in this way, we must admit that this Gbaya tradition is a parallel structure to Christian practice. The Gbaya who practice this rite do not perceive the gospel as a "new mat"; it does not meet their need in this case.

The celebration of Christian mourning rites, however, is an example of how the Gbaya church may indeed weave a new mat over an old mat; and the same kind of accommodation and creativity needs to be developed more fully to serve all the needs of the Gbaya people. The strength of Yaya's rite illustrates, on the other hand, the very present need in the Gbaya church to express the power of the gospel ritually in Gbaya villages. The blacksmith's washing has all the potential for transformation into a specifically Christian rite of reconciliation wherein Jesus our *soré*-cool-thing is present for us in his word and in the bread of life in the Christian sacraments.

Further, Yaya's rite is but one of many that represent the problems and the promise of the church in Africa: the existence of parallel religious systems among the Gbaya and countless other peoples is problematic. The lifting up of all life in and through Jesus our *soré*-cool-thing, in whom all human needs are met, promises that the rites and symbols of the church are sufficient to all needs. The missiological task requires that we be quite clear about what it is that the church brings to the Gbaya, and what in fact we expect to discover among them. Life and shalom come to people from God through the *soré* tree and what it symbolizes, and there is no conflict between God the creator, God the redeemer, and God the life-giving Spirit.

Therefore, what is revealed through the *soré* tree and what is revealed in the revelation of grace and salvation through Jesus Christ come from the same source; yet it is always specifically the gospel that gives us this new way of seeing *soré* and reveals that its final intention has always been to evoke faith in Jesus Christ. *Soré* is in the Gbaya culture to draw them to God's deed in Jesus; the gospel begins when the word is made flesh and comes to dwell at the heart of human life. It is not this instance of *dono* sickness that the gospel overcomes but the fact that we suffer from *dono* sickness. We may and we must work together in Christian mission to weave a new mat over old mats in ways that bring peace to people and glory to God.

THE *SORÉ* WAY TO NEW DISCOVERIES

The contextualization of soteriological themes among the Gbaya emerges from within their contemporary relationships in community and proceeds with the help of a symbolic vocabulary that emerges from their own rites of purification, initiation, reconciliation, and exorcism. Original contextual meanings remain, but they are critiqued, expanded, and transformed: Jesus becomes the new content of *soré* for today's *simbo* persons.

Any number of analogous searches can and should be undertaken to describe the oral and ritual traditions among the Dii, the Bamiléké, the Mbororo, the Dooyaayo, the Tchamba, and the Laka—in short, among all the multiethnic churches of Cameroon and the Central African Republic. Missiological theology must pay attention to the detail of symbolic meanings and relationships that are the context in these places for the incarnation and celebration of the life of Jesus.

And beyond Africa, are there rites of purification, initiation, reconciliation, and exorcism that can be thickly described to become places wherein we are nourished and comforted by the tree of life? How can eschatological salvation in Jesus be meaningfully expressed in other circumstances? What are the deep things we share that may be grafted into him?

Does it make a significant difference, for example, that Gbaya community tends to be considerably more homogeneous than members of a church council in an American city? Or do we Americans also manifest a certain homogeneity in our commitment to the religion of our time? Gbaya Christians and American Christians have in common the description of Jesus in the Bible, which is a symbolic pattern that measures all life and gives hope to all people, the promise and the way to wholeness and peace.

Missiological theology sees the urgency of taking the time to pay attention to the details of our lives in community, and to describe thickly the salvation that is in our ordinary events and social discourse. A method of correlation can be brought to these descriptions wherein the question "Who is Jesus?" is always the crucial question. The Gbaya naming of Jesus as our *soré*-cool-thing is a theological model that others may apply to their own Christian experiences even as it continues to deepen and grow in Africa. The new life of *soré* in the Gbaya church is not an isolated circumstance. Other symbols, analogous to *soré*, also lead our global family into the light of the gospel and eschatological salvation in Jesus—some that are near to us, some in places far away. *Soré*, therefore, calls attention to the need for theological and missiological research in all cultures, and it provides a new way for us to describe the images in our own soteriological arena. Perhaps we, too, shall come to know—by faith and hope in the promise of the Christian gospel—that God is in our midst, in our own culture, reigning and mediating salvation to us in Jesus our *soré*-cool-thing.

Notes

CHAPTER 1

1. See Ellen Hilberth and John Hilberth, *Contribution à l'Ethnographie des Gbaya* (Lund: Berlinska Boktryckeriet, 1968), p. 1; and Philip A. Noss, *Gbaya: Phonologie et Grammaire* (Meiganga, Cameroon: Centre de Traduction Gbaya, 1981), p. 1.

2. Joseph H. Greenberg, "The Languages of Africa," *International Journal of American Linguistics* 29 (January 1963): 106.

3. Yves Blanchard and Philip A. Noss, *Dictionnaire Gbaya-Français: Dialecte Yaayuwee* (Meiganga, Cameroon: Centre de Traduction Gbaya, 1982), pp. vii–viii.

4. Philip Burnham, *Opportunity and Constraint in a Savanna Society: The Gbaya of Meiganga, Cameroon* (London: Academic Press, 1980), p. 129.

5. Philip Noss, "An Interpretation of Gbaya Religious Practice," *International Review of Mission* 61 (October 1972): 364–73.

CHAPTER 6

1. Victor Turner, *The Ritual Process: Structure and Anti-Structure* (Ithaca, N.Y.: Cornell University Press, 1969), pp. 94–95.

CHAPTER 7

1. Philip A. Noss, "The Gbaya Dance of *Diang*," *Practical Anthropology* 18 (1971): 264.

2. Noss, "The Toad and the Frog," in *Gbaya Traditional Literature*. Tapes and transcriptions, Indiana Archives of Traditional Music, Indiana University, Bloomington, Indiana.

3. Noss, "Wanto: The Hero of Gbaya Tradition," *Journal of the Folklore Institute* 8 (January 1972): 9–10.

4. Noss, "The Brother's Quest," in *Gbaya Traditional Literature*.

5. Noss, "Two Brothers," in *Gbaya Traditional Literature*.

6. Noss, "The Gbaya Dance of *Diang*,": 268.

7. Mircea Eliade, *Rites and Symbols of Initiation: The Mysteries of Birth and Rebirth*, trans. Willard R. Trask (New York: Harper & Row, 1958), p. 27.

CHAPTER 10

1. Philip Burnham, *Opportunity and Constraint in a Savanna Society: The Gbaya of Meiganga, Cameroon* (London: Academic Press, 1980), pp. 52–54.

CHAPTER 11

1. Victor Turner, *The Forest of Symbols: Aspects of Ndembu Ritual* (Ithaca, N.Y.: Cornell University Press, 1967), pp. 50–58; and *Revelation and Divination in Ndembu Ritual* (Ithaca, N.Y.: Cornell University Press, 1975), pp. 164–76.

CHAPTER 12

1. Cf. E. O. James, *The Tree of Life: An Archeological Study* (Leiden: E. J. Brill, 1966).

2. Jean Daniélou, *Primitive Christian Symbols*, trans. Donald Attwater (Baltimore, Md.: Helicon Press, 1964), pp. 36–39.

3. Alexander Robert and James Donaldson, eds., *The Ante-Nicene Fathers*, 12 vols. (New York: Charles Scribner's Sons, 1926), 1:242.

4. Ambrose, "The Grain of the Mustard Seed," *The Sunday Sermons of the Great Fathers*, 2 vols., trans. and ed. M. F. Toal (London: Longmans, Green & Co., 1957), 1:348–51.

5. Gregory of Nyssa, "On the Making of Man," *The Nicene and Post-Nicene Fathers*, 2nd series, 8 vols., ed. Philip Schaff and Henry Wace (Grand Rapids, Mich.: Wm. B. Eerdmans, 1954), 5:409–11.

6. Augustine of Hippo, *The City of God*, ed. Vernon J. Bourke (Garden City, N.Y.: Doubleday Image Books, 1961), pp. 287–88.

7. Bonaventure, *The Soul's Journey into God, The Tree of Life, The Life of St. Francis*, trans. and ed. Ewert Cousins, in Classics of Western Spirituality (New York: Paulist Press, 1978), pp. 199–275.

8. *Soré* is related to the cross as the tree of life in Paradise is related to the cross. Neither is a metaphor for the other, but the meanings of both are analogically unified in Christ. To say that this relationship is metonymical means that the relationship is based on "conceptual contiguity, mutual participation, and temporal diachronic sequence." See Gerhard Ladner, "Medieval and Modern Understanding of Symbolism: A Comparison," *Speculum* 54 (April 1979): 237.

CHAPTER 13

1. Cf. W. Pannenberg, "Analogy and Doxology," in *Basic Questions in Theology*, vol. 1, trans. George H. Kehm (Philadelphia, Pa.: Fortress Press, 1970), pp. 225–26.

2. Ibid., pp. 228–38.

3. Martin Luther, *The Small Catechism* (Minneapolis, Minn.: Augsburg Publishing House, 1979), p. 24.

4. Cf. Paul Tillich, *Theology and Culture* (New York: Oxford University Press, Galaxy Book, 1964), p. 41.

Index